THE BANTAM SHAKESPEARE

"It is a boon to have this amount of commentary. The most interesting of all the paperback Shakespeares."

ERIC BENTLEY
Columbia University

"The stage directions will be welcomed by students. . . . We applaud the new Bantam Shakespeare."

THE COLLEGE ENGLISH
ASSOCIATION *Critic*

"The marginal glossary is a genuine contribution to the better understanding of Shakespeare."

JOHN GASSNER
School of Drama
Yale University

"Excellent . . . the best of its kind I have seen, and I honestly think the best ever done."

ERNEST HUNTER WRIGHT
Professor of English Emeritus
Columbia University

"Your edition is quite superb! . . . the publishing coup of the season!"

STEPHEN J. RUSNAK
Chairman, Department of English
Bishop Loughlin Memorial High School

"A concept of editing and publishing as revolutionary as it is simple."

GEORGE FREEDLEY
Curator of the New York Public Library
Theater Collection

THE EDITORS

OSCAR JAMES CAMPBELL established the text for this edition and served as the authority on all points of scholarship. Recognized as one of the leading Shakespearean scholars, he is editor of *The Living Shakespeare*, and author of *Shakespeare's Satire*, *Comical Satyre*, *Shakespeare's Troilus and Cressida*, and numerous other books and articles on literary subjects. Dr. Campbell is now Professor Emeritus of Columbia University; he was formerly Chairman of the English Department.

ALFRED ROTHSCHILD, writer and lecturer, has an original and penetrating approach to many subjects. A lifelong Shakespeare addict, he originated the unique features of the Bantam Shakespeare. He worked on every phase of the project in close contact with the other editors, and supervised the production of the final manuscript.

STUART VAUGHAN is one of the country's most prominent theatrical directors. Formerly Artistic Director of the Phoenix Theatre in New York, he is now at the head of the newly established Seattle Repertory Theatre. He staged the Phoenix' highly successful productions of *Hamlet*, and *Henry IV*, *Parts I* and *II*. He was the first director of the New York Shakespeare Festival productions in Central Park, for which he staged *Romeo and Juliet*, *Macbeth*, *Two Gentlemen of Verona*, *Julius Caesar*, and *Othello*. At the Hechscher Theatre in New York, he also directed *Richard III* and *As You Like It*. Mr. Vaughan supervised in particular the stage directions in this edition, wrote the essay on the Elizabethan theatre, and a number of notes.

KING LEAR

by

WILLIAM SHAKESPEARE

EDITED BY
OSCAR JAMES CAMPBELL
ALFRED ROTHSCHILD
STUART VAUGHAN

BANTAM BOOKS / NEW YORK

KING LEAR

A Bantam Classic / published February 1964

ACKNOWLEDGMENTS

BRADLEY, A. C.: from *Shakespearean Tragedy*; reprinted by permission of Macmillan & Company Ltd., and St. Martin's Press, Inc.

CAMPBELL, LILY BESS: from *Shakespeare's Tragic Heroes, Slaves Of Passion*; reprinted by permission of Cambridge University Press.

GRANVILLE-BARKER, HARLEY: from *Prefaces To Shakespeare*, vol. I; © Copyright 1946 by the Princeton University Press; reprinted by permission of the Princeton University Press, Princeton.

Library of Congress Catalog Card Number: 64-12088
All rights reserved.
© Copyright, 1964, by Bantam Books, Inc.
Published simultaneously in the United States and Canada.

Foreword

BY ALFRED ROTHSCHILD

Still another Shakespeare! To be sure—but a Shakespeare "with a difference."

It all started years ago with a complaint from a high school student. He had seen a performance of *Julius Caesar*, and was intensely excited about it. Then he tried reading the play, and found he just couldn't make any progress. He was disappointed and puzzled. "What makes it so tough?" he asked.

He didn't know he was planting a seed. It was there and then that this edition began to take shape.

The Bantam Shakespeare seeks to provide in a convenient and easily comprehended form as much guidance and information for the student and general reader as is reasonably possible.

This is how we have tried to achieve our objective:

Text

By "text" we mean the words the characters actually speak. While it is true that this text, written in Elizabethan English, contains words and phrases no longer in common usage, allusions to matters and events no longer easily recognized, and various other obscurities, there was never any doubt about one rule: the basic text must not be violated.

So this is not a new text. There are no "improvements," no rewritten lines, no "corrections" of Elizabethan grammar—even though a change might make some lines more easily understood by modern readers. The editors of this edition are all purists—on fundamentals. But it cannot be repeated too often that there is no such thing as a "pure" Shakespeare text—no such thing even as agreement on whether some passages in the plays were written by Shakespeare himself.

There is, however, an authoritative consensus on the basis

of which the so-called "Cambridge Edition" was published about one hundred years ago. William Aldis Wright and William George Clark, the editors, were not, of course, trying to improve Shakespeare. What they did, with infinite care and learning, was to reconcile differences in the original quarto and folio texts, to correct printers' errors, and so on, with due regard to the research and opinions of scholars before them. This Cambridge Edition is now almost universally accepted as the standard reading text.

A special edition of the Cambridge Shakespeare, published under the auspices of the same Cambridge editors, is known as the "Globe" edition, and it is this text that for the purposes of the Bantam Shakespeare is regarded as basically sacrosanct. We have made some changes in punctuation, and also in spelling, particularly in substituting the letter "e" for the apostrophe in words like "aimed," in which the "e" is now always silent. Where we do deviate from the text, which is rarely, we explain why in a Note.

Glossary

Unfamiliar and obscure words in the text of the plays are customarily explained in a glossary at the back of the book, or at the foot of the text page. As a rule, there is no indication that a particular word is "glossed." This means that sometimes the reader will stop to hunt in vain, and sometimes fail to look for an explanation when he should—that is, when the modern meaning of a word differs from its Elizabethan meaning. Take the word "character," for example. It is certainly neither uncommon nor obscure. But as used by Shakespeare in *King Lear* it means "handwriting"; and unless the reader is made aware of this he cannot properly understand the passages in which the word occurs.

Our method is to place an asterisk next to the word that requires clarification, and then to give the equivalent on the same line in the right-hand margin, so that the eye, particularly as it becomes accustomed to the arrangement, can take it in at a glance.

Obviously, these marginal glosses must be kept within certain limits of length, not only for typographical reasons, but also because excessive length would defeat our objective of having the reader absorb the explanation with the least possible interruption of his train of thought.

In some instances, the word in the glossary margin is not simply the modern equivalent of the word marked with an asterisk, as, for instance, on line 13 of the first scene of *Hamlet*. There "rivals" is easily and with reasonable accuracy translated into modern English as "partners." But now take the word "instrument" in the line "Give me the gown. Where is thy instrument?" (*Julius Caesar*, IV, 3, 239.) "Instrument'" is certainly not an unfamiliar word, nor is it used here in an unfamiliar sense. But there is nothing in the preceding lines to indicate that Brutus is referring to a musical instrument. On the stage, this presents no problem, and stage directors through the centuries have known how to convey the information to the audience. But it is different with the reader. He needs help if he is not to be confused and thus lose something of the atmosphere of one of the most charming and effective touches in the play. So we marked "instrument" with an asterisk and printed "*i.e.*, lute" in the margin, fully aware that "lute" is not a definition of "instrument."

It will be noticed that sometimes there is a slight break in the line in which an asterisk occurs. This signifies that the gloss covers more than one word and applies jointly to the two or more words from the break to the asterisk.

Occasionally, two asterisks will be found on one line. When this occurs, the two glosses are separated by a diagonal stroke.

It is interesting to note, incidentally, that very few glosses are needed for an understanding and appreciation of most of the great key passages. This is not an accident: it is part of the genius of Shakespeare. At his greatest, he is at his simplest —or perhaps we should say that he then achieves that simplicity of effect which hides the infinite complexity of perfection.

Stage Directions

Here we have a situation entirely different from that which applies to the text. Stage directions are simply not text at all. They are not part of the poetry, the characterization, the dramatic vigor of the lines, which are the glory of Shakespeare. The stage directions that have come down to us from the quartos and folios are almost certainly only the brief markings in the prompt books used in the early staging of the plays. It was not until nearly one hundred years after

Shakespeare's death that an edition, edited by Nicholas Rowe, was published, incorporating systematic division into acts and scenes, and many new stage directions.

The history of presenting Shakespeare in print is long. Progress has been difficult and slow. It took many years to change even such externals as Elizabethan spelling and typography. The time has come to take a further step forward by bringing other externals such as stage directions up to date.

The obvious function of stage directions in a reading edition is to help the reader follow the action of the play. There should be an adequate description of the scenes and of the way the characters move about. Our rule has been to follow the Globe edition directions, but to amplify them where necessary, to modernize the language, and also to paragraph speeches in accordance with their context. In the few instances where we have deemed it essential to go beyond this in order to help the reader understand what is going on, we have called attention to the change in a Note.

In all cases the stage directions are as simple and direct as we could make them. Mood-setting imagery has no place here, any more than a description of a character's state of mind. That would be tantamount to interpreting the character for the reader. Actually, every effort has been made to avoid interpretation. The purpose is not to get in the reader's way, but to illuminate it. The text must be allowed to speak for itself, so that the reader can make his own interpretation as he progresses with his reading. Not that the Bantam Shakespeare neglects interpretation—on the contrary, it makes a special feature of interpretative comment. But it does so where it belongs: in the appendix.

What must be made clear is the difference between a reading version of a Shakespeare play, where stage directions that interpret character are wrong, and a stage or acting version where they are not only right but also essential—and, indeed, inevitable.

Even though the standard division into scenes and acts admittedly leaves something to be desired, we have adhered to it. Nothing substantial is to be gained by changing or eliminating it, but much to be lost, since it is used in all the important reference works, such as Schmidt's Lexicon and Bartlett's Concordance.

The customary way of printing the passage beginning with line 17 of Act II, Scene 1 of *King Lear* is this:

EDMUND.
    The duke be here tonight? The better! Best!
    This weaves itself perforce into my business.
    My father hath set guard to take my brother;
    And I have one thing, of a queasy question,
    Which I must act: briefness and fortune, work!
    Brother, a word; descend: brother, I say!
              Enter EDGAR.
    My father watches: O sir, fly this place;
    Intelligence is given where you are hid;
    You have now the good advantage of the night:
    Have you not spoken 'gainst the Duke of Cornwall?
    He's coming hither; now i'the night, i'the haste,
    And Regan with him: have you nothing said
    Upon his party 'gainst the Duke of Albany?
    Advise yourself.
EDGAR.   I am sure on't, not a word.
EDMUND.
    I hear my father coming: pardon me;
    In cunning I must draw my sword upon you:
    Draw; seem to defend yourself; now quit you well.
    Yield: come before my father. Light, ho, here!
    Fly, brother. Torches, torches! So, farewell.
                [*Exit* EDGAR.
    Some blood drawn on me would beget opinion
           [*Wounds his arm.*]
    Of my more fierce endeavor: I have seen drunkards
    Do more than this in sport. Father, Father!
    Stop, stop! No help?

Now see what happens when the passage is printed the *Bantam* way—how easy it is to follow the action step by step:

EDMUND.
    The duke be here tonight? The better! Best!
    This weaves itself perforce into my business.
    My father hath set guard to take my brother;
    And I have one thing, of a queasy* question,*   delicate/
    Which I must act: briefness and fortune, work!   nature
                                         20

(*Calling up the stairs.*)
Brother, a word; descend. Brother, I say!
  (EDGAR *comes down from* EDMUND'S *room.*)
My father watches: O sir, fly this place;
Intelligence is given where you are hid;
You have now the good advantage of the night:
Have you not spoken 'gainst the Duke of Cornwall?
He's coming hither; now i'the night, i'the haste,
And Regan with him: have you nothing said
Upon his party* 'gainst the Duke of Albany?
Advise yourself.*

> in his
> favor
> consider

EDGAR.   I am sure on't, not a word.
EDMUND.
I hear my father coming: pardon me;   30
In cunning I must draw my sword upon you:
  (*Draws his sword.*)
Draw; seem to defend yourself.
  (EDGAR *draws, too, and they fence.*)
                    Now quit you* well.

> acquit
> yourself

Yield: come before my father.
                  Light, ho, here!
  (*Aside to* EDGAR.)
Fly, brother.
        Torches, torches!
  (*To* EDGAR *as he leaves.*)
                So, farewell.
Some blood drawn on me would beget opinion
Of my more fierce endeavor.
  (*Wounding his own arm.*)
              I have seen drunkards
Do more than this in sport.
          Father, Father!
Stop, stop! No help?

It should be noted, too, that everything we have added or changed is inherent in the text. Take the stage directions (*Calling up the stairs.*) and (EDGAR *comes down from* EDMUND'S *room.*). We derive the information for these from lines 183 to 185 of Act I, Scene 2 where Edmund says to Edgar, "retire with me to my lodging . . . there's my key," and from line 21 immediately following the first stage direction, "Brother, a word; descend."

This passage also provides a good example of how the glosses function. "Queasy" "question" "upon his party" "advise yourself" "quit you"—these are all terms essential to the meaning of this exciting scene. With the Bantam method of glossing, you do not interrupt your reading five times: the clarifying meaning, fitting into the grammatical construction of the line, is right there under your eye for your instant use. Thus the thread of your thinking is not broken: your mind, to quote from a particularly pregnant comment by Samuel Johnson, is not "refrigerated" by interruptions.

Notes

Here, too, the aim of the Bantam Shakespeare is maximum reader convenience. The words or passages requiring Notes are consecutively numbered. The Notes in the appendix are numbered in rotation, and also identified by the number of the line. Thus, the reader knows at once not only that there is a Note, but also where to find it conveniently and quickly. All the Notes have been written to meet our special objectives. We have tried to keep them succinct, without limiting them in either length or number.

Commentaries

To include a wide range of commentaries with each play in a paperback edition is certainly unusual, and, as far as we know, unique. But the Bantam Shakespeare goes further. Professor Campbell has tied the commentaries together by means of introductory paragraphs. This is important because comment written in the eighteenth century, for example, should not be viewed in the same light as comment written, say, one hundred years later. Some of Voltaire's criticism sounds preposterous today, but the fact is that it cannot be properly evaluated without consideration of the historical and literary background against which it was written.

Format

A great deal of thought has been given to typographical arrangement. The practice of abbreviating character names, so that "Hamlet" becomes "Ham," and "Antony" "Ant," is not only esthetically disturbing but often seriously confusing

—as when you have "Edm" for "Edmund" on one line, and "Edg" for "Edgar" on the next. In the Bantam Shakespeare, the name of the character speaking is printed in full and on a separate line. This not only helps to open up the printing in general, but also has the highly desirable effect of reducing the number of run-over lines. All other details, such as the placing of parenthetical stage directions, and the numbering of the lines, have been handled so as to achieve maximum reading ease.

Other Features

Preceding each play is an essay by Professor Campbell written especially for this edition. It analyzes the play, and gives details regarding the source of the plot, the date of composition, and so on. We have also added an annotated bibliography and a chronological table, both prepared by Professor Campbell. The chronological table, bringing as it does events in Shakespeare's life into relation with other events of the time, makes enlightening and fascinating reading. Even a casual glance reveals that Galileo was born in the same year as Shakespeare; that Shakespeare was thirteen at the time of the publication of Holinshed's *Chronicles of England, Scotland, and Ireland*, on which he drew so heavily for his historical plays; and twenty-four at the time of the defeat of the Spanish Armada.

It is important for the reader to know something about the difference between our modern stage and that for which Shakespeare wrote. An essay on the Elizabethan theater, written by Mr. Stuart Vaughan, has therefore been included.

While the functions of the three editors are clearly defined on the title page, it should be said that the final manuscript emerged as the result of much reviewing of scripts and many conferences involving all the editors. Among these, we must in all fairness include Donald Reis of Bantam Books, whose help in every respect proved invaluable. In actual practice there was no sharp separation of function. So much is here as a result of a harmonious exchange of views and blending of ideas in the action and reaction of open-minded discussion, that it is impossible to tell where one contribution began and the other left off.

About two hundred years ago, Samuel Johnson wrote:

> Let him that is yet unacquainted with the powers of Shake-speare, and who desires to feel the greatest pleasure that the drama can give, read every play from the first scene to the last, with utter negligence of all his commentators. When his fancy is once on the wing, let it not stop at correction or explanation. When his attention is strongly engaged, let it disdain alike to turn aside to the name of Theobald and of Pope. Let him read on through the brightness and obscurity, through integrity and corruption; let him preserve his comprehension of the dialogue and his interest in the fable. And when the pleasures of novelty have ceased, let him attempt exactness and read the commentators. . . .

The advice is good. Countless commentators have written countless words on the precise meaning of countless terms and phrases, with countless varieties of interpretation. It has not been possible, if only because of space limitations, to do more than indicate some of the more prominent controversial issues.

If you want to venture further, you will do well to use our bibliography as a guide. But always remember that the Why and Wherefore of Shakespeare is part of the mystery of the universe. Learn to enjoy him as a poet and a dramatist. Regard him as you would a magnificent view of land and sea, comprehending an infinite variety of light and shade and color, to which you open up your heart and soul and mind, and let it work its wonders upon you.

We are indebted to Mr. George Freedley, curator of the Theater Collection of the New York Public Library and leading authority on the theater, who reviewed our manuscript, and whose wise counsel from the earliest stages of the project was of invaluable help.

Contents

Introduction

BY OSCAR JAMES CAMPBELL

Hamlet is universally regarded as Shakespeare's best play. *King Lear*, of equal but different superlative interest, can be described as the Poet's greatest dramatic poem. On the surface it is the tragedy of an old man driven mad by the violence of wrath and despair, and restored to fitful sanity and precarious peace by his love for Cordelia. But *King Lear* is more than that. It is a profound commentary on life and its values—an exalted morality play set against a backdrop of eternity.

From the time Charles Lamb pronounced his famous dictum: "Lear is essentially impossible to be represented on the stage," his notion has been widely accepted as discerning. Many subsequent critics agree that so transcendental a play loses its essential nature when acted in a theatre. The characters of the play, so Lamb maintained, are objects of meditation and not of curiosity. What they do is of secondary interest to what they represent.

Hence the essential Lear is not the old man "tottering about the stage with a walking stick." This figure we only see with our eyes. As the action develops, we establish a deeper relationship to the character until we completely identify ourselves with him. We gradually become a part of Lear's mind. In Lamb's view, the flesh and blood of no actor can create a character who is as far beyond human ken as Milton's Satan. That is a task for the creative imagination of readers of the tragedy.

A. C. Bradley, the famous nineteenth-century critic, develops this idea in his own penetrating fashion. For him *King Lear* loses its peculiar magnitude when forced into the strait jacket of the stage. Such aspects of the tragedy as its immense scope, its indefinite locale, the vastness of the convulsions both of Nature and of human passion cannot be revealed in the theatre.

Granville-Barker, a distinguished critic and successful producer of Shakespearean plays, takes direct issue with this point of view. He begins by admitting that the Poet, driven by the immensity of his theme, may have given the fellows of his company a play some of the features of which were almost impossible to act. However that may be, Barker points out the additional values which skillful stagecraft contributes to the greatest scenes of the tragedy. Often the sound of the words is almost as important as their meaning. This is particularly true in such a passage as "Blow, winds, and crack your cheeks!" in which not wind-machines but Lear's speech, spoken by an inspired actor, creates the storm. It is Lear, a figure on the stage, being buffeted by the winds and not a reader's conception of his essence that renders him a representative of humanity—pitiful and helpless when pitted against the powers of Nature and those of the great gods of whom its forces are the instruments.

None of these problems bothered the author of the old *King Leir*, Shakespeare's source. He adopted the ending of the traditional tale. There, with the help of the victorious French army, Leir regains his throne from which he reigned peacefully until his death. This ending was not inappropriate to the earlier play, because there Leir, far from being the slave of turbulent passions, is submissive to his daughters' will. Although they outrageously harass him, he remains "the mirror of mild patience, puts up all wrong and never gives reply." Shakespeare, by driving Lear's emotional intensity over into senile dementia, made inevitable the tragic conclusion of the old man's career. In *King Leir*, the King devises the love test, not to serve as a public satisfaction of his vanity, but as a way of trapping Cordeilla (as she is there called) into an undesired marriage with the King of Ireland. The two wicked daughters hire a murderer to kill their father, but a terrific electric storm so frightens the would-be assassin that he does not do the dreadful deed. This incident suggested the purgatorial storm which batters Lear in Shakespeare's drama.

The tragic story of Gloucester is, in all important respects, like that of the Blind King of Paphlagonia in Sidney's *Arcadia*. For a modern audience this second story of a child's cruelty to an aged father (often called an echo plot) fills the play over-full with horror and emotional intensity. Shakespeare had both a philosopher's and a dramatist's reason for associating Gloucester's story with that of Lear. The principal plot rises to a climax in the first act, so that the rest of Lear's story forms a psychological denouement, an exhibition of growing mental anguish up to the moment of his redemption. A series of emotional and spiritual states take the place of deeds. To satisfy every audience's demand for action moving through crises to catastrophe, Shakespeare attached to the tragedy of passion the more conventional plot of a good man led to disaster by the wiles of a villainous calumniator. Yet this plot, unlike that of other plays which boast a subplot, is not a contrast to the main plot but a restatement of it. Both Lear and Gloucester are victims of filial ingratitude and cruelty. The blinding of Gloucester is a physical and Senecan equivalent of the madness of Lear. And both characters pass through purgatorial experiences to reach a wisdom neither has ever known before. Some critics have suggested that this so-called echo plot makes the tragedy more than the report of one singular set of circumstances, that it raises the ingratitude of children and their inhumanity to aged parents to a declaration of universal moral and philosophical significance.

Lear's tragedy has a still deeper meaning. It is a half-stoical, half-Christian morality play depicting a man's redemption through love—the end of a man's agonized search and final discovery of abiding spiritual values. At the beginning of the play Lear's ideals are completely distorted by his love of luxury and of pompous ceremonies. He is dominated by the desire for possessions and is ruled by his passions. In these respects he is the most unstoical of men, for the Stoics taught that love of luxury, shameful in a man of any age, was detestable in the very old. And the quality of all others against which teachers of stoicism thought an old man must carefully guard himself was emotional intemperance. Lear, as we shall see, is purged of these vices through suffering—and this conforms to Stoic philosophy. But he attains not Stoic contentment won through recognition of the ultimate cruelty of things and achieved by withdrawal into the quiet sanctuary of the soul, but rather he reaches the Christian equivalent of that ancient virtue, namely love. Thus he is redeemed, not for life on this earth but for a Christian Heaven, for which the discipline of his suffering has made him ready.

The love test with which the play begins, a folk theme, becomes in Shakespeare's hand a deeply revealing characterizing incident. By exploiting his daughters' supposed affection for the creation of a public show, Lear not only betrays his thirst for adulation and his need to feed his self-esteem, but he also betrays the fact that even love has become to him nothing but an instrument of self-glorification. Incidentally, the rewards which Lear planned to bestow in return for his daughters' expressions of love show him to have become incapable of administering the affairs of a kingdom. For it was one of the principal tenets of Elizabethan political philosophy that to divide a kingdom was to awaken civil war, which would speed the state down the road to ruin. When Lear's carefully planned dramatic scene that was to serve as the climax to his career of pride and vanity fails to issue in the triumph he had expected, the old man suffers tortures of humiliation. Then his injured self-esteem generates anger. Since self-conceit is stronger in old men than in young ones (if we are to accept the verdict of Aristotle and his followers), the injury to it was proportionately painful and the anger proportionately great. This is the passion which dominates Lear throughout most of the play and drives him from one excess to another until he becomes completely mad.

One reason why the love test fails to meet Lear's expectations is that he has been too much occupied with his own ego to understand even those with whom he associates every day. Sympathy is necessary for that, and sympathy is the product of unselfish love. For this reason Lear has never suspected that his two elder daughters are flatterers, calling on adulation whenever they believe it will do them the most good. Though their old father does not realize this, their sister Cordelia does. If we are alienated by her curt "Nothing" given in answer to her father's appeal for an expression of love, we must remember that she speaks partly in scorn and reproof of her evil sisters. Moreover, she "cannot heave [her] heart into [her] mouth," because sincere love loses its nature when it becomes the instrument of flattery.

Lear's reaction to Cordelia's refusal may seem to us extreme until we remember his habitual violence and the pub-

lic humiliation he has just suffered. Furthermore, anger, like
any other passion, when once freed from the control of the
judgment, is infinitely greater than the facts which have
aroused it would seem to warrant. Lear's headlong anger at
the failure of the public love test is a foretaste of the wild
emotional storms which later are to overwhelm him.

For Lear's dramatic career is a history of the ravages of
uncontrolled anger. And Shakespeare's portrayal of the various stages in Lear's tragic journey reveals uncanny knowledge of the symptoms of a disturbed personality on its way
to complete derangement. As soon as Lear's feelings move
beyond righteous indignation, he realizes that his control is
precarious. So he pathetically seeks to retain the illusions
upon which he has built his little universe. When Goneril
rejects him, he rushes to find in Regan's love a center of
mental security. When she too proves false, he abandons
hope of finding a haven of safety anywhere in the protected
world in which he has lived. Then he realizes that the bare
necessities of living have never been enough for him or for
other human beings:

> Our basest beggars
> Are in the poorest thing superfluous:
> Allow not nature more than nature needs,
> Man's life 's as cheap as beast's . . .

Lear has now lost the protection of his regal position, the
trappings that have insulated him from a firsthand knowledge
of life. He is forced to face reality as a plain "unaccommodated" man, and to discover its essence. Therefore, after the
end of the first act, the plot develops Lear's agonized search
for the spiritual truth that will rescue him from the buffeting
of circumstance and re-establish peace and sanity in his violently disordered nature.

The culmination both of Lear's violent passion and of his
wild pursuit of security occurs in the scene on the heath.
The terrifying upheaval in nature is more than a reflection
of the turmoil in Lear's personality. The destructive power
of the tempest is a manifestation of the same cosmic impulse
as the chaos in Lear's soul. The storm thus is more than an
adjunct to the old man's fury; it elevates his passion to the
awful dignity of a natural portent. As Professor Theodore
Spencer points out, Lear's language universalizes his own

experience. He calls upon the wild elements of the storm, the winds, the floods of rain, the thunder, and the lightning to wreak the awful destruction upon all creation that his insane anger has led him to desire. He wishes those forces of ruin to

> Smite flat the thick rotundity o' the world!
> Crack nature's molds, all germens spill at once,
> That make ingrateful man!

Only a little less revealing of the Poet's assumption of a close relationship between the microcosm of man and the macrocosm of Nature is Lear's appeal to the elements to punish human immorality. This is the wildest expression of the anger that has reduced to chaos a normally well-ordered system of emotion as terrifying as the dreadful pother of the tempest which the great gods have caused to erupt above her head.

His recognition of the correspondence between his passion and the fury of the storm fails to soothe the pain of his mad exasperation. For the tempest in his mind "doth from his sense take all feeling else." Yet just as he is about to seek shelter in a hovel, his mind clears for an instant, and he is visited by a flash of social sympathy. He pities all poverty-stricken wretches whose "houseless heads and unfed sides" find no protection from the "pelting of this pitiless storm." This impulse, says A. C. Bradley, is a first sign of Lear's redemption. But Shakespeare does not allow Lear to find salvation in this train of thought, for his momentary control is shattered by Edgar, whose feigned insanity drives Lear back into his madness and sets him again on the road of his frantic quest.

He now has the insane idea of tearing off all his clothes, of surrendering all the protection that the accumulations of civilization and his exalted position have afforded him. He will see what man, naked man, is worth in the presence of the uncontrolled forces of nature. The answer to the question he so passionately asks is a negative one. Nature is no kind mother, comforting and sustaining her foster child, but a hostile force that, with complete indifference, pours torrents of rain on Lear's head and hurls forked lightning at him. His search clearly cannot come to rest in the bosom of nature. Even Tom in his grotesque equivalence of Lear's tragic obsession echoes the futility of this phase of Lear's quest. The old man instead of going quietly into the hovel insists on staying out in the howling storm and cross-examining Tom. "What is your study?" he asks. And Tom replies, "How to prevent the fiend, and to kill vermin." Joseph Wood Krutch suggests that the phrase means "How to achieve both peace of mind and peace of body." This phrase describes in its fantastic fashion the first failure of Lear's search. In nature neither mind nor body can find comfort.

Such pessimism fortunately is not, as some critics have asserted, Shakespeare's reasoned comment on life. Lear does not rest his case in such an atmosphere of gloom. It is in his rediscovery of Cordelia's love that he finds the answer to his quest for peace and security. It is love, unselfish devotion free to everyone, even to the pair when they languish in prison, that is the value which every unaccommodated man can find if he will but seek it. The death of both Lear and Cordelia, certainly dictated by the tragic temper of the action, serves to emphasize the nature of their triumph. To have returned Lear to his throne or even to have saved Cordelia from death so that she might care for her father in prison would have obscured the meaning of this sublime morality play. It is the souls of the two that matter, and in their eternal union their souls are triumphant.

All the characters most closely associated with Lear ironically aggravate his anger and hasten him along the road to his redemption. Kent is the traditionally faithful counselor, an old man, who stands in striking contrast to the flattering daughters. Yet his devotion is uniformly dangerous to his master because of his uncontrolled bursts of righteous indignation. It is his noble desire to protect Lear that drives him to brave the wrath roused by his blunt protests against his master's hideous rashness in disinheriting Cordelia. The violence and impudence of his rebuke merely exaggerate the King's passion and precipitate Kent's own banishment, a major disaster for Lear. This outburst forms the pattern for Kent's action after he has attached himself, disguised as a servant, to the retinue of the King. In this capacity his conduct encourages Lear's tyrannical impulses and explains and half justifies the wicked daughters' determination to check and humiliate their father. Yet Kent persists in remaining at the old man's side, even after his master has gone mad. He follows his monarch through the storm with a tender solicitude that is not unmixed with awe. For to Kent even the insane creature in his charge remains his king, his gracious lord, whose sad steps he accompanies to the brink of the grave. Kent's last speech voices a determination to follow his dear lord into death. Thus though Kent is almost the personification of that unquestioning loyalty to a monarch which was the cornerstone of Tudor patriotism, the very intensity of his devotion is one of the forces which hurry the action to catastrophe.

The Fool is also devoted to Lear, yet his intended encouragements ironically serve only to intensify the old king's regret for his folly in having divested himself of all that he once possessed. A. C. Bradley describes the Fool as "a faithful half-witted lad." Other critics think that he is as old as Lear, having served as his court-fool from the time his master came to the throne. Whether young or old, half-witted or only assuming witlessness, he is faithful to the "business" of his role, that of the traditional court jester. He is consistently impudent. Under the cover of apparent nonsense, to which Lear, half listening, takes only occasional umbrage, the fool shoots his barbed talk. When he fears that he has gone too far in his insolence or when he realizes that Lear is becoming attentive, he darts away from this subject into irrelevance or sheer nonsense, as when he shouts the refrain of some old song like "Whoop, Jug! I love thee." He disappears from the play with the line, "And I'll go to bed at noon," perhaps an indication that his exposure to the storm has been more than his frail old body can endure.

Edgar, though playing his more important part in the tragedy of Gloucester, is also a kind of foil for Lear's madness. His disguise assumed to protect him from Edmund's plot imitates that of a Bedlam beggar, one of the harmless mad folk who were released from Bethlehem hospital for the insane to tramp around the countryside begging alms for their keep. Shakespeare endowed him with grotesque madness partly to draw laughter away from Lear; for to Elizabethans insanity was comic. Therefore, in order to make sure that no member of the Jacobean audience should find Lear's tragic aberration funny, the poet made Edgar's behavior as ridiculously fantastic as any audience could have wished. Yet

Edgar's assumed madness, set against the real madness of Lear and the half-madness of the Fool, produces the effect of universal mental disorder. Such an orgy of unreason is more than a psychological equivalent of the storm on the heath. It also threatens a return of the chaos to which civilized man all his life was thought to be precariously near. Through so wild a purgatory must Lear pass on his road to redemption.

The evil characters in the play are as unnatural as they are wicked. Goneril and Regan by dominating their father turn upside down an important part of the God-ordained social order, the submission of children to parents. To this phase of Lear's folly the Fool continually makes oblique references, as when he says, "May not an ass know when the cart draws the horse?"

Edmund's service to the plot is the old one of a calumniator whose slanders are believed. His motives are not far too seek. In the first place, his father's snickering attitude toward his surreptitiously begotten son deprives Edmund of every shred of human dignity. Why then should he be bound by moral law, which his father had violated in creating him? Furthermore, as a bastard he has no right to inherit property and is thus really an outcast from the entire social system. He is unnatural, then, in not being subject to the laws of nations, the rules of civilized conduct. The Nature that he worships is at the opposite pole from the Nature of the Stoics and of Christian humanism. That was an expression of Reason. Edmund's Nature is the lord of animal instincts, untamed to the uses of society. The adulterous love of Goneril and Regan for Edmund is an invention of Shakespeare's, as are the murder and suicide which close the scandalous little drama of jealousy and lust. This sordid plot further emphasizes the daughters' degeneration from their natural place in the social order.

Edmund's plot to mislead Gloucester exhibits a much less subtle technique of deception than that which Iago employs to deceive Othello. For Gloucester has always been afflicted with tragic moral and spiritual blindness, and so is easily led to mistake good for evil. His credulity thus leads him through injustice to catastrophe. His blinding before the eyes of the spectators is a scene of more than Senecan horror; to us this is a blemish on the play. Yet it marks the top of Regan's fiendish cruelty. She is the first to urge that Cornwall and Edmund "pluck out his eyes." And after Cornwall's heel has ground out one of them, she cries "The other too," and herself strikes dead a servant who protests against the second horror. Here at last she reveals the monster that her woman's form conceals. No sooner are Gloucester's eyes put out than Shakespeare introduces into this scene of savage violence a stab of tragic irony. For at the very moment when Gloucester loses his physical sight, the eyes of his mind are opened. He learns the depth of his blind folly in believing Edmund's calumnies against Edgar. Then, like many a central character in the morality plays, he is driven to utter despair by his conviction of sin and ceases to believe in the gods who keep nicely balanced the proportion between desert and reward:

> As flies to wanton boys, are we to the gods,
> They kill us for their sport.

This is not, as some critics have thought, an expression of Shakespeare's own pessimism, but the blasphemous utterance of a man whose despondency leads him toward suicide. Gloucester tries to kill himself by hurling himself from what Edgar convinces him is a cliff at Dover. Though he only falls forward on the level ground and swoons, Edgar in another disguise is able to convince him that he has actually fallen from a great height, that it was a fiend in the shape of a Bedlam beggar who had tempted him to suicide, and that he owed his preservation to the gods. This experience purges Gloucester of his despair and makes him ready for a Stoical conversion. He cries.

> Henceforth I'll bear
> Affliction till it do cry out itself
> "Enough, enough," and die.

But he has no need to submit to the discipline of adversity for long. The conflict of joy and grief aroused by Edgar's late revelation of himself is too much for Gloucester's "flawed heart" and it bursts "smilingly."

The last act presents the conflict of the English and French forces with all the conventions of the chronicle history play.

There are the familiar alarums and excursions and a stage battle with its inevitable single combat. But these martial events are huddled into a corner while the payment of the wages of sin and folly holds the center of the stage. At the end, the world of Lear and Gloucester lies in desolation, ravaged by the passions of man and Nature which have swept over it, but cleansed as with a purgatorial fire.

Shakespeare's Life and Times

BY OSCAR JAMES CAMPBELL

We have little information about the private life of William Shakespeare. The facts enumerated in the following Chronology seldom reveal any secrets of the poet's personality or of his dramatic achievements. None of his associates in the theatre have left any record of their friend, whom they knew, respected and admired. Nor did any of his contemporaries write even a brief account of his life. This is not strange. In sixteenth-century England only dignitaries of church or state were considered fit subjects for a biography.

The table below does make it clear that the poet was fortunate in the time of his birth, for, in the latter half of the sixteenth century, England basked in the full light of the Renaissance. He was equally fortunate in that the moment of his arrival on the scene coincided with new developments in the theatre. The first public playhouse was built in London when Shakespeare was in his early twenties. And when he began to write plays one company of actors had gained enough eminence and stability to provide a stage on which Shakespeare could bring to fruition all the elements of his genius.

The facts concerning his professional career, though more numerous, do not disclose any of the formative influences upon the design of the dramas or upon their distinctive character. However, these facts, joined with the meager records of the poet's personal life, have established the foundation upon which have been built all later biographies, interpretations and criticisms of Shakespeare and his works.

Chronology

HISTORIC AND LITERARY EVENTS	SHAKESPEARE AND HIS FAMILY
1558 Elizabeth crowned Queen. Thomas Kyd born. Robert Greene born.	
1561 Francis Bacon born.	John Shakespeare elected Chamberlain of Stratford.
1564 Christopher Marlowe born. Galileo Galilei born.	Shakespeare born, April 23; baptized April 26.
1566	Gilbert, Shakespeare's brother, born; died 1612.
1567 Mary, Queen of Scots, dethroned. James VI (later James I of England) crowned.	
1572 Massacre of St. Bartholomew. Ben Jonson born.	
1573 John Donne born.	
1575 Earl of Leicester's entertainment of the Queen at Kenilworth.	
1576 Burbage builds the first public playhouse, The Theatre.	
1577 Drake begins circumnavigation of the earth; finished 1580. Holinshed's *Chronicles of England, Scotland, and Ireland*.	
1579 John Lyly's *Euphues: The Anatomy of Wit*.	

1581
Tenne Tragedies of Seneca.

1582

Shakespeare's marriage.

1583
Philip Massinger born.   Shakespeare's daughter,
The Queen's Company formed.   Susanna, born.

1584
Reginald Scot's *The
   Discovery of Witchcraft.*

1585

Shakespeare's twins,
   Hamnet and Judith, born.

1586
Sir Philip Sidney killed at
   Zutphen.
John Ford born.

1587
Mary, Queen of Scots, beheaded.
Marlowe's *Tamburlaine, I.*
Kyd's *Spanish Tragedy.*

1588
Defeat of the Spanish Armada.
Principal actors of Lord
   Leicester's Company join
   Lord Strange's Men.
Marlowe's *Tamburlaine, II.*
Lyly's *Endimion.*

1589
Henry of Navarre crowned   *Comedy of Errors.*
   King of France as Henry IV.
Greene's *Friar Bacon and
   Friar Bungay.*
Marlowe's *Jew of Malta.*

1590
Sidney's *Arcadia* published.   *Titus Andronicus.*
Spenser's *Faerie Queene (I-III).*   *Henry VI, I.*

1591

Henry VI, II.
Henry VI, III.

1592
Death of Greene.   *Two Gentlemen of Verona.*
Marlowe's *Doctor Faustus* and
  Edward II.

1593
Theatres closed by plague.   *Venus and Adonis.*
Death of Marlowe.   Sonnets begun.
                                     Richard III.

1594
Shakespeare's company becomes   *Rape of Lucrece.*
  the Lord Chamberlain's Men.   *Love's Labour's Lost.*
Death of Kyd.   *Taming of the Shrew.*
                                     King John.

1595
Raleigh's first expedition to   *Richard II.*
  Guiana.   *A Midsummer Night's Dream.*
Spenser's *Amoretti,*   *Merchant of Venice.*
  Epithalamium.
Sidney's *Defense of Poesy*
  published.

1596
Spenser's *The Faerie Queene,*   *Romeo and Juliet.*
  Books IV-VI, *Four Hymns,*   Hamnet Shakespeare dies.
  and *Prothalamium.*

1597
Bacon's *Essays* (first edition).   *Henry IV, I.*
King James's *Demonologie.*   *Merry Wives of Windsor.*
                                     Shakespeare buys and renovates
                                     New Place in Stratford.

1598
Edict of Nantes issued by   *Henry IV, II.*
  Henry IV, giving Huguenots   *Much Ado About Nothing.*
  political rights.
Jonson's *Every Man in His
  Humour* acted.
Seven books of Chapman's
  translation of the *Iliad.*

1599
Death of Spenser.   *Henry V.*
Globe Theatre built.   *Julius Caesar.*
Essex' expedition to Ireland.
Jonson's *Every Man Out of His
  Humour* acted.
Dekker's *Shoemaker's Holiday.*

1600

Fortune Theatre built.   *As You Like It.*
East India Company founded.   *Twelfth Night.*
Children of The Chapel acquire
    a hall in Blackfriars'
    Monastery.

1601

Insurrection and execution of   *Hamlet.*
    Essex.   *Troilus and Cressida.*

1602

Sir Thos. Bodley's Library at   *All's Well That Ends Well.*
    Oxford opened.

1603

Death of Queen Elizabeth.
Accession of James I.
Shakespeare's company
    becomes the King's Men.
Heywood's *A Woman Killed
    with Kindness.*
Jonson's *Sejanus His Fall.*
Florio's translation of
    Montaigne's *Essays.*

1604

Treaty of Peace with Spain.   *Measure for Measure.*
                                              Othello.

1605

The Gunpowder Plot.   *King Lear.*
Middleton's *A Trick to Catch
    the Old One.*

1606

Jonson's *Volpone.*   *Macbeth.*

1607

Settlement of Jamestown,   *Antony and Cleopatra.*
    Virginia.   *Timon of Athens.*
Beaumont's *The Knight of the*   Shakespeare's daughter Susanna
    Burning Pestle.   married to Dr. John Hall.

1608

Burbage leases Blackfriars'   *Coriolanus.*
    Theatre for Shakespeare's   *Pericles, Prince of Tyre.*
    company.
John Milton born.

1609

Beaumont and Fletcher's
  Philaster.

Shakespeare's *Sonnets* published.

1610

Beaumont and Fletcher's
  Maid's Tragedy.

Cymbeline.

1611

Chapman completes translation
  of the *Iliad*.
Authorized version of
  The Bible.

The Winter's Tale.
The Tempest.

1612

Death of Prince Henry.
Beaumont retires from the
  theatre.
Webster's *The White Devil*.
Shelton's translation of
  Don Quixote, Part I.

1613

Globe Theatre burned.
Marriage of Princess Elizabeth
  to the Elector Palatine.

Henry VIII (with Fletcher).
The Two Noble Kinsmen (with
  Fletcher).
Buys a house in Blackfriars.

1614

Globe Theatre rebuilt.
Jonson's *Bartholomew Fair*.
Webster's *The Duchess of
  Malfi*.

1616

Death of Beaumont and
  Cervantes.
Jonson publishes his plays in a
  single volume entitled
  The Works of Ben Jonson.

Marriage of Judith Shakespeare
  to Thomas Quiney.
Death of Shakespeare, April 23.

1623

Publication of the Folio edition
  of Shakespeare's plays.

Death of Anne Hathaway.

Shakespeare's Theatre

BY STUART VAUGHAN

"The play in manuscript is only a blueprint for its performance in the theatre." This thought, whoever first gave voice to it, must have been one of Shakespeare's assumptions, for he took no care about the publishing of his work. He wrote plays to be acted, not to be read. These plays are as related to the theatre of Shakespeare's day as a shooting script is to modern film techniques. The structural evolution of that theatre, and the way it was used, profoundly influenced the nature of the plays themselves.

The simplest theatre of the Middle Ages was the platform of boards placed on trestles in the center of a town square. A frame at the back of the stage provided a place for the actors to be concealed and from which to make their entrances. Sometimes the sides of the platform were curtained off so that the area under the stage could be used for dressing space. The platform was about five feet high in order that the audience standing around on three sides of the stage could see with fair comfort. In such simple surroundings, the text of the play had to tell the audience where the action was placed, and the actors themselves moved the few pieces of furniture in full view of the audience, since there was no provision for a front curtain, nor had anyone yet thought of that idea. Here already are the basic elements of Shakespeare's stage.

When, instead of passing the hat among the gathered audience, admission was charged to the enclosed yard of an inn, the other elements of the Elizabethan theatre had come together. Members of the audience still stood around the stage; but all about the circular courtyard more comfortable places were available—seats placed at the various windows and balconies of the inn, providing more ease and better visibility. In touring, James Burbage, the leading manager of the day,

19

had made enough money to build a real theatre for plays. He had no precedent to follow but the shape of the inn yards he knew so well, and so he made his first building, The Theatre, in the circular shape which became the model for the subsequent public playhouses of this period.

Drawings and descriptions which have come down to us are not very definitive. Deductions from the plays themselves, along with such contemporary information as we do possess, have given us some notion of the form and use of this theatre. There were several tiers of galleries around the yard or "pit." These held the best places, and the occupants of these areas could sit and still see over the heads of the "groundlings" who gathered, standing in the pit, around the stage, which was still about five feet above ground level. The stage projected out into the pit, and was surrounded on at least three sides by audience. The galleries were roofed, and the stage was partially covered by a roof called "the shadow," but the standees in the pit were exposed to the open sky, which was the chief source of light for the plays. Performances took place at three in the afternoon.

There was some kind of permanent architectural background for the stage, with one large opening which revealed an area sometimes called "the inner stage." This opening was probably curtained, and most authorities conjecture that it was used for "discoveries," when the curtain could be drawn back to reveal a tableau, or a scene already set and in progress. It is doubtful that scenes of any length were played there, however, since, in order for the whole audience to see, the action would have been eventually brought down onto the projecting platform, or "forestage." There were at least two other doors, at the right and left of this large opening, which provided access to the stage. There was also an area above this main opening, probably some sort of gallery stretching along the back wall, where scenes could be played. Above that was a gallery for musicians.

Large properties, like beds or thrones, were probably discovered on the inner stage, but there was another means of moving furniture, dead bodies, or set pieces. "Mutes," or nonspeaking actors, were employed. They were probably masked and wore a conventional livery. They were the servants of the stage, and were either accepted as invisible by the audience, or functioned as servants, soldiers, or in similar capacities, carrying out necessary tasks like throne-moving or wine-pouring.

We are not sure what physical changes were made on the stage as the plays proceeded rapidly from, say, forest to castle to shipboard. We know that there were no intermissions or other interruptions in the performance. As actors for one scene left the stage, others for the next scene were already entering. Perhaps signs were hung denoting, for example, "The Boar's Head Tavern," but the dialogue is always so clear about change of locale that these seem hardly necessary. Certainly most objects needed on the stage had to be of a portable nature. Certainly the pattern of physical action must have been in constant flux, like the turning of a wheel, to permit all members of the audience to see. The stage thus presented a continual flow of movement, not a series of static framed pictures.

The actors and the audience were in close contact. Indeed, certain noblemen were permitted to sit on the stage itself, apparently within arms' reach of the action. The actors' costumes were elaborate and expensive, to bear such close and sophisticated scrutiny, but to our eyes they would have presented a strange mixture of attempted historical accuracy and contemporary elegance. Shakespeare's theatre did not try to ignore the problem of presenting Romans who looked like Romans, but apparently neither actors nor public had a very clear idea of what Romans looked like.

We are dealing, then, with an active, exciting spectacle, presented on a very flexible stage which can stimulate the audience's imagination. We go into a movie theatre and are transported by two-dimensional images flashed on a silvered fabric. The Elizabethan audience watched and listened around a wooden platform where as great a transformation was possible through the mind's activity.

The truly complete production of Shakespeare today should permit the same speed of presentation, the same kind of physical action, the same actor-audience intimacy, and a similar imaginative participation on the part of the audience. In the last century elaborate scenic productions became the rule, but great waits for scene changes and large theatres demanding slow elocution necessitated vastly cut versions of the plays. The modern theatre has tried various means of getting back to Shakespeare. The "space stage" technique involves a stage bare of all but steps and platforms. Flexible lighting is relied on for change of locale and emphasis. The "unit set" provides basic walls and other pieces which, by means of simple and rapid adjustments, can be converted into a somewhat differently shaped acting area for each of a number of scenes. Revolving stages change more realistic scenery rapidly. Structural stages have been built which provide simple doors and platforms, giving us Shakespeare's acting space without his décor. Reconstructions of Elizabethan stages have been built and used. Various combinations of all these methods have been tried. Each director will make his own personal choice of method in realizing the particular play he is working on. If he is doing his job well, he will be in search of the best way he can to achieve his author's impact and intention with the means at his disposal in today's theatre.

KING LEAR

CHARACTERS

LEAR, *king of Britain.*
KING OF FRANCE.
DUKE OF BURGUNDY.
DUKE OF CORNWALL, *married to Regan.*
DUKE OF ALBANY, *married to Goneril.*
EARL OF KENT.
EARL OF GLOUCESTER.
EDGAR, *son of Gloucester.*
EDMUND, *bastard son of Gloucester.*
CURAN, *a courtier.*
OSWALD, *steward of Goneril.*
OLD MAN, *tenant of Gloucester.*
DOCTOR.
FOOL.

A CAPTAIN *employed by Edmund.*
GENTLEMAN *attendant on Cordelia.*
A HERALD.
SERVANTS *of Cornwall.*
GONERIL
REGAN   } *daughters of Lear.*
CORDELIA
KNIGHTS *of Lear's train,* CAPTAINS, MESSENGERS, SOLDIERS, *and* ATTENDANTS.

SCENE: *Ancient Britain.*

ACT I

SCENE 1. The Great Hall of Lear's palace.

(KENT and GLOUCESTER enter in conversation, followed by EDMUND, who stands aside.)

KENT.

I thought the king had more affected* the Duke   favored
of Albany than Cornwall.

GLOUCESTER.

It did always seem so to us: but now, in the division of the kingdom, it appears not which of the
dukes he values most; for equalities are so weighed,
that curiosity* in neither can make choice of   scrutiny
either's moiety.*¹   share

KENT.

Is not this your son, my lord?

GLOUCESTER.

His breeding, sir, hath been at my charge:* I have   expense
so often blushed to acknowledge him, that now   10
I am brazed to* it.   brazen about

KENT.

I cannot conceive you.

GLOUCESTER.

Sir, this young fellow's mother could: whereupon
she grew round-wombed, and had, indeed, sir,
a son for her cradle ere she had a husband for
her bed. Do you smell a fault?

KENT.

I cannot wish the fault undone, the issue of it being so proper.*   handsome

25

GLOUCESTER.

But I have, sir, a son by order of law, some year
elder than this, who yet is no dearer in my ac- 20
count: though this knave came something saucily
into the world before he was sent for, yet was his
mother fair; there was good sport at his making,
and the whoreson* must be acknowledged.   bastard
   (*To* EDMUND.)

Do you know this noble gentleman, Edmund?

EDMUND (*stepping forward*).

No, my lord.

GLOUCESTER.

My lord of Kent: remember him hereafter as my
honorable friend.

EDMUND.

My services to your lordship.

KENT.

I must love you, and sue to know you better.   30

EDMUND.

Sir, I shall study deserving.*   *i.e.,* deserving
                                       your love

GLOUCESTER.

He hath been out* nine years, and away he shall   abroad
again. (*The trumpets sound.*) The king is coming.
   (*As the fanfare continues, an* ATTENDANT *enters
   bearing a crown. He is followed by* KING LEAR,
   the Dukes of ALBANY *and* CORNWALL, *the king's
   daughters,* GONERIL, REGAN, *and* CORDELIA, *and* AT-
   TENDANTS.*)

LEAR (*to* GLOUCESTER).

Attend the lords of France and Burgundy,
Gloucester.

GLOUCESTER.

I shall, my liege.
   (GLOUCESTER *leaves, attended by* EDMUND.)

LEAR.

Meantime we shall express our darker purpose.
Give me the map there.

(ATTENDANTS *step forward with a large map*.)

                Know that we have divided
In three our kingdom: and 'tis our fast intent
To shake all cares and business from our age;   40
Conferring them on younger strengths, while we
Unburthened crawl toward death.

                      Our son of Cornwall,
And you, our no less loving son of Albany,
We have this hour a constant will to publish
Our daughters' several dowers, that future strife
May be prevented now. The princes, France and
    Burgundy,
Great rivals in our youngest daughter's love,
Long in our court have made their amorous so-
    journ,
And here are to be answered.

                   Tell me, my daughters—
Since now we will divest us, both of rule,   50
Interest of territory, cares of state—
Which of you shall we say doth love us most
That we our largest bounty may extend
Where nature* doth with merit challenge?[2] Gon-   **natural affection**
    eril,
Our eldest-born, speak first.

GONERIL.

    Sir, I love you more than words can wield* the   **express**
        matter;
    Dearer than eye-sight, space, and liberty;[3]
    Beyond what can be valued, rich or rare;
    No less than life, with grace, health, beauty, honor;
    As much as child e'er loved, or father found;   60
    A love that makes breath poor, and speech un-
        able;
    Beyond all manner of so much I love you.

CORDELIA (*aside*).

    What shall Cordelia do? Love, and be silent.

LEAR (*indicating regions on map*).

    Of all these bounds, even from this line to this,

With shadowy forests and with champains*   plains
   riched,
With plenteous rivers and wide-skirted meads,*   grassland
We make thee lady: to thine and Albany's issue
Be this perpetual.
                What says our second daughter,
Our dearest Regan, wife to Cornwall? Speak.

REGAN.

Sir, I am made   70
Of the self-same metal that my sister is,
And prize* me at her worth. In my true heart   value
I find she names my very deed of* love;   actual
Only she comes too short: that* I profess   in that
Myself an enemy to all other joys,
Which the most precious square* of sense pos-   criterion
   sesses;
And find I am alone felicitate*   happy
In your dear highness' love.

CORDELIA (*aside*).   Then poor Cordelia!
And yet not so; since, I am sure, my love's
More richer than my tongue.   80

LEAR (*again indicating on map*).

To thee and thine hereditary ever
Remain this ample third of our fair kingdom;
No less in space, validity, and pleasure,
Than that conferred on Goneril.
                      Now, our joy,
Although the last, not least; to whose young love
The vines of France and milk of Burgundy
Strive to be interested; what can you say to draw
A third more opulent than your sisters? Speak.

CORDELIA.

Nothing, my lord.

LEAR.

Nothing!   90

CORDELIA.

Nothing.

LEAR.

Nothing will come of nothing: speak again.

CORDELIA.

Unhappy that I am, I cannot heave
My heart into my mouth: I love your majesty
According to my bond:* nor more nor less.   duty

LEAR.

How, how, Cordelia! Mend your speech a little,
Lest it may mar your fortunes.

CORDELIA.   Good my lord,
You have begot me, bred me, loved me: I
Return those duties back as are right fit,
Obey you, love you, and most honor you.   100
Why have my sisters husbands, if they say
They love you all? Haply, when I shall wed,
That lord whose hand must take my plight shall
   carry
Half my love with him, half my care and duty:
Sure, I shall never marry like my sisters,
To love my father all.*   only

LEAR.

But goes thy heart with this?

CORDELIA.   Ay, good my lord.

LEAR.

So young, and so untender?

CORDELIA.

So young, my lord, and true.

LEAR.

Let it be so; thy truth, then, be thy dower—   110
For, by the sacred radiance of the sun,
The mysteries of Hecate,⁴ and the night;
By all the operation* of the orbs*   influence/
From whom we do exist, and cease to be: stars
Here I disclaim all my paternal care,
Propinquity and property* of blood,   identity
And as a stranger to my heart and me
Hold thee, from this, for ever. The barbarous
   Scythian,⁵

Or he that makes his generation* messes*   offspring/food
To gorge his appetite, shall to my bosom   120
Be as well neighbored, pitied, and relieved,
As thou my sometime daughter.

KENT.   Good my liege—

LEAR.

Peace, Kent!
Come not between the dragon and his wrath.⁶
I loved her most, and thought to set my rest
On her kind nursery.*⁷ Hence, and avoid my   care
   sight!
So be my grave my peace, as here I give
Her father's heart from her!
                       Call France; who stirs?
Call Burgundy. (ATTENDANTS *leave.*) Cornwall
   and Albany,
With my two daughters' dowers digest this third: 130
Let pride, which she calls plainness,*marry her.   frankness
I do invest you jointly with my power,
Pre-eminence, and all the large effects*   display
That troop with majesty.
                      Ourself, by monthly course,
With reservation of an hundred knights,
By you to be sustained, shall our abode
Make with you by due turns. Only we still retain
The name, and all the additions* to a king;   titles
The sway, revènue, execution of the rest,
Belovèd sons, be yours: which to confirm,   140
This coronet part betwixt you.
   (*Takes crown from* ATTENDANT *and gives it to*
   CORNWALL *and* ALBANY.)

KENT.   Royal Lear,
Whom I have ever honored as my king,
Loved as my father, as my master followed,
As my great patron thought on in my prayers—

LEAR.

The bow is bent and drawn, make* from the   keep
   shaft.   away

KENT.

Let it fall rather, though the fork* invade   arrowhead
The region of my heart: be Kent unmannerly,
When Lear is mad. What wilt thou do, old man?
Think'st thou that duty shall have dread to speak,
When power to flattery bows? To plainness hon-
  or's bound,   150
When majesty stoops to folly. Reverse thy doom;
And, in thy best consideration, check
This hideous rashness: answer my life my judg-
  ment,
Thy youngest daughter does not love thee least;
Nor are those empty-hearted whose low sound
Reverbs* no hollowness.   reverberates
                                                                  with

LEAR.   Kent, on thy life, no more.

KENT.

My life I never held but as a pawn
To wage* against thy enemies; nor fear to lose it,   stake
Thy safety being the motive.

LEAR.   Out of my sight!

KENT.

See better, Lear; and let me still remain   160
The true blank* of thine eye.   target

LEAR.

Now, by Apollo—

KENT.   Now, by Apollo, king,
Thou swear'st thy gods in vain.

LEAR.   O, vassal! Miscreant!
  (*Laying his hand on his sword.*)

ALBANY.   } Dear sir, forbear.
CORNWALL. }

KENT.

Do;
Kill thy physician, and the fee bestow
Upon thy foul disease. Revoke thy doom;
Or, whilst I can vent clamor from my throat,
I'll tell thee thou dost evil.

LEAR.   Hear me, recreant!
  On thine allegiance, hear me!   170
  Since thou hast sought to make us break our vow,
  Which we durst never yet, and with strained
     pride
  To come between our sentence and our power,
  Which nor our nature nor our place can bear,
  Our potency* made good, take thy reward.   power
  Five days we do allot thee, for provision
  To shield thee from diseases of the world;
  And on the sixth to turn thy hated back
  Upon our kingdom: if, on the tenth day follow-
     ing,
  Thy banished trunk be found in our dominions,   180
  The moment is thy death.
                 Away! By Jupiter,
  This shall not be revoked.[8]

KENT.
  Fare thee well, king: sith thus thou wilt appear,
  Freedom lives hence, and banishment is here.
    (*To* CORDELIA.)
  The gods to their dear shelter take thee, maid,
  That justly think'st, and hast most rightly said!
    (*To* REGAN *and* GONERIL.)
  And your large speeches may your deeds approve
  That good effects may spring from words of
     love.
    (*To all.*)
  Thus Kent, O princes, bids you all adieu;
  He'll shape his old course in a country new.   190
    (*He goes.*)
    (*A flourish of trumpets.* GLOUCESTER *returns
    with the King of* FRANCE *and the Duke of*
    BURGUNDY, *followed by* ATTENDANTS.)

GLOUCESTER.
  Here's France and Burgundy, my noble lord.

LEAR.
  My lord of Burgundy,

We first address towards you, who with this
    king
Hath rivalled for our daughter: what, in the least,
Will you require in present dower with her,
Or cease your quest of love?

BURGUNDY.   Most royal majesty,
I crave no more than what your highness offered,
Nor will you tender less.

LEAR.   Right noble Burgundy,
When she was dear to us, we did hold her so;
But now her price is fall'n. Sir, there she stands: 200
If aught within that little seeming substance,⁹
Or all of it, with our displeasure pieced,
And nothing more, may fitly like your grace,
She's there, and she is yours.

BURGUNDY.   I know no answer.

LEAR.

Will you, with those infirmities she owes,*   owns
Unfriended, new-adopted to our hate,
Dowered with our curse, and strangered with our
    oath,
Take her, or leave her?

BURGUNDY.   Pardon me, royal sir;
Election* makes not up on such conditions.   choice

LEAR.

Then leave her, sir; for, by the power that made
    me,   210
I tell you all her wealth.
   (*To* FRANCE.) For* you, great king,   as for
I would not from your love make such a stray,
To match you where I hate; therefore beseech
    you
To avert* your liking a more worthier way   direct
Than on a wretch whom nature is ashamed
Almost to acknowledge hers.

FRANCE.   This is most strange,
That she, that even but now was your best object,

The argument* of your praise, balm of your   subject
   age,
Most best, most dearest, should in this trice*of   instant
   time
Commit a thing so monstrous, to dismantle   220
So many folds of favor. Sure, her offense
Must be of such unnatural degree,
That monsters it,* or your fore-vouched affection   makes it
                                      monstrous
Fallen into taint:* which to believe of her,   decay
Must be a faith that reason without miracle
Could never plant in me.

CORDELIA.   I yet beseech your majesty—
If for I want that glib and oily art,
To speak and purpose* not; since what I well   mean it
   intend,
I'll do 't before I speak—that you make known
It is no vicious blot, murder, or foulness,   230
No unchaste action, or dishonored step,
That hath deprived me of your grace and favor;
But even for want of that for which I am richer,
A still*-soliciting eye, and such a tongue   ever
As I am glad I have not, though not to have it
Hath lost me in your liking.

LEAR.   Better thou
Hadst not been born than not to have pleased me
   better.

FRANCE.
Is it but this—a tardiness in nature
Which often leaves the history unspoke
That it intends to do? My Lord of Burgundy,   240
What say you to the lady? Love's not love
When it is mingled with regards that stand
Aloof from the entire point.[10] Will you have her?
She is herself a dowry.

BURGUNDY.   Royal Lear,
Give but that portion which yourself proposed,
And here I take Cordelia by the hand,
Duchess of Burgundy.

LEAR.

Nothing: I have sworn; I am firm.

BURGUNDY.

I am sorry, then, you have so lost a father
That you must lose a husband.

CORDELIA.   Peace be with Burgundy!   250
Since that respects* of fortune are his love,   considerations
I shall not be his wife.

FRANCE.

Fairest Cordelia, that art most rich, being poor;
Most choice, forsaken; and most loved, despised!
Thee and thy virtues here I seize upon:
Be it lawful I take up what's cast away.
Gods, gods! 'Tis strange that from their cold'st
    neglect
My love should kindle to inflamed respect.
Thy dowerless daughter, king, thrown to my
    chance,
Is queen of us, of ours, and our fair France: 260
Not all the dukes of waterish Burgundy
Can buy this unprized precious maid of me.
Bid them farewell, Cordelia, though unkind:
Thou losest here, a better where to find.

LEAR.

Thou hast her, France: let her be thine; for we
Have no such daughter, nor shall ever see
That face of hers again. Therefore be gone
Without our grace, our love, our benison.*   blessing
    Come, noble Burgundy.
    (*A flourish of trumpets.* LEAR *leaves, followed
    by the court. Only the King of* FRANCE, GONERIL,
    REGAN, *and* CORDELIA *remain.*)

FRANCE.

Bid farewell to your sisters.   270

CORDELIA.

The jewels of our father, with washed eyes
Cordelia leaves you: I know you what you are;
And like a sister am most loath to call

Your faults as they are named. Use well our
    father:
To your professèd bosoms I commit him.   *professing*
But yet, alas, stood I within his grace,
I would prefer* him to a better place.   *recommend*
So, farewell to you both.

REGAN.
Prescribe not us our duties.

GONERIL.   Let your study
Be to content your lord, who hath received you   280
At fortune's alms.[11] You have obedience scanted,
And well are worth the want that you have
    wanted.[12]

CORDELIA.
Time shall unfold what plaited* cunning hides: *folded*
Who cover faults, at last shame them derides.
Well may you prosper!

FRANCE.   Come, my fair Cordelia.
    (*The King of* FRANCE *and* CORDELIA *go.*)

GONERIL.
Sister, it is not a little I have to say of what most
nearly appertains to us both. I think our father
will hence tonight.

REGAN.
That's most certain, and with you; next month   290
with us.

GONERIL.
You see how full of changes his age is; the obser-
vation we have made of it hath not been little: he
always loved our sister most; and with what poor
judgment he hath now cast her off appears too
grossly.*   *obviously*

REGAN.
'Tis the infirmity of his age: yet he hath ever but
slenderly known himself.

GONERIL.
The best and soundest of his time* hath been but   *lifetime*
rash; then must we look to receive from his age,   299

not alone the imperfections of long-engraffed* condition, but therewithal the unruly wayward-nesss that infirm and choleric years bring with them.

REGAN.

Such unconstant starts* are we like to have from him as this of Kent's banishment.

GONERIL.

There is further compliment* of leave-taking be-tween France and him. Pray you, let's hit to-gether:* if our father carry authority with such dispositions as he bears, this last surrender of his will but offend us.

REGAN.

We shall further think on 't.

GONERIL.

We must do something, and i' the heat.*
(*They leave.*)

Margin glosses: engrafted / sudden whims / ceremony / agree / 310 / while the iron is hot

SCENE 2. The Earl of Gloucester's castle. A courtyard.

(EDMUND *enters with a letter in his hand.*)

EDMUND.

Thou, nature, art my goddess; to thy law
My services are bound. Wherefore should I
Stand in the plague* of custom, and permit
The curiosity* of nations to deprive me,
For that I am some twelve or fourteen moonshines
Lag of* a brother? Why bastard? Wherefore
   base?
When my dimensions are as well compact,
My mind as generous, and my shape as true,
As honest* madam's issue? Why brand they us
With base? With baseness? Bastardy? Base,
   base?

Margin glosses: the victim / fine distinctions / behind / chaste / 10

Who, in the lusty stealth of nature, take
More composition and fierce quality
Than doth, within a dull, stale, tired bed,
Go to the creating a whole tribe of fops,
Got 'tween asleep and wake? Well, then,
Legitimate Edgar, I must have your land:
Our father's love is to the bastard Edmund
As to the legitimate: fine word—legitimate!
Well, my legitimate, if this letter speed,*   succeeds
And my invention thrive, Edmund the base   20
Shall top the legitimate. I grow; I prosper:
Now, gods, stand up for bastards!

   (GLOUCESTER *enters from the far side of the court.*)

GLOUCESTER.

Kent banished thus! And France in choler*   anger
   parted!
And the king gone tonight! Subscribed* his   signed
   power!   away
Confined to exhibition!* All this done   an allowance
Upon the gad!*   spur of the
                                                   moment
   (*Seeing* EDMUND.)
                  Edmund, how now! What news?

EDMUND (*as if attempting to conceal the letter*).

So please your lordship, none.

GLOUCESTER.

Why so earnestly seek you to put up that letter?

EDMUND.

I know no news, my lord.

GLOUCESTER.

What paper were you reading?   30

EDMUND.

Nothing, my lord.

GLOUCESTER.

No? What needed, then, that terrible dispatch*   haste
of it into your pocket? The quality of nothing
hath not such need to hide itself. Let's see: come,
if it be nothing, I shall not need spectacles.

EDMUND.

I beseech you, sir, pardon me: it is a letter from
my brother, that I have not all o'er-read; and for
so much as I have perused, I find it not fit for
your o'er-looking.   40

GLOUCESTER.

Give me the letter, sir.

EDMUND.

I shall offend, either to detain or give it. The contents, as in part I understand them, are to blame.

GLOUCESTER.

Let's see, let's see.

EDMUND (*handing the letter over*).

I hope, for my brother's justification, he wrote this
but as an essay* or taste of my virtue.   test

GLOUCESTER (*reads*).

"This policy and* reverence of age makes the   of
world bitter to the best of our times; keeps our   50
fortunes from us till our oldness cannot relish
them. I begin to find an idle and fond* bondage   foolish
in the oppression of aged tyranny; who sways, not
as it hath power, but as it is suffered. Come to me,
that of this I may speak more. If our father would
sleep till I waked him, you should enjoy half his
revenue for ever, and live the beloved of your
brother,   EDGAR."

Hum—conspiracy!—"Sleep till I waked him—
you should enjoy half his revenue"—My son
Edgar! Had he a hand to write this? A heart   60
and brain to breed it in?—
    When came this to you? Who brought it?

EDMUND.

It was not brought me, my lord; there's the cunning of it; I found it thrown in at the casement of
my closet.*   room

GLOUCESTER.

You know the character* to be your brother's?   handwriting

EDMUND.

If the matter were good, my lord, I durst swear it
were his; but, in respect of that, I would fain think
it were not.   70

GLOUCESTER.

It is his.

EDMUND.

It is his hand, my lord; but I hope his heart is not
in the contents.

GLOUCESTER.

Hath he never heretofore sounded you in this
business?

EDMUND.

Never, my lord: but I have heard him oft maintain
it to be fit, that, sons at perfect age,* and fathers   of age
declining, the father should be as ward to the son,
and the son manage his revenue.

GLOUCESTER.

O villain, villain! His very opinion in the letter!   80
Abhorred villain! Unnatural, detested, brutish villain! Worse than brutish! Go, sirrah, seek him;
I'll apprehend him: abominable villain! Where is
he?

EDMUND.

I do not well know, my lord. If it shall please you
to suspend your indignation against my brother
till you can derive from him better testimony of
his intent, you shall run a certain course; where,*   whereas
if you violently proceed against him, mistaking
his purpose, it would make a great gap in your   90
own honor, and shake in pieces the heart of his
obedience. I dare pawn down my life for him,
that he hath wrote this to feel* my affection to   test
your honor, and to no further pretense of danger.*   dangerous
                                                          intent
GLOUCESTER.

Think you so?

EDMUND.

If your honor judge it meet, I will place you

where you shall hear us confer of this, and by an
auricular assurance have your satisfaction; and that   100
without any further delay than this very evening.

GLOUCESTER.

He cannot be such a monster—

EDMUND.

Nor is not, sure.

GLOUCESTER.

To his father, that so tenderly and entirely loves
him. Heaven and earth! Edmund, seek him out;
wind me* into him, I pray you: frame the busi-   worm
ness after your own wisdom. I would unstate my-   yourself
self, to be in a due resolution.[13]

EDMUND.

I will seek him, sir, presently; convey* the busi-   manage
ness as I shall find means, and acquaint you withal.   111

GLOUCESTER.

These late eclipses in the sun and moon portend
no good to us: though the wisdom of nature* can   i.e.,
reason it thus and thus, yet nature finds itself   science
scourged by the sequent effects:[14] love cools,
friendship falls off, brothers divide; in cities,
mutinies;* in countries, discord; in palaces, trea-   riots
son; and the bond cracked 'twixt son and father.
This villain of mine comes under the prediction:
there's son against father; the king falls from bias   120
of nature; there's father against child. We have
seen the best of our time: machinations, hollowness, treachery, and all ruinous disorders, follow
us disquietly to our graves.

   Find out this villain, Edmund; it shall lose thee
nothing; do it carefully. And the noble and true-
hearted Kent banished! His offense, honesty! 'Tis
strange.

   (*He goes.*)

EDMUND.

This is the excellent foppery* of the world, that,   folly
when we are sick in fortune—often the surfeit

of* our own behavior—we make guilty of our indiges-
tion from disasters the sun, the moon, and the stars: as if we were villains by necessity; fools by heavenly compulsion; knaves, thieves, and treachers,* by spherical traitors predominance;[15] drunkards, liars, and adulterers, by an enforced obedience of planetary influence; and all that we are evil in, by a divine thrusting on: an admirable evasion of whoremaster man, to lay his goatish* disposition to the charge of a star! lustful My father compounded with my mother under 140 the dragon's tail; and my nativity was under Ursa major; so that it follows, I am rough and lecherous. Tut, I should have been that* I am, had the what maidenliest star in the firmament twinkled on my bastardizing. Edgar—

(EDGAR *enters from the opposite side of the court.*)

and pat he comes like the catastrophe of the old comedy: my cue is villainous melancholy, with a sigh like Tom o' Bedlam.[16] O, these eclipses do portend these divisions! Fa, sol, la, mi.

EDGAR.

How now, brother Edmund! What serious con- 150 templation are you in?

EDMUND.

I am thinking, brother, of a prediction I read this other day, what should follow these eclipses.

EDGAR.

Do you busy yourself about that?

EDMUND.

I promise you, the effects he writes of succeed unhappily; as of unnaturalness between the child and the parent; death, dearth, dissolutions of ancient amities; divisions in state, menaces and maledic- 160 tions against king and nobles; needless diffidences,* suspicions banishment of friends, dissipation of cohorts,* troops nuptial breaches, and I know not what.

EDGAR.

How long have you been a sectary* astronomical?   devotee

EDMUND.

Come, come; when saw you my father last?

EDGAR.

Why, the night gone by.

EDMUND.

Spake you with him?

EDGAR.

Ay, two hours together.   170

EDMUND.

Parted you in good terms? Found you no displeasure in him by word or countenance?

EDGAR.

None at all.

EDMUND.

Bethink yourself wherein you may have offended
him: and at my entreaty forbear* his presence till   avoid
some little time hath qualified the heat of his displeasure; which at this instant so rageth in him,
that with the mischief of your person it would
scarcely allay.

EDGAR.

Some villain hath done me wrong.   180

EDMUND.

That's my fear. I pray you, have a continent*   restrained
forbearance till the speed of his rage goes slower;
and, as I say, retire with me to my lodging, from
whence I will fitly bring you to hear my lord
speak. (*Giving him a key.*) Pray ye, go; there's
my key: if you do stir abroad, go armed.

EDGAR.

Armed, brother!

EDMUND.

Brother, I advise you to the best; go armed: I am
no honest man if there be any good meaning towards you: I have told you what I have seen and   190

heard; but faintly, nothing like the image and hor-
ror* of it: pray you, away.   horrible
                                                                truth
EDGAR.

Shall I hear from you anon?

EDMUND.

I do serve you in this business.
   (EDGAR *goes.*)
A credulous father! And a brother noble,
Whose nature is so far from doing harms,
That he suspects none; on whose foolish honesty
My practices ride easy! I see the business.
Let me, if not by birth, have lands by wit:
All with me's meet that I can fashion fit.   200
   (*He leaves.*)

SCENE 3. Chamber in the Duke of Albany's palace.

(GONERIL *enters with* OSWALD, *her steward.*)

GONERIL.

Did my father strike my gentleman for chiding of
his fool?

OSWALD.

Yes, madam.

GONERIL.

By day and night he wrongs me; every hour
He flashes into one gross crime* or other,   fault
That sets us all at odds: I'll not endure it:
His knights grow riotous, and himself upbraids us
On every trifle. When he returns from hunting,
I will not speak with him; say I am sick:
If you come slack* of former services,   fall short
You shall do well; the fault of it I'll answer.   10
   (*Hunting horns sound from the courtyard.*)

OSWALD.

He's coming, madam; I hear him.

GONERIL.

Put on what weary negligence you please,
You and your fellows; I'd have it come to question:*   force the issue
If he dislike it, let him to our sister,
Whose mind and mine, I know, in that are one,
Not to be overruled. Idle old man,
That still would manage those authorities
That he hath given away! Now, by my life,
Old fools are babes again; and must be used
With checks* as* flatteries—when they are   rebukes/as well as
    seen abused.
Remember what I tell you.   21

OSWALD.   Well, madam.

GONERIL.

And let his knights have colder looks among you;
What grows of it, no matter; advise your fellows
    so:
I would breed from hence occasions, and I shall
That I may speak: I'll write straight to my sister,
To hold my very course. Prepare for dinner.
    (*They leave.*)

SCENE 4. The hall in Albany's palace.

(KENT *enters, disguised in gray beard and rough country dress.*)

KENT.

If but as well I other accents borrow,
That can my speech defuse,* my good intent   disguise
May carry through itself to that full issue
For which I razed* my likeness.* Now, banished   erased/identity
    Kent,
If thou canst serve where thou dost stand condemned,
So may it come, thy master, whom thou lovest,
Shall find thee full of labors.

(*Hunting horns sound again.* LEAR *enters, with* KNIGHTS *and* ATTENDANTS.)

LEAR.

Let me not stay a jot for dinner; go get it ready.
    (*As an* ATTENDANT *leaves, turning to* KENT.)
How now! What art thou?   10

KENT (*using a rural dialect*).

A man, sir.

LEAR.

What dost thou profess?* What wouldst thou is your
with us?   profession

KENT.

I do profess to be no less than I seem; to serve him
truly that will put me in trust; to love him that is
honest; to converse* with him that is wise, and associate
says little; to fear judgment; to fight when I cannot choose; and to eat no fish.[17]

LEAR.

What art thou?

KENT.

A very honest-hearted fellow, and as poor as the
king.   20

LEAR.

If thou be as poor for a subject as he is for a king,
thou art poor enough. What wouldst thou?

KENT.

Service.

LEAR.

Who wouldst thou serve?

KENT.

You.

LEAR.

Dost thou know me, fellow?

KENT.

No, sir; but you have that in your countenance
which I would fain call master.   30

LEAR.

What's that?

KENT.

Authority.

LEAR.

What services canst thou do?

KENT.

I can keep honest counsel, ride, run, mar a curious*   elaborate
tale in telling it, and deliver a plain message bluntly:
that which ordinary men are fit for, I am qualified
in; and the best of me is diligence.

LEAR.

How old art thou?

KENT.

Not so young, sir, to love a woman for singing,   40
nor so old to dote on her for any thing: I have
years on my back forty-eight.

LEAR.

Follow me; thou shalt serve me: if I like thee no
worse after dinner, I will not part from thee yet.
    Dinner, ho, dinner! Where's my knave? My
fool? Go you, and call my fool hither.
        (ATTENDANT *leaves*.)
        (*To* OSWALD *as he enters*.)
You, you, sirrah, where's my daughter?

OSWALD.

So please you—(*Without stopping,* OSWALD *goes
    out*.)

LEAR.

What says the fellow there? Call the clotpoll*   blockhead
back. (*A* KNIGHT *follows* OSWALD *out*.) Where's   51
my fool, ho? I think the world's asleep.
        (*The* KNIGHT *returns*.)
How now! Where's that mongrel?

KNIGHT.

He says, my lord, your daughter is not well.

LEAR.

Why came not the slave back to me when I called
him.

KNIGHT.

Sir, he answered me in the roundest* manner, he
would not.

plainest

LEAR.

He would not!

60

KNIGHT.

My lord, I know not what the matter is; but, to
my judgment, your highness is not entertained
with that ceremonious affection as you were wont;
there's a great abatement of kindness appears* as
well in the general dependents as in the duke himself also and your daughter.

that appears

LEAR.

Ha! Sayest thou so?

KNIGHT.

I beseech you, pardon me, my lord, if I be mis-
taken; for my duty cannot be silent when I think
your highness wronged.

70

LEAR.

Thou but rememberest* me of mine own conception:* I have perceived a most faint* neglect of
late; which I have rather blamed as mine own
jealous curiosity* than as a very pretense and purpose of unkindness: I will look further into 't.
But where's my fool? I have not seen him this two
days.

remindest

idea/ cold

suspicions

KNIGHT.

Since my young lady's going into France, sir, the
fool hath much pined away.

80

LEAR.

No more of that; I have noted it well. (*To an*
ATTENDANT.) Go you, and tell my daughter I
would speak with her. (*To another* ATTENDANT.)
Go you, call hither my fool.
 (*Both* ATTENDANTS *leave.*)
 (OSWALD *re-enters.*)
O, you sir, you, come you hither, sir: who am I,
sir?

OSWALD.

My lady's father.

LEAR.

"My lady's father"! My lord's knave: You whoreson dog! You slave! You cur!

OSWALD.

I am none of these, my lord; I beseech your par-
don.   90

LEAR.

Do you bandy looks with me, you rascal? (*Strikes*
OSWALD.)

OSWALD.

I'll not be struck, my lord.

KENT.

Nor tripped neither, you base football player.
    (*Tripping him.*)

LEAR (*to* KENT).

I thank thee, fellow; thou servest me, and I'll love
thee.

KENT (*to* OSWALD).

Come, sir, arise, away! I'll teach you differences:*   *i.e., in*
away, away! If you will measure your lubber's*   *rank
length again, tarry: but away! Go to; have you   *lout's*
wisdom? So. (*Pushing* OSWALD *out.*)   101

LEAR.

Now, my friendly knave, I thank thee: there's
earnest* of thy service.   *advance*
    (*The* FOOL *enters as* LEAR *gives* KENT *some*   *pay*
    money.)

FOOL.

Let me hire him too: here's my coxcomb.18
    (*Offering* KENT *his cap.*)

LEAR.

How now, my pretty knave! How dost thou?

FOOL (*to* KENT).

Sirrah, you were best take my coxcomb.

KENT.

Why, fool?   110

FOOL.

Why, for taking one's part that's out of favor:
nay, an thou canst not smile as the wind sits,
thou'lt catch cold shortly:[19] there, take my coxcomb: why, this fellow has banished two on 's
daughters, and did the third a blessing against his
will; if thou follow him, thou must needs wear my
coxcomb. (*To* LEAR.) How now, nuncle![20]
Would I had two coxcombs and two daughters!

LEAR.

Why, my boy?

FOOL.

If I gave them all my living, I'd keep my coxcombs   120
myself. (*Offers his cap to* LEAR.) There's mine;
beg another of thy daughters.

LEAR.

Take heed, sirrah; the whip.[21]

FOOL.

Truth's a dog must to kennel; he must be whipped
out, when Lady the brach may stand by the fire
and stink.[22]

LEAR.

A pestilent gall to me!

FOOL.

Sirrah, I'll teach thee a speech.

LEAR.

Do.

FOOL.

Mark it, nuncle: 130
   Have more than thou showest,
   Speak less than thou knowest,
   Lend less than thou owest,*   ownest
   Ride more than thou goest,*   walkest
   Learn more than thou trowest,*   believest
   Set* less than thou throwest;   stake
   Leave thy drink and thy whore,
   And keep in-a-door,*   indoors

And thou shalt have more
    Than two tens to a score.   140

KENT.
    This is nothing, fool.

FOOL.
    Then 'tis like the breath of an unfeed lawyer; you
    gave me nothing for 't. Can you make no use of
    nothing, nuncle?

LEAR.
    Why, no, boy; nothing can be made out of nothing.

FOOL (*to* KENT).
    Prithee, tell him, so much the rent of his land
    comes to: he will not believe a fool.

LEAR.
    A bitter fool!   150

FOOL (*to* LEAR).
    Dost thou know the difference, my boy, between
    a bitter fool and a sweet fool?

LEAR.
    No, lad; teach me.

FOOL.
    That lord that counseled thee
        To give away thy land,
    Come place him here by me,
        Do thou for him stand:
    The sweet and bitter fool
        Will presently appear;
    The one in motley here,   160
        The other found out there.

LEAR.
    Dost thou call me fool, boy?

FOOL.
    All thy other titles thou hast given away; that
    thou wast born with.

KENT.
    This is not altogether fool, my lord.

FOOL.
    No, faith, lords and great men will not let me; if

I had a monopoly out,* they would have part on   *granted*
't: and ladies too, they will not let me have all fool   *me*
to myself; they'll be snatching.[23] Give me an egg,   170
nuncle, and I'll give thee two crowns.[24]

LEAR.

What two crowns shall they be?

FOOL.

Why, after I have cut the egg i' the middle, and
eat up the meat, the two crowns of the egg. When
thou clovest thy crown i' the middle, and gavest
away both parts, thou borest thy ass on thy back
o'er the dirt:[25] thou hadst little wit in thy bald
crown when thou gavest thy golden one away.
If I speak like myself* in this, let him be whipped   *i.e., a*
that first finds it so.   *fool*
                                           180
(*Singing.*)

   Fools had ne'er less wit in a year;
      For wise men are grown foppish,[26]
   They know not how their wits to wear,
      Their manners are so apish.

LEAR.

When were you wont to be so full of songs,
sirrah?

FOOL.

I have used it, nuncle, ever since thou madest thy
daughters thy mother: for when thou gavest them
the rod, and put'st down thine own breeches,   190
(*Singing.*)

   Then they for sudden joy did weep,[27]
      And I for sorrow sung,
   That such a king should play bo-peep,*   *hide-and-*
      And go the fools among.   *seek*

Prithee, nuncle, keep a schoolmaster that can teach
thy fool to lie: I would fain learn to lie.

LEAR.

An you lie, sirrah, we'll have you whipped.

FOOL.

I marvel what kin thou and thy daughters are:

they'll have me whipped for speaking true, thou'lt   200
have me whipped for lying; and sometimes I am
whipped for holding my peace. I had rather be
any kind o' thing than a fool: and yet I would not
be thee, nuncle; thou hast pared thy wit o' both
sides, and left nothing i' the middle. (*As* GONERIL
enters.) Here comes one o' the parings.

LEAR.

How now, daughter! What makes that frontlet
on? Methinks you are too much of late i' the
frown.

FOOL.

Thou wast a pretty fellow when thou hadst no   210
need to care for her frowning; now art an O*   *i.e.,* zero
without a figure. I am better than thou art now:
I am a fool, thou art nothing. (*To* GONERIL.) Yes,
forsooth, I will hold my tongue; so your face bids
me, though you say nothing. Mum, mum,
  He that keeps nor crust nor crumb,
  Weary of all, shall want some.
  (*Pointing to* LEAR.) That's a shealed pcascod.*   shelled
                                                                    peapod

GONERIL.

Not only, sir, this your all-licensed fool,   220
But other of your insolent retinue
Do hourly carp and quarrel; breaking forth
In rank and not-to-be-endurèd riots. Sir,
I had thought, by making this well known unto
  you,
To have found a safe redress; but now grow fear-
  ful,
By what yourself too late have spoke and done,
That you protect this course, and put it on*   encourage it
By your allowance; which if you should, the fault
Would not 'scape censure, nor the redresses sleep,
Which, in the tender of a wholesome weal,[28]   230
Might in their working do you that offense,
Which else were shame, that then necessity
Will call discreet proceeding.[29]

FOOL.

For, you know, nuncle,
    The hedge-sparrow fed the cuckoo so long,
    That it had it head bit off by it young.
So, out went the candle, and we were left darkling.

LEAR.

Are you our daughter?

GONERIL.

Come, sir,
I would you would make use of that good wis-
    dom,   240
Whereof* I know you are fraught;* and put   with which/
    away   freighted
These dispositions, that of late transform you
From what you rightly are.

FOOL.

May not an ass know when the cart draws the
horse? Whoop, Jug! I love thee.³⁰

LEAR.

Doth any here know me? This is not Lear:
Doth Lear walk thus? Speak thus? Where are
    his eyes?
Either his notion* weakens, his discernings   understanding
Are lethargied— Ha! waking?* 'Tis not so.   am I awake
Who is it that can tell me who I am?   250

FOOL.

Lear's shadow.

LEAR.

I would learn that; for, by the marks of sover-
eignty, knowledge, and reason, I should be false
persuaded I had daughters.

FOOL.

Which* they will make an obedient father.   whom

LEAR.

Your name, fair gentlewoman?

GONERIL.

This admiration,* sir, is much o' the savour   pretense
Of other your new pranks. I do beseech you

To understand my purposes aright: 260
As you are old and reverend, you should be wise.
Here do you keep a hundred knights and squires;
Men so disordered, so deboshed* and bold,   debauched
That this our court, infected with their manners,
Shows like a riotous inn: epicurism and lust
Make it more like a tavern or a brothel[31]
Than a graced palace. The shame itself doth
   speak.
For instant remedy: be then desired
By her, that else will take the thing she begs,   269
A little to disquantity* your train;   reduce
And the remainder, that shall still depend,*   attend
To be such men as may besort* your age,   befit
And know themselves and you.

LEAR.   Darkness and devils!
   (*To* ATTENDANTS.)
Saddle my horses; call my train together.
   (*To* GONERIL.)
Degenerate bastard! I'll not trouble thee:
Yet have I left a daughter.

GONERIL.
You strike my people; and your disordered rabble
Make servants of their betters.
   (*The Duke of* ALBANY *enters.*)

LEAR.
Woe, that too late repents—
   (*To* ALBANY.) O, sir, are you come?
Is it your will? Speak, sir.
   (*Calling to* ATTENDANTS.) Prepare my horses.   280
Ingratitude, thou marble-hearted fiend,
More hideous when thou show'st thee in a child
Than the sea-monster![32]

ALBANY.   Pray, sir, be patient.

LEAR (*to* GONERIL).
Detested kite! Thou liest:
My train are men of choice and rarest parts,
That all particulars of duty know,

And in the most exact regard support
The worships* of their name. O most small
  fault,   honor
How ugly didst thou in Cordelia show!
That, like an engine, wrenched my frame of
  nature[33]   290
From the fixed place; drew from my heart all love,
And added to the gall. O Lear, Lear, Lear!
Beat at this gate,
  (*Striking his head.*) that let thy folly in,
And thy dear judgment out!
                    Go, go, my people.

ALBANY.
My lord, I am guiltless, as I am ignorant
Of what hath moved you.

LEAR.   It may be so, my lord.
Hear, nature, hear; dear goddess, hear!
Suspend thy purpose, if thou didst intend
To make this creature fruitful!
Into her womb convey sterility!   300
Dry up in her the organs of increase;
And from her derogate* body never spring   blighted
A babe to honor her! If she must teem,*   be fruitful
Create her child of spleen;* that it may live,   malice
And be a thwart disnatured torment to her!
Let it stamp wrinkles in her brow of youth;
With cadent* tears fret channels in her cheeks;   flowing
Turn all her mother's pains and benefits
To laughter and contempt; that she may feel
How sharper than a serpent's tooth it is   310
To have a thankless child!
                   Away, away!
  (*He rushes out.*)

ALBANY.
Now, gods that we adore, whereof comes this?

GONERIL.
Never afflict yourself to know the cause;
But let his disposition have that scope
That dotage gives it.

(LEAR *re-enters.*)

LEAR.

What, fifty of my followers at a clap!
Within a fortnight!

ALBANY.   What's the matter, sir?

LEAR.

I'll tell thee.

(*To* GONERIL.) Life and death! I am ashamed
That thou hast power to shake my manhood
   thus,
That these hot tears, which break from me
   perforce,   320
Should make thee worth them. Blasts and fogs
   upon thee![34]
The untented woundings of a father's curse[35]
Pierce every sense about thee! Old fond eyes,
Beweep this cause again, I'll pluck ye out,
And cast you, with the waters that you lose,
To temper clay. Yea, is it come to this?
Let it be so: yet have I left a daughter,
Who, I am sure, is kind and comfortable:*   comforting
When she shall hear this of thee, with her nails
She'll flay thy wolvish visage. Thou shalt find   330
That I'll resume the shape which thou dost think
I have cast off for ever: thou shalt, I warrant thee.

(LEAR *leaves, followed by* KENT *and* ATTEND-
ANTS.)

GONERIL.

Do you mark that, my lord?

ALBANY.

I cannot be so partial, Goneril,
To the great love I bear you—

GONERIL.

Pray you, content.

                 What, Oswald, ho!

(*To the* FOOL.)

You sir, more knave than fool, after your master.

FOOL (*following* LEAR).

Nuncle Lear, nuncle Lear, tarry and take the
fool with thee.[86]

(*Stopping at the door.*)

A fox, when one has caught her,   340
And such a daughter,
Should sure to the slaughter,
If my cap would buy a halter:
So the fool follows after.

(*He goes.*)

GONERIL.

This man hath had good counsel—a hundred
knights!

'Tis politic* and safe to let him keep   prudent
At point* a hundred knights: yes, that, on every   fully
dream,   armed
Each buzz,* each fancy, each complaint, dislike,   rumor
He may enguard* his dotage with their powers,   guard
And hold our lives in* mercy.   at his

                          Oswald, I say!   350

ALBANY.

Well, you may fear too far.

GONERIL.   Safer than trust too far:
Let me still take away the harms I fear,
Not fear still to be taken:[37] I know his heart.
What he hath uttered I have writ my sister:
If she sustain him and his hundred knights,
When I have showed the unfitness—

(OSWALD *enters.*)   How now, Oswald!

What, have you writ that letter to my sister?

OSWALD.

Yes, madam.

GONERIL.

Take you some company, and away to horse:
Inform her full of my particular fear;   360
And thereto add such reasons of your own
As may compact* it more. Get you gone;   strengthen
And hasten your return.

(OSWALD *leaves*.) No, no, my lord,
This milky gentleness and course of yours
Though I condemn not, yet, under pardon,
You are much more attasked* for want of   taken to
    wisdom   task
Than praised for harmful mildness.

ALBANY.
How far your eyes may pierce I cannot tell:
Striving to better, oft we mar what's well.

GONERIL.
Nay, then—   370

ALBANY.
Well, well;   the event.*   *i.e., wait
    (*They leave the hall.*)   and see

SCENE 5. In front of Albany's palace.

(LEAR, KENT, *and the* FOOL *enter.*)

LEAR (*to* KENT).
Go you before to Gloucester with these letters.
Acquaint my daughter no further with any thing
you know than comes from her demand out of
the* letter. If your diligence be not speedy, I   inherent
shall be there afore you.   in

KENT.
I will not sleep, my lord, till I have delivered your
letter.
    (*He goes.*)

FOOL.
If a man's brains were in 's heels, were 't not in
danger of kibes?*   chilblains

LEAR.
Ay, boy.   10

FOOL.
Then, I prithee, be merry; thy wit shall ne'er go
slip-shod.*   in slippers

LEAR.

Ha, ha, ha!

FOOL.

Shalt see thy other daughter will use thee kindly;[38]
for though she's as like this as a crab's like an
apple, yet I can tell what I can tell.

LEAR.

Why, what canst thou tell, my boy?

FOOL.

She will taste as like this as a crab does to a crab.
Thou canst tell why one's nose stands i' the mid-
dle on's face?   20

LEAR.

No.

FOOL.

Why, to keep one's eyes of either side's nose; that
what a man cannot smell out, he may spy into.

LEAR.

I did her wrong—

FOOL.

Canst tell how an oyster makes his shell?

LEAR.

No.

FOOL.

Nor I neither; but I can tell why a snail has a
house.   30

LEAR.

Why?

FOOL.

Why, to put his head in; not to give it away to
his daughters, and leave his horns without a case.

LEAR.

I will forget my nature. So kind a father! Be my
horses ready?

FOOL.

Thy asses are gone about 'em. The reason why
the   seven stars* are no more than seven is a   *i.e.,
pretty reason.   Pleiades

LEAR.

Because they are not eight?   40

FOOL.

Yes, indeed: thou wouldst make a good fool.

LEAR.

To take 't again perforce!* Monster ingratitude!   by force

FOOL.

If thou wert my fool, nuncle, I'd have thee
beaten for being old before thy time.

LEAR.

How's that?

FOOL.

Thou shouldst not have been old till thou hadst
been wise.

LEAR.

O, let me not be mad, not mad, sweet heaven!   50
Keep me in temper: I would not be mad!
  (*A* GENTLEMAN *of* LEAR's *train enters.*)
How now! are the horses ready?

GENTLEMAN.

Ready, my lord.

LEAR (*to the* FOOL).

Come, boy.

FOOL.

She that's a maid now, and laughs at my departure,
Shall not be a maid long, unless things be cut
  shorter.
  (*They go.*)

ACT II

SCENE 1. Night. A courtyard within the castle of the Earl of Gloucester. Various doors lead to other parts of the castle, and stairs lead up to Edmund's quarters.

(EDMUND *enters, meeting* CURAN.)

EDMUND.
Save thee, Curan.

CURAN.
And you, sir. I have been with your father, and given him notice that the Duke of Cornwall and Regan his duchess will be here with him this night.

EDMUND.
How comes that?

CURAN.
Nay, I know not. You have heard of the news abroad; I mean the whispered ones, for they are yet but ear-kissing* arguments?   whis-pered

EDMUND.
Not I: pray you, what are they?   10

CURAN.
Have you heard of no likely wars toward* 'twixt the Dukes of Cornwall and Albany?   in prospect

EDMUND.
Not a word.

CURAN.
You may do, then, in time. Fare you well, sir.
    (*He goes.*)

EDMUND.

The duke be here tonight? The better! Best!
This weaves itself perforce into my business.
My father hath set guard to take my brother;
And I have one thing, of a queasy* question,*   delicate/
Which I must act: briefness and fortune, work!   nature
   (*Calling up the stairs.*)   20

Brother, a word; descend. Brother, I say!
   (EDGAR *comes down from* EDMUND's *room.*)
My father watches: O sir, fly this place;
Intelligence is given where you are hid;
You have now the good advantage of the night:
Have you not spoken 'gainst the Duke of Corn-
   wall?
He's coming hither; now, i' the night, i' the haste,
And Regan with him: have you nothing said
Upon his party* 'gainst the Duke of Albany?   in his
Advise yourself.*   favor
    consider

EDGAR.   I am sure on 't, not a word.

EDMUND.

I hear my father coming: pardon me;   30
In cunning I must draw my sword upon you:
   (*Draws his sword.*)
Draw; seem to defend yourself.
   (EDGAR *draws, too, and they fence.*)
            Now quit you* well.   acquit
Yield: come before my father.   yourself

                   Light, ho, here!
   (*Aside to* EDGAR.)
Fly, brother.
          Torches, torches!
   (*To* EDGAR *as he leaves.*) So, farewell.
Some blood drawn on me would beget opinion
Of my more fierce endeavor.
   (*Wounding his own arm.*) I have seen drunkards
Do more than this in sport.[39]
              Father, father!
Stop, stop! No help?

(GLOUCESTER and SERVANTS with torches enter.)

GLOUCESTER.

Now, Edmund, where's the villain?

EDMUND.

Here stood he in the dark, his sharp sword out,   40
Mumbling of wicked charms, conjuring the moon
To stand auspicious mistress—

GLOUCESTER.   But where is he?

EDMUND.

Look, sir, I bleed.

GLOUCESTER.   Where is the villain, Edmund?

EDMUND.

Fled this way, sir. When by no means he could—

GLOUCESTER (to some SERVANTS.)

Pursue him, ho! Go after. (They go.)
                              By no means what?

EDMUND.

Persuade me to the murder of your lordship;
But that I told him, the revenging gods
'Gainst parricides did all their thunders bend:*   aim
Spoke, with how manifold and strong a bond
The child was bound to the father; sir, in fine,   50
Seeing how loathly opposite* I stood   opposed
To his unnatural purpose, in fell* motion,   fierce
With his preparèd sword, he charges home
My unprovided* body, lanced mine arm: undefended
But when he saw my best alarumed spirits,
Bold in the quarrel's right, roused to the en-
    counter,
Or whether gasted* by the noise I made,   frightened
Full suddenly he fled.

GLOUCESTER.   Let him fly far:
Not in this land shall he remain uncaught;
And found—dispatch.* The noble duke my   finish
    master,   him!
                                                             60
My worthy arch and patron,* comes tonight: chief
                                                             patron
By his authority I will proclaim it,
That he which finds him shall deserve our thanks,

Bringing the murderous coward to the stake;
He that conceals him, death.

EDMUND.

When I dissuaded him from his intent,
And found him pight* to do it, with curst*   determined/
   speech   irate
I threatened to discover him: he replied,
"Thou unpossessing bastard! Dost thou think,
If I would stand against thee, would the reposal   70
Of any trust, virtue, or worth in thee
Make thy words faithed?* No: what I should   believed
   deny—
As this I would; ay, though thou didst produce
My very character*—I'd turn it all   hand-
                                                                                      writing
To thy suggestion, plot, and damned practice:
And thou must make a dullard of the world,
If they not thought the profits of my death
Were very pregnant and potential spurs
To make thee seek it."⁴⁰

GLOUCESTER.   Strong and fastened* villain!   confirmed
Would he deny his letter? I never got* him.   begot
   (Trumpet calls sound at the gate.)
Hark, the duke's trumpets! I know not why he
   comes.   81
All ports I'll bar; the villain shall not 'scape;
The duke must grant me that: besides, his picture*   i.e.,
I will send far and near, that all the kingdom   description
May have due note of him. And of my land,
Loyal and natural boy, I'll work the means
To make thee capable.*   legal heir
   *(The Duke of CORNWALL and REGAN enter, fol-
   lowed by ATTENDANTS.)*

CORNWALL.

How now, my noble friend! Since I came hither,
Which I can tell but now, I have heard strange
   news.

REGAN.

If it be true, all vengeance comes too short   90

Which can pursue the offender. How dost, my
  lord?

GLOUCESTER.

O, madam, my old heart is cracked, is cracked!

REGAN.

What, did my father's godson seek your life?
He whom my father named? Your Edgar?

GLOUCESTER.

O, lady, lady, shame would have it hid!

REGAN.

Was he not companion with the riotous knights
That tend upon my father?

GLOUCESTER.

I know not, madam: 'tis too bad, too bad.

EDMUND.

Yes, madam, he was of that consort.*   gang

REGAN.

No marvel, then, though he were ill affected: 100
'Tis they have put him on the old man's death,
To have the expense* and waste of his revènues.   spending
I have this present evening from my sister
Been well informed of them; and with such cau-
  tions,
That if they come to sojourn at my house,
I'll not be there.

CORNWALL.   Nor I, assure thee, Regan.
Edmund, I hear that you have shown your father
  A child-like* office.   i.e., filial

EDMUND.   'Twas my duty, sir.

GLOUCESTER.

He did bewray* his practice; and received   reveal
This hurt you see, striving to apprehend him.   110

CORNWALL.

Is he pursued?

GLOUCESTER.   Ay, my good lord.

CORNWALL.

If he be taken, he shall never more

Be feared of doing harm: make your own purpose,*   plans

How in my strength you please.41

                           For you, Edmund,
Whose virtue and obedience doth this instant
So much commend itself, you shall be ours:
Natures of such deep trust we shall much need;
You we first seize on.

EDMUND.   I shall serve you, sir,
Truly, however else.

GLOUCESTER.   For him I thank your grace.

CORNWALL.

You know not why we came to visit you—   120

REGAN.

Thus out of season, threading dark-eyed night:
Occasions, noble Gloucester, of some poise,*   weight
Wherein we must have use of your advice:
Our father he hath writ, so hath our sister,
Of differences, which I least thought it fit
To answer from* our home; the several messen- away
  gers   from
From hence attend* dispatch.   wait for
                         Our good old friend,
Lay comforts to your bosom; and bestow
Your needful counsel to our business,
Which craves the instant use.*   action

GLOUCESTER.   I serve you, madam: 130
Your graces are right welcome.
    (*All leave.*)

SCENE 2. In front of Gloucester's castle.

(KENT *and* OSWALD *enter from separate directions.*)

OSWALD.

Good dawning to thee, friend: art of this house?

KENT.

Ay.

OSWALD.

Where may we set our horses?

KENT.

I' the mire.

OSWALD.

Prithee, if thou lovest me, tell me.

KENT.

I love thee not.

OSWALD.

Why, then, I care not for thee.

KENT.

If I had thee in Lipsbury pinfold, I would make
thee care for me.[42]   10

OSWALD.

Why dost thou use me thus? I know thee not.

KENT.

Fellow, I know thee.

OSWALD.

What dost thou know me for?

KENT.

A knave; a rascal; an eater of broken meats; a
base, proud, shallow, beggarly, three-suited,[43]
hundred-pound, filthy, worsted-stocking knave;
a lily-livered, action-taking knave, a whoreson,
glass-gazing, superserviceable, finical rogue; one-   20
trunk-inheriting slave; one that wouldst be a
bawd, in way of good service, and art nothing
but the composition of a knave, beggar, coward,
pander, and the son and heir of a mongrel bitch:
one whom I will beat into clamorous whining, if
thou deniest the least syllable of thy addition.*   description

OSWALD.

Why, what a monstrous fellow art thou, thus to
rail on one that is neither known of thee nor
knows thee!

KENT.

What a brazen-faced varlet art thou, to deny   30
thou knowest me! Is it two days ago since I

tripped up thy heels, and beat thee before the
king? Draw, you rogue: for, though it be night,
yet the moon shines; I'll make a sop o' the moonshine of you:⁴⁴ draw, you whoreson cullionly*   vile
barber-monger,⁴⁵ draw.
   (*Drawing his sword.*)

OSWALD.

Away! I have nothing to do with thee.

KENT.

Draw, you rascal: you come with letters against
the king; and take vanity the puppet's part⁴⁶
against the royalty of her father: draw, you   40
rogue, or I'll so carbonado* your shanks: draw,   slash
you rascal; come your ways.

OSWALD.

Help, ho! Murder! Help!

KENT.

Strike, you slave; stand, rogue, stand; you neat*   dainty
slave, strike. (*Beating him.*)

OSWALD.

Help, ho! Murder! Murder!
   (EDMUND *enters from the castle, with drawn
   sword, followed by* CORNWALL, REGAN, GLOU-
   CESTER, *and* ATTENDANTS.)

EDMUND.

How now! What's the matter?

KENT.

With you, goodman* boy, an you please: come,   presump-
I'll flesh* ye: come on, young master.   tuous
                                 initiate

GLOUCESTER.

Weapons! Arms! What's the matter here?   50

CORNWALL.

Keep peace, upon your lives;
He dies that strikes again. What is the matter?

REGAN.

The messengers from our sister, and the king.

CORNWALL.

What is your difference? Speak.

OSWALD.

I am scarce in breath, my lord.

KENT.

No marvel, you have so bestirred your valor.
You cowardly rascal, nature disclaims in thee: a
tailor made thee.   60

CORNWALL.

Thou art a strange fellow: a tailor make a man?

KENT.

Ay, a tailor, sir: a stone-cutter or a painter could
not have made him so ill, though he had been but
two hours at the trade.

CORNWALL.

Speak yet, how grew your quarrel?

OSWALD.

This ancient ruffian, sir, whose life I have spared
at suit of his gray beard—

KENT.

Thou whoreson zed! Thou unnecessary letter! [47]
My lord, if you will give me leave, I will tread   70
this unbolted* villain into mortar, and daub the   unsifted
walls of a jakes* with him. Spare my gray beard,   privy
you wagtail? [48]

CORNWALL.

Peace, sirrah!
You beastly knave, know you no reverence?

KENT.

Yes, sir; but anger hath a privilege.

CORNWALL.

Why art thou angry?

KENT.

That such a slave as this should wear a sword,
Who wears no honesty. Such smiling rogues as
    these,
Like rats, oft bite the holy cords a-twain   80
Which are too intrinse* t' unloose; [49] smooth every   intricate
    passion
That in the natures of their lords rebel;

Bring oil to fire, snow to their colder moods;
Renege, affirm, and turn their halcyon beaks[50]
With every gale and vary of their masters,
Knowing nought, like dogs, but following.
A plague upon your epileptic* visage![51]　　　　　　*i.e., con-
　(*To* OSWALD.)　　　　　　　　　　　　　　　　　　torted

Smile you my speeches, as I were a fool?*　　　　　　jester
Goose, if I had you upon Sarum plain,
I'd drive ye cackling home to Camelot.[52]　　　　　　90

CORNWALL.

What, art thou mad, old fellow?

GLOUCESTER.

How fell you out? Say that.

KENT.

No contraries hold more antipathy
Than I and such a knave.

CORNWALL.

Why dost thou call him knave? What's his
　offense?

KENT.

His countenance likes* me not.　　　　　　　　　　pleases

CORNWALL.

No more, perchance, does mine, nor his, nor hers.

KENT.

Sir, 'tis my occupation to be plain:
I have seen better faces in my time
Than stands on any shoulder that I see　　　　　　100
Before me at this instant.

CORNWALL (*to the others*). This is some fellow,
Who, having been praised for bluntness, doth affect
A saucy roughness, and constrains the garb
Quite from his nature:[53] he cannot flatter, he,
An honest mind and plain, he must speak truth!
An they will take it, so; if not, he's plain.
These kind of knaves I know, which in this plain-
　ness
Harbor more craft and more corrupter ends

Than twenty silly ducking observants* obsequious
That stretch their duties nicely.   courtiers
               110

KENT.

Sir, in good sooth, in sincere verity,
Under the allowance of your great aspect,
Whose influence, like the wreath of radiant fire
On flickering Phœbus' front—⁵⁴

CORNWALL.   What mean'st by this?

KENT.

To go out of my dialect, which you discommend
so much. I know, sir, I am no flatterer: he that
beguiled you in a plain accent was a plain knave;
which for my part I will not be, though I should
win your displeasure to entreat me to 't. 120

CORNWALL (*to* OSWALD).

What was the offense you gave him?

OSWALD.

I never gave him any:
It pleased the king his master very late
To strike at me, upon his misconstruction;
When he, conjunct,* and flattering his displeasure, joining
Tripped me behind; being down, insulted, railed, with
And put upon him such a deal of man,
That worthied him, got praises of the king
For him attempting who was self-subdued;
And, in the fleshment* of this dread exploit, fierceness
Drew on me here again.⁵⁵   131

KENT.   None of these rogues and cowards
But Ajax is their fool.

CORNWALL (*to* ATTENDANTS). Fetch forth the stocks!
  (*To* KENT.)
You stubborn ancient knave, you reverend brag-
  gart,
We'll teach you—

KENT.   Sir, I am too old to learn:
Call not your stocks for me: I serve the king;
On whose employment I was sent to you:
You shall do small respect, show too bold malice

Against the grace and person of my master,
Stocking his messenger.

CORNWALL (*to* ATTENDANTS).

Fetch forth the stocks! (ATTENDANTS *leave*.)
               As I have life and honor,   140
There shall he sit till noon.

REGAN.

Till noon! Till night, my lord; and all night too.

KENT.

Why, madam, if I were your father's dog,
You should not use me so.

REGAN.   Sir, being his knave, I will.

CORNWALL.

This is a fellow of the self-same color
Our sister speaks of. Come, bring away* the stocks!   out
    (ATTENDANTS *bring out the stocks*.)

GLOUCESTER.

Let me beseech your grace not to do so:
His fault is much, and the good king his master
Will check him for 't: your purposed low correc-
    tion
Is such as basest and contemned'st wretches   150
For pilferings and most common trespasses
Are punished with: the king must take it ill,
That he's so slightly valued in his messenger,
Should have him thus restrained.

CORNWALL.   I'll answer that.

REGAN.

My sister may receive it much more worse,
To have her gentleman abused, assaulted,
For following her affairs.
    (*To* ATTENDANTS.)   Put in his legs.
    (KENT *is put in the stocks*.)
Come, my good lord, away.
    (EDMUND, REGAN, CORNWALL, OSWALD, *and* AT-
    TENDANTS *leave*.)

GLOUCESTER.

I am sorry for thee, friend; 'tis the duke's pleasure,

Whose disposition, all the world well knows,   160
Will not be rubbed nor stopped:[56] I'll entreat for
  thee.

KENT.

Pray, do not, sir: I have watched and traveled
  hard;
Some time I shall sleep out, the rest I'll whistle.
A good man's fortune may grow out at heels.
Give you good morrow!

GLOUCESTER.

The duke's to blame in this; 'twill be ill taken.
  (*He goes.*)

KENT.

Good king, that must approve the common saw,*   familiar
Thou out of heaven's benediction comest   saying
To the warm sun![57]
Approach, thou beacon to this under globe,   170
That by thy comfortable beams I may
Peruse this letter!
  (*Trying to read a letter he has taken from his
  pocket.*)   Nothing almost sees miracles
But misery:[58] I know 'tis from Cordelia,
Who hath most fortunately been informed
Of my obscurèd course;* and shall find time   *i.e.,* disguise
From this enormous state,* seeking to give   *i.e.,* con-
Losses their remedies.   fusion
               All weary and o'erwatched,
Take vantage, heavy eyes, not to behold
This shameful lodging.
Fortune, good night: smile once more; turn thy
  wheel!   180
  (*He goes to sleep.*)

SCENE 3. The open country.

(EDGAR *enters.*)

EDGAR.

I heard myself proclaimed;[59]
And by the happy* hollow of a tree   *happily*
Escaped the hunt. No port is free; no place,   *found*
That guard, and most unusual vigilance,
Does not attend* my taking. Whiles I may 'scape,   *seek*
I will preserve myself: and am bethought*   *decided*
To take the basest and most poorest shape
That ever penury, in contempt of man,
Brought near the beast: my face I'll grime with
  filth;[60]
Blanket my loins; elf* all my hair in knots;   *tangle*
And with presented nakedness out-face   11
The winds and persecutions of the sky.
The country gives me proof and precedent
Of Bedlam beggars, who, with roaring voices,
Strike in their numbed and mortified* bare arms   *without*
Pins, wooden pricks, nails, sprigs of rosemary;   *feeling*
And with this horrible object,* from low farms,   *spectacle*
Poor pelting* villages, sheep-cotes, and mills,   *paltry*
Sometime with lunatic bans, sometime with prayers,
Enforce their charity.
                Poor Turlygod! poor Tom!   20
That's something yet: Edgar I nothing am.
  (*He goes.*)

SCENE 4. In front of Gloucester's castle.

(KENT *is in the stocks.* LEAR *enters from a distance, with the* FOOL *and* GENTLEMAN.)

LEAR.
'Tis strange that they should so depart from home,
And not send back my messenger.

GENTLEMAN.   As I learned,
The night before there was no purpose in them
Of this remove.*   removal

KENT.   Hail to thee, noble master!

LEAR (*discovering* KENT *in the stocks*).
Ha!
Makest thou this shame thy pastime?

KENT.   No, my lord.

FOOL.
Ha, ha! He wears cruel garters.[61] Horses are tied
by the heads, dogs and bears by the neck, monkeys
by the loins,[62] and men by the legs: when a man's
over-lusty at legs, then he wears wooden nether-   10
stocks.*   stockings

LEAR.
What's he that hath so much thy place mistook
To set thee here?

KENT.   It is both he and she;
Your son and daughter.

LEAR.
No.

KENT.
Yes.

LEAR.
No, I say.

KENT.
I say, yea.

LEAR.
No, no, they would not.

KENT.

  Yes, they have.   20

LEAR.

  By Jupiter, I swear, no.

KENT.

  By Juno, I swear, ay.

LEAR.   They durst not do 't;

  They could not, would not do 't; 'tis worse than
    murder,

  To do upon respect* such violent outrage: deliberately

  Resolve me,* with all modest haste, which way   explain

  Thou mightst deserve, or they impose, this usage,

  Coming from us.

KENT.   My lord, when at their home

  I did commend your highness' letters to them,

  Ere I was risen from the place that showed

  My duty kneeling, came there a reeking post,*   messenger

  Stewed in his haste, half breathless, panting forth   31

  From Goneril his mistress salutations;

  Delivered letters, spite of intermission,*   *i.e.*, inter-
                            rupting me

  Which presently they read: on whose contents,

  They summoned up their meiny,* straight took   menials
    horse;

  Commanded me to follow, and attend

  The leisure of their answer; gave me cold looks:

  And meeting here the other messenger,

  Whose welcome, I perceived, had poison'd mine—

  Being the very fellow that of late   40

  Display'd so saucily against your highness—

  Having more man than wit about me, drew:

  He raised the house with loud and coward cries.

  Your son and daughter found this trespass worth

  The shame which here it suffers.

FOOL.

  Winter's not gone yet, if the wild-geese fly that
way.

    Fathers that wear rags

      Do make their children blind;

But fathers that bear bags*   *i.e.,* are rich
   Shall see their children kind.   51
Fortune, that arrant whore,
Ne'er turns the key to* the poor.   *i.e.,* to
                                         let in
But, for all this, thou shalt have as many dolors*   griefs
for thy daughters as thou canst tell in a year.

LEAR.

O, how this mother swells up toward my heart!
Hysterica passio,[63] down, thou climbing sorrow,
Thy element's below!
                Where is this daughter?

KENT.

With the earl, sir, here within.

LEAR.   Follow me not;
Stay here.   60
   (*He goes into the castle.*)

GENTLEMAN.

Made you no more offense, but what you speak of?

KENT.

None.
How chance the king comes with so small a train?

FOOL.

An thou hadst been set i' the stocks for that question, thou hadst well deserved it.

KENT.

Why, fool?

FOOL.

We'll set thee[64] to school to an ant, to teach thee
there's no laboring i' the winter. All that follow
their noses are led by their eyes but blind men;   70
and there's not a nose among twenty but can smell
him that's stinking. Let go thy hold when a great
wheel runs down a hill, lest it break thy neck with
following it; but the great one that goes up the
hill, let him draw thee after. When a wise man
gives thee better counsel, give me mine again: I
would have none but knaves follow it, since a
fool gives it.

That sir which serves and seeks for gain,
  And follows but for form,   80
Will pack* when it begins to rain,   run away
  And leave thee in the storm.
But I will tarry; the fool will stay,
  And let the wise man fly:
The knave turns fool that runs away;
  The fool no knave, perdy.⁶⁵

KENT.

Where learned you this, fool?

FOOL.

Not i' the stocks, fool.

  (LEAR *returns, with* GLOUCESTER.)

LEAR.

Deny* to speak with me? They are sick? They   refuse
  are weary?
They have traveled all the night? Mere fetches;*   pretexts
The images of revolt and flying off.   91
Fetch me a better answer.

GLOUCESTER.   My dear lord,
You know the fiery quality of the duke;
How unremovable and fixed he is
In his own course.

LEAR.

Vengeance! Plague! Death! Confusion!
Fiery? What quality? Why, Gloucester, Glou-
  cester,
I'd speak with the Duke of Cornwall and his wife.

GLOUCESTER.

Well, my good lord, I have informed them so.

LEAR.

Informed them! Dost thou understand me, man?   100

GLOUCESTER.

Ay, my good lord.

LEAR.

The king would speak with Cornwall; the dear
  father

Would with his daughter speak, commands her
    service:
Are they inform'd of this? My breath and blood!
Fiery? The fiery duke? Tell the hot duke that—
No, but not yet: may be he is not well:
Infirmity doth still neglect* all office   *cause neglect of*
Whereto our health is bound; we are not ourselves
When nature, being oppressed, commands the
    mind
To suffer with the body: I'll forbear;   110
And am fall'n out with my more headier* will,   *impulsive*
To take the indisposed and sickly fit
For the sound man.
    (*Indicating* KENT.) Death on my state! Wherefore
Should he sit here? This act persuades me
That this remotion* of the duke and her   *remoteness*
Is practice* only. Give me my servant forth.   *trickery*
Go tell the duke and's wife I'd speak with them.
Now, presently:* bid them come forth and hear   *at once*
    me,
Or at their chamber-door I'll beat the drum
Till it cry sleep to death.*   *murder sleep*

GLOUCESTER.
I would have all well betwixt you.   121
    (*He goes into the castle.*)

LEAR.
O me, my heart, my rising heart! But, down!

FOOL.
Cry to it, nuncle, as the cockney did to the eels
when she put 'em i' the paste alive; she knapped
'em o' the coxcombs with a stick, and cried, "Down,
wantons, down!" 'Twas her brother that, in pure
kindness to his horse, buttered his hay.[66]
    (CORNWALL, REGAN, *and* SERVANTS *come out of
    the castle with* GLOUCESTER.)

LEAR.
Good morrow to you both.

CORNWALL.   Hail to your grace!

REGAN.

I am glad to see your highness.   130

LEAR.

Regan, I think you are; I know what reason
I have to think so: if thou shouldst not be glad,
I would divorce me from thy mother's tomb,
Sepulchring an adultress.[67]
   (*To* KENT, *who has been released from the stocks.*)
                         O, are you free?
Some other time for that.
                         Belovèd Regan,
Thy sister's naught;* O Regan, she hath tied   wicked
Sharp-toothed unkindness, like a vulture, here:
   (*His hand on his heart.*)
I can scarce speak to thee; thou'lt not believe
With how depraved a quality— O Regan!

REGAN.

I pray you, sir, take patience: I have hope   140
You less know how to value her desert
Than she to scant her duty.

LEAR.   Say, how is that?

REGAN.

I cannot think my sister in the least
Would fail her obligation: if, sir, perchance
She have restrained the riots of your followers,
'Tis on such ground, and to such wholesome end,
As clears her from all blame.

LEAR.

My curses on her!

REGAN.   O, sir, you are old;
Nature in you stands on the very verge
Of her confine: you should be ruled and led   150
By some discretion, that discerns your state
Better than you yourself. Therefore, I pray you,
That to our sister you do make return;
Say you have wronged her, sir.

LEAR.   Ask her forgiveness?
Do you but mark how this becomes the house:

I should ask forgiveness

"Dear daughter, I confess that I am old;
Age is unnecessary: on my knees I beg
That you'll vouchsafe me raiment, bed, and food."

REGAN.   *sounds good*

Good sir, no more; these are unsightly tricks:
Return you to my sister.

LEAR.   Never, Regan: 160
She hath abated me of half my train;
Looked black upon me; struck me with her tongue,
Most serpentlike, upon the very heart:
All the stored vengeances of heaven fall
On her ingrateful top! Strike her young bones,[68]
You taking* airs, with lameness!   malignant

CORNWALL.   Fie, sir, fie!

LEAR.

You nimble lightnings, dart your blinding flames
Into her scornful eyes! Infect her beauty,
You fen-sucked fogs, drawn by the powerful suns,
To fall and blast her pride!   170

REGAN.

O the blest gods! so will you wish on me,
When the rash mood is on.

LEAR.

No, Regan, thou shalt never have my curse: *491*
Thy tender-hefted* nature shall not give   tender-
Thee o'er to harshness: her eyes are fierce; but   swayed
   thine
Do comfort and not burn. 'Tis not in thee
To grudge my pleasures, to cut off my train,
To bandy hasty words, to scant my sizes,*   allowances
And in conclusion to oppose the bolt
Against my coming in: thou better know'st   180
The offices of nature, bond of childhood,
Effects of courtesy, dues of gratitude.
Thy half o' the kingdom hast thou not forgot,
Wherein I thee endowed.

REGAN.   Good sir, to the purpose.*   point

LEAR.

Who put my man i' the stocks?
(*A trumpet sounds.*)

CORNWALL.　　　　　What trumpet's that?

REGAN.

I know 't, my sister's: this approves* her letter,　　　confirms
That she would soon be here.
　　　(*To* OSWALD *as he enters.*)　Is your lady come?

LEAR.

This is a slave, whose easy-borrowed pride
Dwells in the fickle grace of her he follows.
Out, varlet,* from my sight!　　　　　　knave

CORNWALL.　　　　　　　What means your grace?

LEAR.

Who stocked my servant?　Regan, I have good　　190
　hope
Thou didst not know on 't.

　　　　　　　　　　　Who comes here?
　　　(GONERIL *enters, and* REGAN *goes to greet her.*)
　　O heavens,
If you do love old men, if your sweet sway
Allow* obedience, if yourselves are old,　　　approve
Make it your cause; send down, and take my part!
　　　(*To* GONERIL.)
Art not ashamed to look upon this beard?
O Regan, wilt thou take her by the hand?

GONERIL.

Why not by the hand, sir?　How have I offended?
All's not offense that indiscretion finds
And dotage terms so.

LEAR.　　　　　　O sides, you are too tough;　　200
Will you yet hold?　How came my man i' the
　stocks?

CORNWALL.

I set him there, sir: but his own disorders
Deserved much less advancement.*　　　honor

LEAR.　　　　　　　You! Did you?

REGAN. ~~I'll take~~ *sho* *care of her ded & 50 servt*

I pray you, father, being weak, seem so.
If, till the expiration of your month,
You will return and sojourn with my sister,
Dismissing half your train, come then to me:
I am now from home, and out of that provision
Which shall be needful for your entertainment.*   maintenance

LEAR. *- no way*

Return to her, and fifty men dismissed?   210
No, rather I abjure all roofs, and choose
To wage* against the enmity o' the air;   wage war
To be a comrade with the wolf and owl—
Necessity's sharp pinch! Return with her?
Why, the hot-blooded France, that dowerless took
Our youngest born, I could as well be brought
To knee* his throne, and, squire-like, pension beg   kneel before
To keep base life afoot. Return with her?
Persuade me rather to be slave and sumpter*   pack horse
To this detested groom. (*Pointing at* OSWALD.)

GONERIL.   At your choice, sir.   220

LEAR.

I prithee, daughter, do not make me mad:
I will not trouble thee, my child. Farewell:
We'll no more meet, no more see one another:
But yet thou art my flesh, my blood, my daughter;
Or rather a disease that's in my flesh,
Which I must needs call mine: thou art a boil,
A plague-sore, an embossèd* carbuncle,   swollen
In my corrupted blood.

               But I'll not chide thee;
Let shame come when it will, I do not call it:
I do not bid the thunder-bearer shoot,   230
Nor tell tales of thee to high-judging Jove:
Mend when thou canst; be better at thy leisure:
I can be patient; I can stay with Regan,
I and my hundred knights.

REGAN.   Not altogether so:
I looked not for you yet, nor am provided

For your fit welcome. Give ear, sir, to my sister;
For those that mingle reason with your passion*   violence
Must be content to think you old, and so—
But she knows what she does.

LEAR.   Is this well spoken?

REGAN.

I dare avouch* it, sir: what, fifty followers?   affirm
Is it not well? What should you need of more?   241
Yea, or so many, sith that both charge and danger
Speak 'gainst so great a number? How, in one
    house,
Should many people, under two commands,
Hold amity? 'Tis hard; almost impossible.

GONERIL.

Why might not you, my lord, receive attendance
From those that she calls servants or from mine?

REGAN.

Why not, my lord? If then they chanced to slack*   neglect
    you,
We could control them. If you will come to me—
For now I spy a danger—I entreat you   250
To bring but five and twenty: to no more   25
Will I give place or notice.

LEAR.

I gave you all—

REGAN.   And in good time you gave it.   sould to togh
                                                            luets

LEAR.

Made you my guardians, my depositaries;
But kept a reservation to be followed
With such a number. What, must I come to you   25?
With five and twenty, Regan? Said you so?

REGAN.

And speak 't again, my lord; no more with me.   Thate
                                                        i f

LEAR.

Those wicked creatures yet do look well-favored,
When others are more wicked; not being the
    worst   260
Stands in some rank of praise.

(*To* GONERIL.)

        I'll go with thee:
Thy fifty yet doth double five-and-twenty,
And thou art twice her love.

GONERIL.   Hear me, my lord:
What need you five and twenty, ten, or five,
To follow in a house where twice so many
Have a command to tend you?

REGAN.   What need one?

LEAR.

O, reason not the need: our basest beggars
Are in the poorest thing superfluous:[69]
Allow not nature more than nature needs,
Man's life 's as cheap as beast's: thou art a lady; 270
If only to go warm were gorgeous,
Why, nature needs not what thou gorgeous wear'st,
Which scarcely keeps thee warm. But, for true
 need—
You heavens, give me that patience, patience I need!
You see me here, you gods, a poor old man,
As full of grief as age; wretched in both!
If it be you that stir these daughters' hearts
Against their father, fool* me not so much   **weaken**
To bear it tamely; touch me with noble anger,
And let not women's weapons, water-drops,   280
Stain my man's cheeks!
      No, you unnatural hags,
I will have such revenges on you both,
That all the world shall—I will do such things—
What they are, yet I know not; but they shall be
The terrors of the earth. You think I'll weep;
No, I'll not weep: *Notare*
I have full cause of weeping; but this heart
Shall break into a hundred thousand flaws,* **fragments**
Or ere I'll weep.
    O fool, I shall go mad!
  (LEAR, GLOUCESTER, KENT, *and the* FOOL *leave.*)

CORNWALL.

Let us withdraw; 'twill be a storm.   290

REGAN.

he turns her father!

This house is little: the old man and his people
Cannot be well bestowed.

GONERIL.

'Tis his own blame;* hath* put himself from rest,
And must needs taste his folly.

fault/
he hath

REGAN.

For his particular,* I'll receive him gladly,
But not one follower.

him alone

GONERIL.   So am I purposed.
Where is my lord of Gloucester?

— their meanness
is revealed

CORNWALL.

Followed the old man forth: he is returned.

 (GLOUCESTER *returns. Tempest, thunder, and*
 lightning.)

GLOUCESTER.

The king is in high rage.

CORNWALL.   Whither is he going?

GLOUCESTER.

He calls to horse; but will I know not whither.   300

CORNWALL.

'Tis best to give him way;* he leads himself.   *let him go*

GONERIL.

My lord, entreat him by no means to stay.

GLOUCESTER.

Alack, the night comes on, and the bleak winds
Do sorely ruffle;* for many miles about   *bluster*
There's scarce a bush.

REGAN.   O, sir, to willful men,
The injuries that they themselves procure
Must be their schoolmasters.   Shut up your doors:
He is attended with a desperate train;
And what they may incense him to, being apt
To have his ear abused, wisdom bids fear.   310

CORNWALL.

Shut up your doors, my lord; 'tis a wild night:
My Regan counsels well: come out o' the storm.

 (*They all go into the castle.*)

ACT III

SCENE 1. Wild, bleak, open country. The
storm rages.

(KENT *and a* GENTLEMAN *enter from different
directions.*)

KENT.
 Who's there, besides foul weather?
GENTLEMAN (*as he joins* KENT).
 One minded like the weather, most unquietly.
KENT.
 I know you. Where's the king?
GENTLEMAN.
 Contending with the fretful element;
 Bids the wind blow the earth into the sea,
 Or swell the curled waters 'bove the main,*   land
 That things might change or cease; tears his white
   hair,
 Which the impetuous blasts, with eyeless* rage,   blind
 Catch in their fury, and make nothing of;
 Strives in his little world of man to out-scorn   10
 The to-and-fro-conflicting wind and rain.
 This night, wherein the cub-drawn* bear would   sucked
   couch,   dry
 The lion and the belly-pinched wolf
 Keep their fur dry, unbonneted he runs,
 And bids what will take all.[70]
KENT.   But who is with him?
GENTLEMAN.
 None but the fool; who labors to out-jest
 His heart-struck injuries.[71]

KENT.   Sir, I do know you;
   And dare, upon the warrant of my note,*   knowledge
   Commend a dear thing to you. There is division,
   Although as yet the face of it be covered   20
   With mutual cunning, 'twixt Albany and Corn-
     wall;
   Who have—as who have not, that their great stars
   Throned and set high?—servants, who seem no
     less,
   Which are to France the spies and speculations*   observers
   Intelligent* of our state; what hath been seen,   giving
   Either in snuffs* and packings* of the dukes,   information
                                                          resentments/
   Or the hard rein which both of them have borne   plots
   Against the old kind king; or something deeper,
   Whereof perchance these are but furnishings;*   trimmings
   But, true it is, from France there come a power*   army
   Into this scattered kingdom; who already,   31
   Wise in* our negligence, have secret feet   aware of
   In some of our best ports, and are at point*   fully
   To show their open banner.   armed
                  Now to you:
   If on my credit* you dare build so far   your trust
   To make your speed to Dover, you shall find   in me
   Some that will thank you, making just report
   Of how unnatural and bemadding sorrow
   The king hath cause to plain.*   complain
   I am a gentleman of blood and breeding;   40
   And, from some knowledge and assurance, offer
   This office to you.

GENTLEMAN.
   I will talk further with you.

KENT (giving him a purse). No, do not.
   For confirmation that I am much more
   Than my out-wall,* open this purse, and take   garb
   What it contains. If you shall see Cordelia—
   As fear not but you shall—show her this ring;
   And she will tell you who your fellow is
   That yet you do not know.

Fie on this storm!

I will go seek the king.   50

GENTLEMAN.

Give me your hand: have you no more to say?

KENT.

Few words, but, to* effect, more than all yet;   in

That, when we have found the king—in which
   your pain*   effort

That way, I'll this*—he that first lights on him   go this way

Holla the other.

(*They leave in different directions.*)

SCENE 2. Another part of the heath.
The storm continues.

(LEAR *enters, followed by the* FOOL.)

LEAR.

Blow, winds, and crack your cheeks! Rage!
  Blow!

You cataracts and hurricanoes,* spout   water-
                                        spouts

Till you have drenched our steeples, drowned
   the cocks!

You sulphurous and thought-executing fires,

Vaunt-couriers to oak-cleaving thunderbolts,

Singe my white head! And thou, all-shaking
   thunder,

Smite flat the thick rotundity o' the world!

Crack nature's molds, all germens* spill at once,   seeds

That make ingrateful man![72]   9

FOOL.

O nuncle, court holy-water* in a dry house is   *i.e.,*
                                            flattery

better than this rain-water out o' door. Good
nuncle, in, and ask thy daughters' blessing: here's
a night pities neither wise man nor fool.

LEAR.

Rumble thy bellyful! Spit, fire! Spout, rain!

Mon subject to nature

Nor rain, wind, thunder, fire, are my daughters:
I tax not you, you elements, with unkindness;
I never gave you kingdom, called you children,
You owe me no subscription:* then let fall   submission
Your horrible pleasure: here I stand, your slave,
A poor, infirm, weak, and despised old man: 20
But yet I call you servile ministers,*   agents
That have with two pernicious daughters joined
Your high engendered battles 'gainst a head
So old and white as this. O! O! 'Tis foul!

FOOL.

He that has a house to put 's head in has a good
head-piece.
    The cod-piece that will house[73]
      Before the head has any,
    The head and he shall louse;
      So beggars marry many.   30
    The man that makes his toe
      What he his heart should make[74]
    Shall of a corn cry woe,
      And turn his sleep to wake.
For there was never yet fair woman but she made
mouths* in a glass.*   faces/
                                                     mirror
LEAR.

No, I will be the pattern of all patience;
I will say nothing.
    (KENT *enters at a distance.*)

KENT.

Who's there?

FOOL.

Marry, here's grace and a cod-piece; that's a wise   40
man and a fool.

KENT (*joining them*).

Alas, sir, are you here? Things that love night
Love not such nights as these; the wrathful skies
Gallow* the very wanderers of the dark,   terrify
And make them keep their caves: since I was man,
Such sheets of fire, such bursts of horrid thunder,

Such groans of roaring wind and rain, I never
Remember to have heard: man's nature cannot
carry*   bear
The affliction nor the fear.

LEAR.   Let the great gods,
That keep this dreadful pother* o'er our heads,   uproar
Find out their enemies now. Tremble, thou
wretch,   51
That hast within thee undivulgèd crimes,
Unwhipped of justice: hide thee, thou bloody
hand;
Thou perjured, and thou simular* man of virtue   simulated
That art incestuous: caitiff,* to pieces shake,   wretch
That under covert and convenient seeming*   hypocrisy
Hast practiced on man's life: close pent-up guilts,
Rive* your concealing continents,* and cry   rip open/
                                                       containers
These dreadful summoners grace.75 I am a man
More sinned against than sinning.

KENT.   Alack, bare-headed!   60
Gracious my lord, hard by here is a hovel;
Some friendship will it lend you 'gainst the
tempest:
Repose you there; while I to this hard house—
More harder than the stones whereof 'tis raised,
Which even but now, demanding after* you,   asking for
Denied me to come in—return, and force
Their scanted courtesy.

LEAR.   My wits begin to turn.
Come on, my boy: how dost, my boy? Art cold?
I am cold myself. Where is this straw, my
fellow?
The art of our necessities is strange,   70
That can make vile* things precious.76 Come,   worthless
your hovel.
Poor fool and knave, I have one part in my heart
That's sorry yet for thee.

FOOL (*singing*).
He that has and a little tiny wit—

    With hey, ho, the wind and the rain—
Must make content with his fortunes fit,[77]
    For the rain it raineth every day.

LEAR.

True, my good boy. Come, bring us to this
hovel.

(LEAR *and* KENT *leave*.)

FOOL.

This is a brave night to cool a courtesan.
I'll speak a prophecy ere I go:
    When priests are more in word than matter;
    When brewers mar their malt with water;
    When nobles are their tailors' tutors;
    No heretics burned, but wenches' suitors;
    When every case in law is right;
    No squire in debt, nor no poor knight;
    When slanders do not live in tongues;
    Nor cutpurses come not to throngs;
    When usurers tell* their gold i' the field; count
    And bawds and whores do churches build;
    Then shall the realm of Albion* Britain
    Come to great confusion:
    Then comes the time, who lives to see 't,
    That going* shall be used with feet. walking
This prophecy Merlin shall make; for I live before
his time.[78]

(*He follows the others.*)

80

90

SCENE 3. Gloucester's castle.

(GLOUCESTER *enters with* EDMUND.)

GLOUCESTER.

Alack, alack, Edmund, I like not this unnatural
dealing. When I desired their leave that I might
pity him, they took from me the use of mine own
house; charged me, on pain of their perpetual

displeasure, neither to speak of him, entreat for him, nor any way sustain him.

EDMUND.

Most savage and unnatural!

GLOUCESTER.

Go to; say you nothing. There's a division be- twixt the dukes; and a worse matter than that: I have received a letter this night; 'tis dangerous to be spoken; I have locked the letter in my closet: these injuries the king now bears will be revenged home; there's part of a power already footed:* we must incline to* the king. I will seek him, and privily relieve him: go you and maintain talk with the duke, that my charity be not of him perceived: if he ask for me, I am ill, and gone to bed. Though I die for it, as no less is threatened me, the king my old master must be relieved. There is some strange thing toward, Edmund; pray you, be careful.

    (*He goes.*)

10

landed/
side with

20

EDMUND.

This courtesy, forbid thee, shall the duke
Instantly know; and of that letter too:
This seems a fair deserving, and must draw me
That which my father loses; no less than all:
The younger rises when the old doth fall.
    (*He leaves.*)

SCENE 4. In front of a hovel on the heath.
The storm continues.

(LEAR *and* KENT *enter, with the* FOOL.)

KENT.

Here is the place, my lord; good my lord, enter:
The tyranny of the open night's too rough
For nature to endure.

LEAR.   Let me alone.

KENT.

  Good my lord, enter here.

LEAR.   Wilt break my heart?

KENT.

  I had rather break mine own. Good my lord,
    enter.

LEAR.

  Thou think'st 'tis much that this contentious
    storm

  Invades us to the skin: so 'tis to thee;

  But where the greater malady is fixed,

  The lesser is scarce felt. Thou 'dst shun a bear;

  But if thy flight lay toward the raging sea,   10

  Thou 'ldst meet the bear i' the mouth.* When   *i.e.,* brave
    the mind's free,   the bear

  The body's delicate:* the tempest in my mind   sensitive

  Doth from my senses take all feeling else

  Save what beats there.   Filial ingratitude!

  Is it not as* this mouth should tear this hand   as if

  For lifting food to 't? But I will punish home:

  No, I will weep no more.   In such a night

  To shut me out!   Pour on; I will endure.

  In such a night as this! O Regan, Goneril!

  Your old kind father, whose frank heart gave
    all—   20

  O, that way madness lies; let me shun that;

  No more of that.

KENT.   Good my lord, enter here.

LEAR.

  Prithee, go in thyself; seek thine own ease:

  This tempest will not give me leave to ponder

  On things would hurt me more.

                                But I'll go in.

(To the FOOL.*)*

In, boy; go first. You houseless poverty—
Nay, get thee in. I'll pray, and then I'll sleep.
   (The FOOL *goes into the hovel.)*
Poor naked wretches, wheresoe'er you are,
That bide* the pelting of this pitiless storm,   endure
How shall your houseless heads and unfed sides,   30
Your looped and windowed* raggedness, defend   full of
   you   holes
From seasons such as these? O, I have ta'en
Too little care of this! Take physic, pomp;
Expose thyself to feel what wretches feel,
That thou mayst shake the superflux* to them,   your
And show the heavens more just.   superfluity

EDGAR *(inside the hovel).*

Fathom and half,[79] fathom and half! Poor Tom!
   (The FOOL *runs out of the hovel.)*

FOOL.

Come not in here, nuncle, here's a spirit. Help
me, help me!

KENT.

Give me thy hand. Who's there?   40

FOOL.

A spirit, a spirit: he says his name's poor Tom.

KENT *(calling into the hovel).*

What art thou that dost grumble there i' the
straw? Come forth.
   *(*EDGAR *comes out, disguised as a madman, half-
   naked and filthy.)*

EDGAR *(disguising his speech).*

Away! The foul fiend follows me!
Through the sharp hawthorn blows the cold
   wind.
Hum! Go to thy cold bed, and warm thee.

LEAR.

Hast thou given all to thy two daughters?
And art thou come to this?   50

EDGAR.

Who gives anything to poor Tom?[80] Whom the
foul fiend hath led through fire and through
flame, through ford and whirlipool, o'er bog and
quagmire; that hath laid knives under his pillow,
and halters in his pew; set ratsbane by his por-
ridge; made him proud of heart, to ride on a bay
trotting-horse over four-inched bridges, to course
his own shadow for a traitor. Bless thy five wits!

Tom's a-cold—O, do de, do de, do de. Bless thee
from whirlwinds, star-blasting, and taking!* Do
poor Tom some charity, whom the foul fiend
vexes: there could I have him now—and there—
there again, and there.

(The storm still rages.)

LEAR.

What, have his daughters brought him to this
pass?

Couldst thou save nothing? Didst thou give them
all?

FOOL.

Nay, he reserved a blanket, else we had been all
shamed.

LEAR.

Now, all the plagues that in the pendulous air
Hang fated o'er men's faults, light on thy daughters!

KENT.

He hath no daughters, sir.

LEAR.

Death, traitor! Nothing could have subdued
nature
To such a lowness but his unkind daughters.
Is it the fashion, that discarded fathers
Should have thus little mercy on their flesh?[81]
Judicious punishment! 'Twas this flesh begot
Those pelican daughters.[82]

EDGAR.

Pillicock sat on Pillicock-hill:
Halloo, halloo, loo, loo!

FOOL.

This cold night will turn us all to fools and mad-
men.   80

EDGAR.

Take heed o' the foul fiend:[83] obey thy parents;
keep thy word justly; swear not; commit not*   *i.e.,
with man's sworn spouse; set not thy sweet heart   adultery
on proud array. Tom's a-cold.

LEAR.

What hast thou been?

EDGAR.

A serving-man, proud in heart and mind; that
curled my hair; wore gloves in my cap; served
the lust of my mistress' heart, and did the act of   90
darkness with her; swore as many oaths as I spake
words, and broke them in the sweet face of
heaven: one that slept in the contriving of lust,
and waked to do it: wine loved I deeply, dice
dearly; and in woman out-paramoured the Turk:
false of heart, light of ear,* bloody of hand; hog   *credu-
in sloth, fox in stealth, wolf in greediness, dog in   lous
madness, lion in prey. Let not the creaking of
shoes nor the rustling of silks betray thy poor
heart to woman: keep thy foot out of brothels,
thy hand out of plackets,* thy pen from lenders'   *petticoat
books, and defy the foul fiend.   slits
Still through the hawthorn blows the cold wind: 102
Says suum, mun, ha, no, nonny.
Dolphin my boy, my boy, sessa! Let him trot by.
    (*The storm rages.*)

LEAR.

Why, thou wert better in thy grave than to
answer with thy uncovered body this extremity
of the skies. Is man no more than this? Consider
him well. Thou owest the worm no silk, the

beast no hide, the sheep no wool, the cat* no　　civet cat
perfume. Ha! here's three on 's are sophisticated!
Thou art the thing itself: unaccommodated man is
no more but such a poor, bare, forked animal as
thou art. Off, off, you lendings! Come, unbutton
here. *baring self*

(*Starts to rip off his clothes.*)

FOOL.

Prithee, nuncle, be contented; 'tis a naughty
night to swim in. Now a little fire in a wild field
were like an old lecher's heart: a small spark, all
the rest on 's body cold. Look, here comes a
walking fire.

(GLOUCESTER, *from a distance, enters with a
torch.*)

EDGAR.

This is the foul fiend Flibbertigibbet:[84] he begins　　120
at curfew, and walks till the first cock; he gives
the web and the pin,* squints the eye, and makes　　cataract
the hare-lip; mildews the white wheat, and hurts
the poor creature of earth.

　　Saint Withold footed thrice the old;
　　He met the night-mare,* and her nine-fold;　　incubus
　　　　Bid her alight,
　　　　And her troth plight,
　　And, aroint thee, witch, aroint thee!*　　away with
　　　　　　　　　　　　　　　　　　　　　thee

KENT.

How fares your grace?　　130

LEAR.

What's he?

KENT (*calling out*).

Who's there? What is 't you seek?

GLOUCESTER.

What are you there? Your names?

EDGAR.

Poor Tom; that eats the swimming frog, the toad,
the tadpole, the wall-newt* and the water; that　　lizard
in the fury of his heart, when the foul fiend rages,

eats cow-dung for sallets;* swallows the old rat   salads
and the ditch-dog; drinks the green mantle of the
standing pool; who is whipped from tithing* to   parish
tithing, and stock-punished, and imprisoned; who   141
hath had three suits to his back, six shirts to his
body, horse to ride, and weapon to wear;

   But mice and rats, and such small deer,
   Have been Tom's food for seven long year.

Beware my follower.* Peace, Smulkin; peace, thou *i.e., attend-
fiend!   ant fiend*

GLOUCESTER (*recognizing* LEAR).

What, hath your grace no better company?

EDGAR.

The prince of darkness is a gentleman:
Modo he's called, and Mahu.

GLOUCESTER.

Our flesh and blood is grown so vile, my lord,   150
That it doth hate what gets* it.   begets

EDGAR.

Poor Tom 's a-cold.

GLOUCESTER.

Go in with me: my duty cannot suffer*   allow me
To obey in all your daughters' hard commands:
Though their injunction be to bar my doors,
And let this tyrannous night take hold upon you,
Yet have I ventured to come seek you out,
And bring you where both fire and food is ready.

LEAR.

First let me talk with this philosopher.
   (*To* EDGAR.)
What is the cause of thunder?   160

KENT (*to* LEAR).

Good my lord, take his offer; go into the house.

LEAR.

I'll talk a word with this same learned Theban.
   (*To* EDGAR.)
What is your study?

EDGAR.

How to prevent* the fiend, and to kill vermin.   forestall

LEAR.

Let me ask you one word in private.

KENT (*to* GLOUCESTER).

Importune him once more to go, my lord;

His wits begin to unsettle.

GLOUCESTER.

Canst thou blame him?

   (*The storm rages.*)

His daughters seek his death; ah, that good Kent!

He said it would be thus, poor banished man!

Thou say'st the king grows mad; I'll tell thee,
   friend,   170

I am almost mad myself: I had a son,

Now outlawed from my blood; he sought my life,

But lately, very late: I loved him, friend:

No father his son dearer: truth to tell thee,

The grief hath crazed my wits. What a night's
   this!

   (*To* LEAR.)

I do beseech your grace—

LEAR.   O, cry you mercy,* sir,   beg your pardon

   (*To* EDGAR.)

Noble philosopher, your company.

EDGAR.

Tom 's a-cold.

GLOUCESTER (*to* EDGAR).

In, fellow, there, into the hovel: keep thee warm.

LEAR.

Come, let's in all.

KENT (*to* LEAR). This way, my lord.

LEAR (*indicating* EDGAR).   With him;   180

   I will keep still with my philosopher.

KENT (*to* GLOUCESTER).

Good my lord, soothe* him; let him take the   indulge
   fellow.

GLOUCESTER (*to* KENT).

Take him you on.

KENT (*to* EDGAR).

Sirrah, come on; go along with us.

LEAR (*to* EDGAR).

Come, good Athenian.

GLOUCESTER.

No words, no words: hush.

EDGAR.

Child Rowland to the dark tower came,
His word was still—Fie, foh, and fum,
  I smell the blood of a British man.[85]
  (*They all go into the hovel.*)

Scene 5. A chamber in Gloucester's castle.

(CORNWALL *enters with* EDMUND.)

CORNWALL.

I will have my revenge ere I depart his house.

EDMUND.

How, my lord, I may be censured,* that nature   *judged*
thus gives way to loyalty, something fears me* to   *I fear*
think of.

CORNWALL.

I now perceive, it was not altogether your brother's
evil disposition made him seek his death; but a pro-
voking merit, set a-work by a reprovable badness in himself.   9

EDMUND.

How malicious is my fortune, that I must repent
to be just!* This is the letter he spoke of, which *regret being righteous*
approves* him an intelligent party* to the advan- *proves/spy*
tages of France. O heavens! that this treason were
not, or not I the detector!

CORNWALL.

Go with me to the duchess.

EDMUND.

If the matter of this paper be certain, you have
mighty business in hand.

CORNWALL.

True or false, it hath made thee earl of Gloucester.
Seek out where thy father is, that he may be
ready for our apprehension.*

19
i.e., of him

EDMUND (*aside*).

If I find him comforting the king, it will stuff his
suspicion more fully. (*To* CORNWALL.) I will per-
severe in my course of loyalty, though the conflict be sore between that and my blood.

CORNWALL.

I will lay trust upon thee; and thou shalt find a
dearer father in my love.

(*They go.*)

SCENE 6. Inside the hovel.[86]

(GLOUCESTER, LEAR, KENT, FOOL, *and* EDGAR *enter.*)

GLOUCESTER (*aside, to* KENT).

Here is better than the open air; take it thank-
fully. I will piece out the comfort with what addition I can: I will not be long from you.

KENT (*aside, to* GLOUCESTER).

All the power of his wits have given way to
his impatience: the gods reward your kindness!

(GLOUCESTER *goes.*)

EDGAR.

Frateretto* calls me; and tells me Nero is an angler
in the lake of darkness.[87] Pray, innocent,* and beware the foul fiend.

i.e.,
a fiend
simpleton

FOOL.

Prithee, nuncle, tell me whether a madman be a
gentleman or a yeoman?

10
*Nero
all
mad*

LEAR.

A king, a king!

FOOL.

No, he's a yeoman that has a gentleman to his
son; for he's a mad yeoman that sees his son a
gentleman before him.[88]

LEAR.

To have a thousand with red burning spits
Come hissing in upon 'em—

EDGAR.

The foul fiend bites my back.

FOOL.

He's mad that trusts in the tameness of a wolf, a
horse's health, a boy's love, or a whore's oath.   20

LEAR.

It shall be done; I will arraign them[89] straight.
    (*To* EDGAR.)
Come, sit thou here, most learned justicer;
    (*To the* FOOL.)
Thou, sapient sir, sit here. Now, you she foxes!

EDGAR.

Look, where he stands and glares!
Wantest thou eyes at trial, madam?
    Come o'er the bourn, Bessy, to me,[90]—

FOOL.

    Her boat hath a leak,
        And she must not speak
    Why she dares not come over to thee.   30

EDGAR.

The foul fiend haunts poor Tom in the voice of
a nightingale. Hopdance cries in Tom's belly for
two white herring.[91] Croak* not, black angel;   rumble
I have no food for thee.

KENT (*to* LEAR).

How do you, sir? Stand you not so amazed:
Will you lie down and rest upon the cushions?

LEAR.

I'll see their trial first. Bring in the evidence.
    (*To* EDGAR.)
Thou robed man of justice, take thy place;

(*To the* FOOL.)
And thou, his yoke-fellow of equity,
Bench by his side.
    (*To* KENT.)   You are o' the commission,   40
Sit you too.

EDGAR.

Let us deal justly.
  Sleepest or wakest thou, jolly shepherd?
    Thy sheep be in the corn;
  And for one blast of thy minikin* mouth,   pretty
    Thy sheep shall take no harm.   little
Pur! The cat is gray.

LEAR.

Arraign her first; 'tis Goneril. I here take my
oath before this honorable assembly, she kicked
the poor king her father.   50

FOOL.

Come hither, mistress. Is your name Goneril?

LEAR.

She cannot deny it.

FOOL.

Cry you mercy, I took you for a joint-stool.

LEAR.

And here's another, whose warped looks proclaim
What store* her heart is made on. Stop her there!   stuff
Arms, arms, sword, fire! Corruption in the place!
False justicer, why hast thou let her 'scape?

EDGAR.

Bless thy five wits!   60

KENT.

O pity!
  (*To* LEAR.) Sir, where is the patience now,
That you so oft have boasted to retain?

EDGAR (*aside*).

My tears begin to take his part so much,
They'll mar my counterfeiting.

LEAR.

The little dogs and all,

Tray, Blanch, and Sweet-heart, see, they bark at
me.

EDGAR.

Tom will throw his head at them.
Avaunt, you curs!
Be thy mouth or black or white,
Tooth that poisons if it bite;   70
Mastiff, greyhound, mongrel grim,
Hound or spaniel, brach* or lym,*   bitch/
Or bobtail tike* or trundle-tail,   bloodhound
Tom will make them weep and wail: cur
For, with throwing thus my head,
Dogs leap the hatch,* and all are fled.   half door
Do de, de, de. Sessa! Come, march to wakes and
fairs and market-towns. Poor Tom, thy horn is
dry.⁹²

LEAR.

Then let them anatomize Regan; see what breeds   80
about her heart. Is there any cause in nature that
makes these hard hearts? (To EDGAR.) You, sir,
I entertain* for one of my hundred; only I do not   engage
like the fashion of your garments: you will say
they are Persian* attire; but let them be changed.   i.e., gor-
                                                      geous
KENT.

Now, good my lord, lie here and rest awhile.

LEAR.

Make no noise, make no noise; draw the curtains:
so, so, so. We'll go to supper i' the morning.
(As he lies down.) So, so, so.   91

FOOL.

And I'll go to bed at noon.
(GLOUCESTER returns.)

GLOUCESTER.

Come hither, friend: where is the king my master?

KENT (aside, to GLOUCESTER).

Here, sir; but trouble him not, his wits are gone.

GLOUCESTER (aside, to KENT).

Good friend, I prithee, take him in thy arms;

I have o'erheard a plot of death upon* him: against
There is a litter ready; lay him in 't,
And drive towards Dover, friend, where thou shalt
   meet
Both welcome and protection. Take up thy master:
If thou shouldst dally half an hour, his life,   100
With thine, and all that offer to defend him,
Stand in assured loss: take up, take up;
And follow me, that will to some provision*   *i.e.,* for
Give thee quick conduct.   safety

KENT.   Oppressed nature sleeps:
This rest might yet have balmed thy broken sinews,
Which, if convenience will not allow,
Stand in hard* cure.   are hard
                      to
   (*To the* FOOL.)   Come, help to bear thy master;
Thou must not stay behind.

GLOUCESTER.   Come, come, away.
   (*They leave the hovel,* KENT *and the* FOOL *carrying* LEAR. EDGAR *remains behind.*)

EDGAR.

When we our betters see bearing our woes,
We scarcely think our miseries our foes.   110
Who alone suffers, suffers most i' the mind,
Leaving free things and happy shows* behind: appearances
But then the mind much sufferance doth o'erskip,
When grief hath mates, and bearing fellowship.
How light and portable* my pain seems now,   endurable
When that which makes me bend makes the king
   bow,
He childed as I fathered!⁹³
               Tom, away!
Mark the high noises;* and thyself bewray*   disturbances/
                      reveal
When false opinion, whose wrong thought
   defiles thee,
In thy just proof, repeals and reconciles thee.⁹⁴   120
What will hap more tonight, safe 'scape the king!
Lurk, lurk.*   hide
   (*He goes.*)

SCENE 7. A chamber in Gloucester's castle.

(CORNWALL *enters with* GONERIL, EDMUND, REGAN, *and some* SERVANTS.)

CORNWALL (*to* GONERIL, *giving her a letter*).
Post speedily to my lord your husband; show him
this letter: the army of France is landed. (*To*
SERVANTS.) Seek out the villain Gloucester.
(*Some of the* SERVANTS *leave.*)

REGAN.
Hang him instantly.

GONERIL.
Pluck out his eyes.

CORNWALL.
Leave him to my displeasure. Edmund, keep you
our sister company: the revenges we are bound to
take upon your traitorous father are not fit for
your beholding. Advise the duke, where you are
going, to a most festinate* preparation: we are   hurried
bound to the like. Our posts shall be swift and in-   11
telligent betwixt us. (*To* GONERIL.) Farewell,
dear sister. (*To* EDMUND.) Farewell, my lord of
Gloucester.[95]
(*To* OSWALD *as he enters.*)
How now! Where's the king?

OSWALD.
My lord of Gloucester hath conveyed him hence:
Some five or six and thirty of his knights,
Hot questrists* after him, met him at gate: seekers
Who, with some other of the lords dependents,
Are gone with him towards Dover; where they
    boast
To have well-armèd friends.

CORNWALL.   Get horses for your mistress.   20

GONERIL (*to* CORNWALL *and* REGAN).
Farewell, sweet lord, and sister.

CORNWALL.

    Edmund, farewell.

      (GONERIL, EDMUND, *and* OSWALD *leave.*)

      (*To other* SERVANTS.) Go seek the traitor Glou-
        cester,

    Pinion him like a thief, bring him before us.

      (SERVANTS *go.*)

    Though well we may not pass upon his life

    Without the form of justice, yet our power

    Shall do a courtesy to our wrath, which men

    May blame, but not control.[96]

                        Who's there? The traitor?

      (GLOUCESTER *is brought in by* SERVANTS.)

REGAN.

    Ingrateful fox! 'Tis he.

CORNWALL.

    Bind fast his corky* arms.   shriveled

GLOUCESTER.

    What mean your graces? Good my friends, con-
      sider   30

    You are my guests: do me no foul play, friends.

CORNWALL.

    Bind him, I say.

REGAN (*as the* SERVANTS *bind his arms behind him*).

              Hard, hard.

      (*To* GLOUCESTER.) O filthy traitor!

GLOUCESTER.

    Unmerciful lady as you are, I'm none.

CORNWALL.

    To this chair bind him.

      (*The* SERVANTS *bind* GLOUCESTER *to a chair.*)

                       Villain, thou shalt find—

      (REGAN *plucks his beard.*)

GLOUCESTER.

    By the kind gods, 'tis most ignobly done

    To pluck me by the beard.

REGAN.

    So white, and such a traitor!

GLOUCESTER.   Naughty lady,
  These hairs, which thou dost ravish from my
    chin,
  Will quicken,* and accuse thee: I am your host: become
  With robbers' hands my hospitable favors*   alive
                                                         features
  You should not ruffle thus. What will you do?   41

CORNWALL.
  Come, sir, what letters had you late from France?

REGAN.
  Be simple answerer, for we know the truth.

CORNWALL.
  And what confederacy have you with the traitors
  Late footed in the kingdom?

REGAN.
  To whose hands have you sent the lunatic king?
  Speak.

GLOUCESTER.
    I have a letter guessingly set down,
  Which came from one that's of a neutral heart,
  And not from one opposed.

CORNWALL.   Cunning.

REGAN.   And false.

CORNWALL.
  Where hast thou sent the king?   50

GLOUCESTER.
  To Dover.

REGAN.
  Wherefore to Dover? Wast thou not charged at
    peril—

CORNWALL.
  Wherefore to Dover? Let him first answer that.

GLOUCESTER.
  I am tied to the stake, and I must stand the course.[97]

REGAN.
  Wherefore to Dover, sir?

GLOUCESTER.
  Because I would not see thy cruel nails
  Pluck out his poor old eyes; nor thy fierce sister

In his anointed flesh stick boarish fangs.[98]
The sea, with such a storm as his bare head
In hell-black night endured, would have buoyed
    up,   60
And quenched the stellèd* fires: stellar
Yet, poor old heart, he holp* the heavens to rain.   helped
If wolves had at thy gate howled that stern time,
Thou shouldst have said "Good porter, turn the
    key,"
All cruels else subscribed: but I shall see
The winged vengeance overtake such children.[99]

CORNWALL.
See 't shalt thou never. Fellows, hold the chair.
Upon these eyes of thine I'll set my foot.
    (*The* SERVANTS *tip the chair back and* CORNWALL
    grinds his heel into one of GLOUCESTER'S *eyes.*)

GLOUCESTER.
He that will think to live till he be old,
Give me some help! O cruel! O you gods!   70

REGAN.
One side will mock another; the other too.

CORNWALL.
If you see vengeance—

FIRST SERVANT (*stopping* CORNWALL, *who is about to
    proceed*).

                     Hold your hand, my lord:
I have served you ever since I was a child;
But better service have I never done you
Than now to bid you hold.

REGAN.   How now, you dog!

FIRST SERVANT.
If you did wear a beard upon your chin,
I'd shake it on this quarrel. What do you mean?

CORNWALL.
My villain!
    (*They draw their swords and fight.*)

FIRST SERVANT.
Nay, then, come on, and take the chance of anger.

REGAN (*to a* SERVANT).

Give me thy sword. A peasant stand up thus!   80
   (*Taking a sword, she stabs the* FIRST SERVANT *in
   the back.*)

FIRST SERVANT.

O, I am slain! My lord, you have one eye left
To see some mischief on him. O!
   (*He dies.*)

CORNWALL.

Lest it see more, prevent it.
   (*Stamping out* GLOUCESTER's *other eye.*)
                              Out, vile jelly!
Where is thy luster now?

GLOUCESTER.

All dark and comfortless. Where's my son
   Edmund?
Edmund, enkindle all the sparks of nature,
To quit* this horrid act.   repay

REGAN.   Out, treacherous villain!
Thou call'st on him that hates thee: it was he
That made the overture* of thy treasons to us;   disclosure
Who is too good to pity thee.   90

GLOUCESTER.

O my follies! Then Edgar was abused.
Kind gods, forgive me that, and prosper him!

REGAN.

Go thrust him out at gates, and let him smell
His way to Dover.
   (*One of the* SERVANTS *unties* GLOUCESTER *from
   the chair.*)
   (*To* CORNWALL.)
How is 't, my lord? How look you?

CORNWALL.

I have received a hurt: follow me, lady.
   (*To* SERVANTS.)
Turn out that eyeless villain.
   (*Indicating dead* SERVANT.) Throw this slave
Upon the dunghill.

(GLOUCESTER *is led out and body removed.*)
                    Regan, I bleed apace:
Untimely comes this hurt: give me your arm.
    (*He goes, supported by* REGAN.)

SECOND SERVANT.

I'll never care what wickedness I do,
If this man come to good.

THIRD SERVANT.   If she live long,   100
And in the end meet the old course of death,
Women will all turn monsters.

SECOND SERVANT.

Let's follow the old carl, and get the Bedlam*   lunatic
To lead him where he would: his roguish madness
Allows itself to anything.

THIRD SERVANT.

Go thou: I'll fetch some flax and whites of eggs
To apply to his bleeding face. Now, heaven help
    him!
    (*They leave.*)

ACT IV

Scene 1. A desolate heath.

(EDGAR *enters, still disguised as Mad Tom.*)

EDGAR.

    Yet better thus, and known to be contemned,*   held in
                                                              contempt
    Than still contemned and flattered. To be worst,
    The lowest and most dejected thing of fortune,
    Stands still in esperance,* lives not in fear: hope
    The lamentable change is from the best;
    The worst returns to laughter. Welcome, then,
    Thou unsubstantial air that I embrace!
    The wretch that thou hast blown unto the worst
    Owes nothing to thy blasts.

                            But who comes here?
    (*The blinded* GLOUCESTER *enters, led by an* OLD
    MAN.)

    My father, poorly led? World, world, O world!   10
    But that thy strange mutations make us hate thee,
    Life would not yield to age.[100]

OLD MAN (*to* GLOUCESTER).

    O, my good lord, I have been your tenant, and
    your father's tenant, these fourscore years.

GLOUCESTER.

    Away, get thee away; good friend, be gone:
    Thy comforts can do me no good at all;
    Thee they may hurt.

OLD MAN.

    Alack, sir, you cannot see your way.

GLOUCESTER.

    I have no way, and therefore want no eyes;   20

I stumbled when I saw: full oft 'tis seen,
Our means secure us, and our mere defects
Prove our commodities.*101   O dear son Edgar,   benefits
The food of thy abusèd father's wrath!
Might I but live to see thee in my touch,
I'd say I had eyes again!

OLD MAN (*aware of* EDGAR's *presence*).
                              How now! Who's there?

EDGAR (*aside*).
O gods! Who is 't can say "I am at the worst"?
I am worse than e'er I was.

OLD MAN.   'Tis poor mad Tom.

EDGAR (*aside*).
And worse I may be yet: the worst is not
So long as we can say "This is the worst."   30

OLD MAN.
Fellow, where goest?

GLOUCESTER (*to the* OLD MAN).
                              Is it a beggar-man?

OLD MAN.
Madman and beggar too.

GLOUCESTER.
He has some reason, else he could not beg.
I' the last night's storm I such a fellow saw;
Which made me think a man a worm: my son
Came then into my mind; and yet my mind
Was then scarce friends with him: I have heard
    more since.
As flies to wanton boys, are we to the gods,
They kill us for their sport.

EDGAR (*aside*).   How should this be?
Bad is the trade that must play fool to sorrow,   40
Angering itself and others.
    (*To* GLOUCESTER.)
                              Bless thee, master!

GLOUCESTER.
Is that the naked fellow?

OLD MAN.   Ay, my lord.

GLOUCESTER (*to the* OLD MAN).

Then, prithee, get thee gone: if, for my sake,
Thou wilt o'ertake us, hence a mile or twain,
I' the way toward Dover, do it for ancient love;
And bring some covering for this naked soul,
Who I'll entreat to lead me.

OLD MAN.   Alack, sir, he is mad.

GLOUCESTER.

'Tis the times' plague, when madmen lead the
blind.
Do as I bid thee, or rather do thy pleasure;
Above the rest, be gone.   50

OLD MAN.

I'll bring him the best 'parel that I have,
Come on 't what will.
   (*He goes.*)

GLOUCESTER.

Sirrah, naked fellow—

EDGAR.

Poor Tom 's a-cold.
   (*Aside.*)   I cannot daub* it further.   dissemble

GLOUCESTER.

Come hither, fellow.

EDGAR (*aside*).

And yet I must.
   (*Approaching* GLOUCESTER.)
                              Bless thy sweet eyes, they bleed.

GLOUCESTER.

Know'st thou the way to Dover?

EDGAR.

Both stile and gate, horse-way and foot-path. Poor
Tom hath been scared out of his good wits: bless
thee, good man's son, from the foul fiend! Five   60
fiends have been in poor Tom at once; of lust, as
Obidicut; Hobbididance, prince of dumbness;
Mahu, of stealing; Modo, of murder; Flibbertigibbet, of mopping and mowing,* who since possesses   grimacing

chambermaids and waiting-women. So, bless thee,
master!

GLOUCESTER.

Here, take this purse, thou whom the heavens'
   plagues
Have humbled to all strokes: that I am wretched
Makes thee the happier: heavens, deal so still!
Let the superfluous and lust-dieted man,   70
That slaves your ordinance, that will not see
Because he doth not feel, feel your power quickly;
So distribution should undo excess,102
And each man have enough. Dost thou know
   Dover?

EDGAR.

Ay, master.

GLOUCESTER.

There is a cliff, whose high and bending head
Looks fearfully in* the confined deep: fear-arousing
                                                      into
Bring me but to the very brim of it,
And I'll repair the misery thou dost bear
With something rich about me: from that place   80
I shall no leading need.

EDGAR.   Give me thy arm:
Poor Tom shall lead thee.
   (*They go.*)

SCENE 2. Before the Duke of Albany's palace.

(GONERIL *and* EDMUND *enter.*)

GONERIL.

Welcome, my lord: I marvel our mild husband
Not met us on the way.
   (*To* OSWALD *as he comes out of the palace.*)
                         Now, where's your master?

OSWALD.

Madam, within; but never man so changed.
I told him of the army that was landed;

He smiled at it: I told him you were coming;
His answer was "The worse": of Gloucester's
   treachery,
And of the loyal service of his son,
When I informed him, then he called me sot,*   fool
And told me I had turned the wrong side out:
What most he should dislike seems pleasant to
   him;   10
What like, offensive.
GONERIL (*to* EDMUND).
                   Then shall you go no further.
It is the cowish* terror of his spirit,   cowardly
That dares not undertake: he'll not feel wrongs
Which tie him to an answer. Our wishes* on   *i.e.,* what we
   the way   wished for
May prove effects.* Back, Edmund, to my brother;   happen
Hasten his musters and conduct his powers:
I must change arms at home, and give the distaff
Into my husband's hands. This trusty servant
Shall pass between us: ere long you are like to
   hear,
If you dare venture in your own behalf,   20
A mistress's command. Wear this.[103]
   (*Gives him a favor.*)   Spare speech;
Decline your head.
   (*Kisses him.*)   This kiss, if it durst speak,
Would stretch thy spirits up into the air:
Conceive,* and fare thee well.   understand
EDMUND.
Yours in the ranks of death.
GONERIL.   My most dear Gloucester!
  (EDMUND *leaves.*)
  O, the difference of man and man!
  To thee a woman's services are due:
  My fool usurps my body.
OSWALD.   Madam, here comes my lord.
   (*As* ALBANY *comes from the palace,* OSWALD
   goes back in.)

GONERIL.

I have been worth the whistle.

ALBANY.   O Goneril!
You are not worth the dust which the rude wind   30
Blows in your face. I fear* your disposition: *fear for*
That nature, which contemns its origin,
Cannot be bordered certain in itself;104
She that herself will sliver and disbranch
From her material sap, perforce must wither
And come to deadly use.

GONERIL.

No more; the text is foolish.

ALBANY.

Wisdom and goodness to the vile seem vile;
Filths savor but themselves.105 What have you
   done?
Tigers, not daughters, what have you performed?   40
A father, and a gracious agèd man,
Whose reverence even the head-lugged bear
   would lick
Most barbarous, most degenerate—have you
   madded.*   *made mad*
Could my good brother suffer you to do it?
A man, a prince, by him so benefited!
If that the heavens do not their visible spirits
Send quickly down to tame these vile offenses,
It will come,
Humanity must perforce prey on itself,
Like monsters of the deep.

GONERIL.   Milk-livered man!   50
That bearest a cheek for blows, a head for
   wrongs:
Who hast not in thy brows an eye discerning
Thine honor from thy suffering; that not knowest
Fools* do those villains pity who are punished   *i.e.,*
Ere they have done their mischief. Where's thy   *only fools*
   drum?
France spreads his banners in our noiseless* land,   *unre-*
   sisting

With plumèd helm thy state begins to threat;*   be threat-
                                                  ened
Whiles thou, a moral* fool, sit'st still, and criest   moral-
                                                  izing
"Alack, why does he so?"

ALBANY.   See thyself, devil!

Proper* deformity seems not in the fiend   appro-
                                                  priate
So horrid as in woman.

GONERIL.   O vain fool!   61

ALBANY.

Thou changed and self-covered thing, for shame,
Be-monster not thy feature.[106] Were 't my fitness
To let these hands obey my blood,
They are apt enough to dislocate and tear
Thy flesh and bones: howe'er* thou art a fiend,   however
                                                  much
A woman's shape doth shield thee.

GONERIL.

Marry, your manhood now[107]—
    (*A* MESSENGER *enters, bearing a letter.*)

ALBANY.

What news?

MESSENGER.

O, my good lord, the Duke of Cornwall's dead;   70
Slain by his servant, going to put out
The other eye of Gloucester.

ALBANY.   Gloucester's eyes!

MESSENGER.

A servant that he bred, thrilled with remorse,*   pity
Opposed against the act, bending* his sword   directing
To his great master; who, thereat enraged,
Flew on him, and amongst them felled* him dead;   they
                                                  felled
But not without that harmful stroke, which since
Hath plucked him after.

ALBANY.   This shows you are above,
You justicers, that these our nether crimes
So speedily can venge! But, O poor Gloucester!   80
Lost he his other eye?

MESSENGER.   Both, both, my lord.
    (*Gives letter to* GONERIL.)

This letter, madam, craves a speedy answer;
'Tis from your sister.

GONERIL (*aside*).

                One way I like this well; *still plotting*
But being widow, and my Gloucester with her,
May all the building in my fancy pluck
Upon my hateful life:[108] another way,
The news is not so tart.—I'll read, and answer.
    (*Goes into the palace.*)

ALBANY.

Where was his son when they did take his eyes?

MESSENGER.

Come with my lady hither.

ALBANY.   He is not here.   90

MESSENGER.

No, my good lord; I met him back* again.   going
                                 back

ALBANY.

Knows he the wickedness?

MESSENGER.

Ay, my good lord; 'twas he informed against
    him;
And quit the house on purpose, that their pun-
    ishment
Might have the freer course.

ALBANY.   Gloucester, I live
To thank thee for the love thou showedst the
    king,
And to revenge thine eyes.   Come hither, friend;
Tell me what more thou know'st.
    (*They go.*)

SCENE 3. The French camp near Dover.

(KENT *enters with a* GENTLEMAN.)

KENT.

Why the King of France is so suddenly gone
back know you the reason?

GENTLEMAN.

Something he left imperfect in the state, which
since his coming forth is thought of; which im-
ports* to the kingdom so much fear and danger,   portends
that his personal return was most required and
necessary.

KENT.

Who hath he left behind him general?

GENTLEMAN.

The Marshal of France, Monsieur La Far.   10

KENT.

Did your letters pierce the queen to any demon-
stration of grief?

GENTLEMAN.

Ay, sir; she took them, read them in my presence;
And now and then an ample tear trilled* down   trickled
Her delicate cheek: it seemed she was a queen
Over her passion;* who, most rebel-like,   grief
Sought to be king o'er her.

KENT.   O, then it moved her.

GENTLEMAN.

Not to a rage: patience and sorrow strove
Who should express her goodliest. You have seen
Sunshine and rain at once: her smiles and tears   20
Were like a better way: those happy smilets,*   little
That played on her ripe lip, seemed not to know   smiles
What guests were in her eyes; which parted
      thence,
As pearls from diamonds dropped. In brief,
Sorrow would be a rarity most beloved,
If all could so become it.

KENT.   Made she no verbal question?

GENTLEMAN.

'Faith, once or twice she heaved the name of
      "father"
Pantingly forth, as if it pressed her heart;
Cried "Sisters! sisters! Shame of ladies! Sisters!

Kent! Father! Sisters! What, i' the storm?
   I' the night?   30
Let pity not be believed!" There she shook
The holy water from her heavenly eyes,
And clamor* moistened: then away she started   cries of
To deal with grief alone.   grief

KENT.   It is the stars,
The stars above us, govern our conditions;
Else one self* mate and mate could not beget   one and
Such different issues. You spoke not with her   the same
   since?

GENTLEMAN.
No.

KENT.
Was this before the king returned?

GENTLEMAN.   No, since.

KENT.
Well, sir, the poor distressèd Lear's i' the town;   40
Who sometime, in his better tune,* remembers   intervals
What we are come about, and by no means
Will yield* to see his daughter.   assent

GENTLEMAN.   Why, good sir?

KENT.   *he's humbled*

A sovereign* shame so elbows him: his own   compelling
   unkindness,
That stripped her from his benediction, turned
   her
To foreign casualties,* gave her dear rights   hazards
To his dog-hearted daughters, these things sting
His mind so venomously, that burning shame
Detains him from Cordelia.

GENTLEMAN.   Alack, poor gentleman!

KENT.
Of Albany's and Cornwall's powers you heard
   not?   50

GENTLEMAN.
'Tis so, they are afoot.

KENT.

    Well, sir, I'll bring you to our master Lear,
    And leave you to attend him: some dear* cause   important
    Will in concealment wrap me up awhile;
    When I am known aright, you shall not grieve
    Lending* me this acquaintance. I pray you, go   affording
    Along with me.
       (*They leave.*)

SCENE 4. Another part of the French camp.

(CORDELIA *and a* DOCTOR *enter, accompanied by*
SOLDIERS *with drums and banners.*)

CORDELIA.

    Alack, 'tis he: why, he was met even now
    As mad as the vexed sea; singing aloud;
    Crowned with rank fumiter and furrow-weeds,
    With burdocks, hemlock, nettles, cuckoo-
      flowers,[109]
    Darnel, and all the idle weeds that grow
    In our sustaining corn.*   wheat
      (*To an* OFFICER.)   A century* send forth;   100 soldiers
    Search every acre in the high-grown field,
    And bring him to our eye.
      (*The* OFFICER *leaves.*)
      (*To the* DOCTOR.)
                 What can* man's wisdom   can be done by
    In the restoring his bereaved sense?
    He that helps him take all my outward worth.   10

DOCTOR.

    There is means, madam:
    Our foster-nurse of nature is repose,
    The which he lacks; that to provoke* in him,   induce
    Are many   simples operative,* whose power   effective herbs
    Will close the eye of anguish.

CORDELIA.   All blest secrets,

    All you unpublished* virtues of the earth,   unknown

Spring with my tears! be aidant and remediate*   remedial
In the good man's distress!
   (*To the* DOCTOR.)   Seek, seek for him;
Lest his ungoverned rage dissolve the life
That wants the means* to lead it.   reason
   (DOCTOR *and some* SOLDIERS *go as a* MESSENGER
   enters.)

MESSENGER.   News, madam;   20
The British powers are marching hitherward.

CORDELIA.
'Tis known before; our preparation stands
In expectation of them.
   (*Dismissing the* MESSENGER.)
              O dear father,
It is thy business that I go about;
Therefore great France
My mourning and important tears hath pitied.
No blown* ambition doth our arms incite,   swollen
But love, dear love, and our aged father's right:
Soon may I hear and see him!
   (*She leaves, followed by remaining* SOLDIERS.)

SCENE 5. Before Gloucester's castle.

   (REGAN *enters with* OSWALD, *who carries a
letter.*)

REGAN.
But are my brother's powers set forth?

OSWALD.   Ay, madam.

REGAN.
Himself in person there?

OSWALD.   Madam, with much ado:
Your sister is the better soldier.

REGAN.
Lord Edmund spake not with your lord at home?

OSWALD.
No, madam.

REGAN.

What might import* my sister's letter to him?   mean

OSWALD.

I know not, lady.

REGAN.

'Faith, he is posted* hence on serious matter.   has hurried
It was great ignorance,* Gloucester's eyes   stupidity
   being out,
To let him live: where he arrives he moves   10
All hearts against us: Edmund, I think, is gone,
In pity of his misery, to dispatch*   take
His nighted life; moreover, to descry
The strength o' the enemy.

OSWALD.

I must needs after him, madam, with my letter.

REGAN.

Our troops set forth tomorrow: stay with us;
The ways are dangerous.

OSWALD.   I may not, madam:
My lady charged my duty in this business.

REGAN.

Why should she write to Edmund? Might not you
Transport her purposes by word? Belike,   20
Something—I know not what: I'll love thee much,
Let me unseal the letter.

OSWALD.   Madam, I had rather—

REGAN.

I know your lady does not love her husband;
I am sure of that: and at her late being here
She gave strange oeillades* and most speaking   ogles
   looks
To noble Edmund. I know you are of* her   in
   bosom.*   confidence

OSWALD.

I, madam?

REGAN.

I speak in understanding; you are, I know 't:
Therefore I do advise you, take this note: 29

My lord is dead; Edmund and I have talked;*   agreed
And more convenient* is he for my hand   suitable
Than for your lady's: you may gather more.
If you do find him, pray you, give him this;
  (*Gives him a letter.*)
And when your mistress hears thus much from
  you,
I pray, desire her call her wisdom to her.
  So, fare you well.
If you do chance to hear of that blind traitor,
Preferment* falls on him that cuts him off.   advancement

OSWALD.
Would I could meet him, madam! I should
  show
What party I do follow.

REGAN.   Fare thee well.   40
  (OSWALD *leaves, and* REGAN *goes into the castle.*)

SCENE 6. The fields near Dover.

(EDGAR, *in peasant dress, enters, leading* GLOU-
CESTER.)

GLOUCESTER.
When shall we come to the top of that same hill?
EDGAR.
You do climb up it now: look, how we labor.
GLOUCESTER.
Methinks the ground is even.
EDGAR.   Horrible steep.
  Hark, do you hear the sea?
GLOUCESTER.   No, truly.
EDGAR.
Why, then, your other senses grow imperfect
By your eyes' anguish.
GLOUCESTER.   So may it be, indeed:
Methinks thy voice is altered; and thou speakest
In better phrase and matter than thou didst.

EDGAR.

You're much deceived: in nothing am I changed
But in my garments.

GLOUCESTER.

Methinks you're better spoken.   10

EDGAR.

Come on, sir; here's the place: stand still. How
    fearful
And dizzy 'tis, to cast one's eyes so low!
The crows and choughs* that wing the midway   blackbirds
    air
Show scarce so gross* as beetles: half way down   large
Hangs one that gathers samphire, dreadful
    trade!110
Methinks he seems no bigger than his head:
The fishermen, that walk upon the beach,
Appear like mice; and yond tall anchoring bark,
Diminished to her cock;* her cock, a buoy   tender
Almost too small for sight: the murmuring surge,   20
That on the unnumbered idle pebbles chafes,
Cannot be heard so high. I'll look no more;
Lest my brain turn, and the deficient sight
Topple* down headlong.   topple me

GLOUCESTER.   Set me where you stand.

EDGAR.

Give me your hand: you are now within a foot
Of the extreme verge: for all beneath the moon
Would I not leap upright.

GLOUCESTER.   Let go my hand.
Here, friend, 's another purse; in it a jewel
Well worth a poor man's taking: fairies and gods
Prosper it with thee!111
    (Giving purse to EDGAR.)
                        Go thou farther off;   30
Bid me farewell, and let me hear thee going.

EDGAR (moving some distance away as he speaks).

Now fare you well, good sir.

GLOUCESTER.   With all my heart.

EDGAR (*aside*).

Why I do trifle thus with his despair
Is done to cure it.

GLOUCESTER (*kneeling*).

              O you mighty gods!
This world I do renounce, and, in your sights,
Shake patiently my great affliction off:
If I could bear it longer, and not fall
To quarrel with* your great opposeless*   rebel against/
  wills,   irresistible
My snuff* and loathèd part of nature should   wick
Burn itself out. If Edgar live, O, bless him!   40
Now, fellow, fare thee well.

    (*He falls forward, and then faints.*)

EDGAR.   Gone, sir: farewell.
And yet I know not how conceit* may rob   imagination
The treasury of life, when life itself
Yields to the theft: had he been where he thought,
By this, had thought been past.

    (*Going to* GLOUCESTER.)   Alive or dead?
Ho, you sir! Friend! Hear you, sir! Speak!
Thus might he pass* indeed: yet he revives.   die
What are you, sir?

GLOUCESTER (*reviving*). Away, and let me die.

EDGAR (*in a different voice*).

Hadst thou been aught but gossamer,* feathers,   cobweb
  air,
So many fathom down precipitating,   50
Thou 'dst shivered* like an egg: but thou dost shattered
  breathe;
Hast heavy substance; bleed'st not; speak'st; art
  sound.
Ten masts at each* make not the altitude   stood on
Which thou hast perpendicularly fell: each other
Thy life's a miracle. Speak yet again.

GLOUCESTER.

But have I fallen, or no?

EDGAR.

From the dread summit of this chalky bourn.*   boundary
Look up a-height; the shrill-gorged* lark so far   throated
Cannot be seen or heard: do but look up.

GLOUCESTER.

Alack, I have no eyes.   60
Is wretchedness deprived that benefit,
To end itself by death? 'Twas yet some comfort,
When misery could beguile* the tyrant's rage,   cheat
And frustrate his proud will.

EDGAR (helping him up).   Give me your arm:
Up: so. How is 't? Feel you your legs? You stand.

GLOUCESTER.

Too well, too well.

EDGAR.   This is above all strangeness.
Upon the crown o' the cliff, what thing was that
Which parted from you?

GLOUCESTER.   A poor unfortunate beggar.

EDGAR.

As I stood here below, methought his eyes
Were two full moons; he had a thousand noses,   70
Horns whelked* and waved like the enridgèd   twisted
sea:
It was some fiend; therefore, thou happy father,
Think that the clearest* gods, who make them   glorious
honors
Of men's impossibilities, have preserved thee.

GLOUCESTER.

I do remember now: henceforth I'll bear
Affliction till it do cry out itself
"Enough, enough," and die. That thing you speak of,
I took it for a man; often 'twould say
"The fiend, the fiend." He led me to that place.

EDGAR.

Bear free and patient thoughts.
    But who comes here?   80
(LEAR enters, fantastically dressed with wild
flowers.)

The safer* sense will ne'er accommodate* saner/dress
His master thus.

LEAR.

No, they cannot touch me for coining;* counter-
I am the king himself. feiting

EDGAR.

O thou side-piercing sight!

LEAR.

Nature's above art in that respect.[112] There's
your press-money. That fellow handles his bow
like a crow-keeper: draw me a clothier's yard.
Look, look, a mouse! Peace, peace; this piece of
toasted cheese will do 't. There's my gauntlet; 90
I'll prove it on a giant. Bring up the brown bills.
O, well flown, bird! I' the clout, i' the clout:
hewgh! Give the word.

EDGAR.

Sweet marjoram.

LEAR.

Pass.

GLOUCESTER.

I know that voice.

LEAR.

Ha! Goneril, with a white beard! They flattered
me like a dog; and told me I had white hairs in
my beard ere the black ones were there. To say
"ay" and "no" to everything that I said!—"Ay" 100
and "no" too was no good divinity. When the
rain came to wet me once, and the wind to make
me chatter; when the thunder would not peace* *i.e.,* cease
at my bidding; there I found 'em, there I smelt
'em out. Go to, they are not men o' their words:
they told me I was every thing; 'tis a lie, I am
not ague-proof.

GLOUCESTER.

The trick of that voice I do well remember:
Is 't not the king?

LEAR.   Ay, every inch a king:

When I do stare, see how the subject quakes.   110
I pardon that man's life. What was thy cause?
Adultery?
Thou shalt not die: die for adultery! No:
The wren goes to 't, and the small gilded fly
Does lecher in my sight.
Let copulation thrive; for Gloucester's bastard son
Was kinder to his father than my daughters
Got 'tween the lawful sheets.
To 't, luxury,* pell-mell! for I lack soldiers.   lust
Behold yond simpering dame,   120
Whose face between her forks presages snow;*   *i.e.*, purity
That minces virtue, and does shake the head
To hear of pleasure's name;
The fitchew,* nor the soiled* horse, goes to 't   skunk/
With a more riotous appetite.   full-fed
Down from the waist they are Centaurs,[113]
Though women all above:
But* to the girdle do the gods inherit,*   only/rule
Beneath is all the fiends';
There's hell, there's darkness, there's the sul-
  phurous pit,   130
Burning, scalding, stench, consumption; fie, fie,
fie! Pah, pah! Give me an ounce of civet,* good   perfume
apothecary, to sweeten my imagination: there's
money for thee.

GLOUCESTER.

O, let me kiss that hand!

LEAR.

Let me wipe it first; it smells of mortality.

GLOUCESTER.

O ruined piece of nature!* This great world   masterpiece
Shall so wear out to nought. Dost thou know me?

LEAR.

I remember thine eyes well enough. Dost thou
squiny* at me? No, do thy worst, blind Cupid;   squint

I'll not love. Read thou this challenge; mark but   141
the penning of it.

GLOUCESTER.

Were all the letters suns, I could not see one.

EDGAR.

I would not take* this from report; it is,   believe
And my heart breaks at it.

LEAR.

Read.

GLOUCESTER.

What, with the case* of eyes?   socket

LEAR.

O, ho, are you there with me? No eyes in your
head, nor no money in your purse? Your eyes
are in a heavy case, your purse in a light: yet   150
you see how this world goes.

GLOUCESTER.

I see it feelingly.

LEAR.

What, art mad? A man may see how this world
goes with no eyes. Look with thine ears: see how
yond justice rails upon yond simple thief. Hark,
in thine ears: change places; and, handy-dandy,
which is the justice, which is the thief?114 Thou
hast seen a farmer's dog bark at a beggar?

GLOUCESTER.

Ay, sir.   160

LEAR.

And the creature run from the cur? There thou
mightst behold the great image of authority: a
dog's obeyed in office.
Thou rascal beadle, hold thy bloody hand!
Why dost thou lash that whore? Strip thine own
back;
Thou hotly lust'st to use her in that kind*   manner
For which thou whipp'st her. The usurer hangs
the cozener.*   sharper
Through tattered clothes small vices do appear;

Robes and furred gowns hide all. Plate sin with
  gold,
And the strong lance of justice hurtless breaks;   170
Arm it in rags, a pigmy's straw does pierce it.
None does offend, none, I say, none; I'll able*   authorize
  'em:
Take that of me, my friend, who have the power
To seal the accuser's lips. Get thee glass eyes;
And, like a scurvy* politician, seem   vile
To see the things thou dost not. Now, now, now,
  now:
Pull off my boots: harder, harder: so.

EDGAR.
  O, matter and impertinency* mixed!   incoherence
  Reason in madness!

LEAR.
  If thou wilt weep my fortunes, take my eyes.   180
  I know thee well enough; thy name is Gloucester:
  Thou must be patient; we came crying hither:
  Thou know'st, the first time that we smell the air,
  We wawl* and cry. I will preach to thee: mark.   wail

GLOUCESTER.
  Alack, alack the day!

LEAR.
  When we are born, we cry that we are come
  To this great stage of fools: this' a good block;*   hat
  It were a delicate stratagem, to shoe
  A troop of horse with felt: I'll put 't in proof;*   try it
  And when I have stol'n upon these sons-in-law,   190
  Then, kill, kill, kill, kill, kill, kill!
    (*A* GENTLEMAN *enters with* ATTENDANTS.)

GENTLEMAN.
  O, here he is: lay hand upon him. Sir,
    (ATTENDANTS *hold* LEAR's *arms.*)
  Your most dear daughter—

LEAR.
  No rescue? What, a prisoner? I am even

The natural fool of fortune. Use me well;
You shall have ransom. Let me have surgeons;
I am cut to the brains.

GENTLEMAN.   You shall have anything.

LEAR.

No seconds? All myself?
Why, this would make a man a man of salt,
To use his eyes for garden water-pots,   200
Ay, and laying autumn's dust.

GENTLEMAN.   Good sir—

LEAR.

I will die bravely, like a bridegroom. What!
I will be jovial: come, come; I am a king,
My masters, know you that.

GENTLEMAN.

You are a royal one, and we obey you.

LEAR.

Then there's life in 't. Nay, if you get it, you
shall get it with running. Sa, sa, sa, sa.

(*Breaks from the* ATTENDANT *and runs off,*
ATTENDANTS *in pursuit.*)

GENTLEMAN.

A sight most pitiful in the meanest wretch—
Past speaking of in a king! Thou hast one daugh-
   ter,
Who redeems nature from the general* curse   universal
Which twain have brought her to.   211

EDGAR (*to the* GENTLEMAN).

Hail, gentle sir.

GENTLEMAN.   Sir, speed you; what's your will?

EDGAR.

Do you hear aught, sir, of a battle toward?*   at hand

GENTLEMAN.

Most sure and vulgar:* everyone hears that   common
Which* can distinguish sound.   knowledge
                                                      who

EDGAR.   But, by your favor,
How near's the other army?

GENTLEMAN.

Near and on speedy foot; the main descry*   discovery
Stands on the hourly thought.*   looked for
        any hour

EDGAR.   I thank you, sir: that's all.

GENTLEMAN.

Though that the queen on special cause is here,
Her army is moved on.

EDGAR.   I thank you, sir,   220
    (*The* GENTLEMAN *leaves*.)

GLOUCESTER.

You ever-gentle gods, take my breath from me;
Let not my worser spirit tempt me again
To die before you please!

EDGAR.   Well pray you, father.

GLOUCESTER.

Now, good sir, what are you?

EDGAR.

A most poor man, made tame to fortune's blows;
Who, by the art of known and feeling sorrows,
Am   pregnant to* good pity. Give me your   able to
    hand,   conceive
I'll lead you to some biding.*   abode

GLOUCESTER.   Hearty thanks:
The bounty and the benison of heaven
To boot,* and boot!   besides
    (*They start to leave*, EDGAR *supporting* GLOU-
    CESTER *by the arm, when* OSWALD *enters and*
    threatens GLOUCESTER *with drawn sword*.)

OSWALD.   A proclaimed prize! Most happy!   230
That eyeless head of thine was first framed flesh
To raise my fortunes. Thou old unhappy traitor,
Briefly thyself remember:* the sword is out   repent
That must destroy thee.

GLOUCESTER.   Now let thy friendly hand
Put strength enough to 't.
    (EDGAR *steps between them*.)

OSWALD.   Wherefore, bold peasant,

Darest thou support a published* traitor?   proclaimed
  Hence;
Lest that the infection of his fortune take
Like hold on thee. Let go his arm.

EDGAR (*in broad, country dialect*).

Chill not let go, zir, without vurther 'casion.   240

OSWALD.

Let go, slave, or thou diest!

EDGAR.

Good gentleman, go your gait,115 and let poor
volk pass. An chud ha' bin zwaggered out of my
life, 'twould not ha' bin zo long as 'tis by a vort-
night. Nay, come not near th' old man; keep out,
che vor ye, or ise try whether your costard* or   head
my ballow* be the harder: chill be plain with you.   cudgel

OSWALD.

Out, dunghill!

EDGAR.

Chill pick your teeth, zir: come; no matter vor   250
your foins.

    (*They fight, and* EDGAR *strikes him down.*)

OSWALD.

Slave, thou hast slain me: villain, take my purse:
If ever thou wilt thrive, bury my body;
And give the letters which thou find'st about me
To Edmund earl of Gloucester; seek him out
Upon the British party. O, untimely death!
    (*He dies.*)

EDGAR.

I know thee well: a serviceable villain;
As duteous to the vices of thy mistress
As badness would desire.

GLOUCESTER.   What, is he dead?

EDGAR.

Sit you down, father; rest you.   260

    (*As* GLOUCESTER *sits,* EDGAR *goes through* OSWALD's
    pockets.*)

Let's see these pockets: the letters that he speaks
of
May be my friends. He's dead; I am only sorry
He had no other death's-man.* Let us see: *executioner*
Leave,* gentle wax.   *by your leave*
   (*Unsealing the letter.*) And, manners, blame us
   not:
To know our enemies' minds, we'd rip their hearts;
Their papers, is more lawful.
   (*Reads.*)
"Let our reciprocal vows be remembered. You
have many opportunities to cut him off: if your
will want not, time and place will be fruitfully
offered. There is nothing done, if he return the
conqueror: then am I the prisoner, and his bed my
jail; from the loathed warmth whereof deliver me,
and supply the place for your labor.
      "Your—wife, so I would say—
           "Affectionate servant,
                "GONERIL."

O undistinguished* space of woman's will!*   *limitless/ lust*
A plot upon her virtuous husband's life;
And the exchange my brother! Here, in the sands,   280
Thee I'll rake up,* the post* unsanctified   *bury/ messenger*
Of murderous lechers: and in the mature time
With this ungracious paper strike the sight
Of the death-practiced* duke: for him 'tis well   *death- plotted*
That of thy death and business I can tell.
   (*Tucks the letter away.*)

GLOUCESTER.
The king is mad: how stiff is my vile sense,
That I stand up, and have ingenious* feeling   *keen*
Of my huge sorrows! Better I were distract:*   *insane*
So should my thoughts be severed from my griefs,
And woes by wrong imaginations lose   290
The knowledge of themselves.
EDGAR.   Give me your hand:
   (*A distant drum is heard.*)

Far off, methinks, I hear the beaten drum:
Come, father, I'll bestow you with a friend.
    (EDGAR *leads* GLOUCESTER *off*.)

SCENE 7. Before a tent in the French camp. Soft music plays.[116]

(DOCTOR, *the* GENTLEMAN, *and* SERVANTS *are in attendance.* CORDELIA *and* KENT *enter*.)

CORDELIA.

O thou good Kent, how shall I live and work,
To match thy goodness? My life will be too short,
And every measure fail me.

KENT.

To be acknowledged, madam, is o'erpaid.
All my reports go with the modest truth;
Nor more nor clipped,* but so.   abridged

CORDELIA.   Be better suited:
These weeds* are memories of those worser hours: garments
I prithee, put them off.

KENT.   Pardon me, dear madam;
Yet to be known shortens my made intent:
My boon* I make it, that you know me not   favor
Till time and I think meet.   to me
                                                    11

CORDELIA.

Then be 't so, my good lord.
    (*To the* DOCTOR.)   How does the king?

DOCTOR.

Madam, sleeps still.

CORDELIA.

O you kind gods,
Cure this great breach in his abusèd nature!
The untuned and jarring senses, O, wind up
Of this child-changèd* father!   changed
                                                  into a child
DOCTOR.   So please your majesty
That we may wake the king: he hath slept long.

CORDELIA.

Be governed by your knowledge, and proceed
I' the sway of your own will. Is he arrayed?   20

GENTLEMAN.

Ay, madam; in the heaviness of his sleep
We put fresh garments on him.

(LEAR, *asleep, is borne in by* SERVANTS.)

DOCTOR.

Be by, good madam, when we do awake him;
I doubt not of his temperance.*   self-
                                                          control

CORDELIA.   Very well.

DOCTOR.

Please you, draw near.

(KENT *and* CORDELIA *approach the bed.*)

                          Louder the music there!

CORDELIA.

O my dear father! Restoration hang
Thy medicine on my lips; and let this kiss
Repair those violent harms that my two sisters
Have in thy reverence made!

(*Kisses him.*)

KENT.   Kind and dear princess!

CORDELIA.

Had you not been their father, these white flakes   30
Had challenged pity of them. Was this a face
To be opposed against the warring winds?
To stand against the deep dread-bolted thunder?
In the most terrible and nimble stroke
Of quick, cross lightning? to watch—poor perdu!—
With this thin helm?[117] Mine enemy's dog,
Though he had bit me, should have stood that
      night
Against my fire; and wast thou fain,* poor father,   glad
To hovel thee with swine, and rogues* forlorn,   vagrants
In short and musty straw? Alack, alack!   40
'Tis wonder that thy life and wits at once
Had not concluded all.*   completely

(LEAR *stirs.*)   He wakes; speak to him.

DOCTOR.
Madam, do you; 'tis fittest.

CORDELIA (*to* LEAR).
How does my royal lord? How fares your majesty?

LEAR.
You do me wrong to take me out o' the grave:
Thou art a soul in bliss; but I am bound
Upon a wheel of fire, that mine own tears
Do scald like molten lead.

CORDELIA.   Sir, do you know me?

LEAR.
You are a spirit, I know: when did you die?

CORDELIA.
Still, still, far wide!   50

DOCTOR.
He's scarce awake: let him alone awhile.

LEAR.
Where have I been? Where am I? Fair daylight?
I am mightily abused. I should e'en die with pity,
To see another thus. I know not what to say.
I will not swear these are my hands: let's see;
I feel this pin prick. Would I were assured
Of my condition!

CORDELIA.   O, look upon me, sir,
And hold your hands in benediction o'er me:
No, sir, you must not kneel.

LEAR.   Pray, do not mock me: 59
I am a very foolish fond* old man,   doting
Fourscore and upward, not an hour more nor less;
And, to deal plainly,
I fear I am not in my perfect mind.
Methinks I should know you, and know this man;
Yet I am doubtful: for I am mainly ignorant
What place this is; and all the skill I have
Remembers not these garments; nor I know not
Where I did lodge last night. Do not laugh at me;
For, as I am a man, I think this lady
To be my child Cordelia.

CORDELIA.   And so I am, I am.   70

LEAR.

Be your tears wet? Yes, 'faith. I pray, weep not:
If you have poison for me, I will drink it.
I know you do not love me; for your sisters
Have, as I do remember, done me wrong:
You have some cause, they have not.

CORDELIA.   No cause, no cause.

LEAR.

Am I in France?

KENT.   In your own kingdom, sir.

LEAR.

Do not abuse me.

DOCTOR.

Be comforted, good madam: the great rage,
You see, is killed in him: and yet it is danger
To make him even o'er* the time he has lost.   perceive
Desire him to go in; trouble him no more   81
Till further settling.*   rest

CORDELIA.

Will 't please your highness walk?

LEAR.   You must bear with me:
Pray you now, forget and forgive: I am old and
    foolish.

(LEAR *and* CORDELIA *go into the tent, followed
by the* DOCTOR *and* ATTENDANTS. KENT *and the*
GENTLEMAN *remain.*)

GENTLEMAN.

Holds it true, sir, that the Duke of Cornwall was
so slain?

KENT.

Most certain, sir.

GENTLEMAN.

Who is conductor of his people?

KENT.

As 'tis said, the bastard son of Gloucester.   90

GENTLEMAN.

They say Edgar, his banished son, is with the Earl
of Kent in Germany.

KENT.

Report is changeable. 'Tis time to look about; the
powers of the kingdom approach apace.

GENTLEMAN.

The arbitrement* is like to be bloody. Fare you   decision
well, sir.
(*He goes.*)

KENT.

My point and period* will be throughly wrought,   *i.e.,* fate
Or well or ill, as this day's battle's fought.   99
(*He leaves.*)

ACT V

Scene 1. The British camp near Dover.

(EDMUND *and* REGAN *enter, followed by* GENTLE-
MEN, *and* SOLDIERS *with drawn banners.*)

EDMUND (*to a* GENTLEMAN).
Know of the duke if his last purpose hold,
Or whether since he is advised by aught*   induced
To change the course: he's full of alteration
And self-reproving: bring his constant* pleasure.   settled
    (GENTLEMAN *goes.*)

REGAN.
Our sister's man is certainly miscarried.*   come to grief

EDMUND.
'Tis to be doubted,* madam.   feared

REGAN.   Now, sweet lord,
You know the goodness I intend upon you:
Tell me—but truly—but then speak the truth,
Do you not love my sister?

EDMUND.   In honored love.

REGAN.
But have you never found my brother's way   10
To the forfended* place?   forbidden

EDMUND.   That thought abuses* you.   dishonors

REGAN.
I am doubtful* that you have been conjunct*   suspect/ joined
And bosomed with her, as far as we call hers.

EDMUND.
No, by mine honor, madam.

REGAN.
I never shall endure her: dear my lord,
Be not familiar with her.

144

EDMUND.   Fear me not:
  She and the duke her husband!
    (ALBANY *and* GONERIL *enter, attended by* SOL-
    DIERS *with drums and banners.*)

GONERIL (*aside*).
  I had rather lose the battle than that sister
  Should loosen him and me.

ALBANY (*to* REGAN).
  Our very loving sister, well be-met.   20
    (*To* EDMUND.)
  Sir, this I hear; the king is come to his daughter,
  With others whom the rigor of our state*   administration
  Forced to cry out. Where I could not be honest,*   honorable
  I never yet was valiant: for this business,
  It toucheth us, as France invades our land,
  Not bolds* the king, with others, whom, I fear,   emboldens
  Most just and heavy causes make oppose.

EDMUND.
  Sir, you speak nobly.

REGAN.   Why is this reasoned?

GONERIL.
  Combine together 'gainst the enemy;
  For these domestic and particular* broils   family and
  Are not the question here.   personal

ALBANY.   Let's then determine   31
  With the ancient of war* on our proceedings.   veterans

EDMUND.
  I shall attend you presently at your tent.

REGAN.
  Sister, you'll go with us?

GONERIL.
  No.

REGAN.
  'Tis most convenient;* pray you, go with us.   fitting

GONERIL (*aside*).
  O, ho, I know the riddle.
    (*To* REGAN.)   I will go.

(As they are leaving, EDGAR *enters disguised as peasant.)*

EDGAR *(to* ALBANY*).*

If e'er your grace had speech with man so poor,
Hear me one word.

ALBANY *(to the others as they leave).* I'll overtake you.
(To EDGAR.*)*   Speak.

EDGAR *(giving him the letter).*

Before you fight the battle, ope this letter.   40
If you have victory, let the trumpet sound
For him that brought it: wretched though I seem,
I can produce a champion that will prove
What is avouched there. If you miscarry,
Your business of the world hath so an end,
And machination ceases. Fortune love you!

ALBANY.

Stay till I have read the letter.

EDGAR.   I was forbid it.
When time shall serve, let but the herald cry,
And I'll appear again.

ALBANY.

Why, fare thee well: I will o'erlook* thy paper.   look at
*(*EDGAR *leaves as* EDMUND *returns.)*

EDMUND.

The enemy's in view; draw up your powers.   51
Here is the guess of their true strength and forces
By diligent discovery; but your haste
Is now urged on you.

ALBANY.   We will greet the time.*   meet the
                                                        event
(He goes.)

EDMUND.

To both these sisters have I sworn my love;
Each jealous of the other, as the stung
Are of the adder. Which of them shall I take?
Both? One? Or neither? Neither can be enjoyed,
If both remain alive: to take the widow
Exasperates, makes mad her sister Goneril;   60
And hardly shall I carry out my side,*   plan

Her husband being alive. Now then we'll use
His countenance* for the battle; which being done,   support
Let her who would be rid of him devise
His speedy taking off. As for the mercy
Which he intends to Lear and to Cordelia,
The battle done, and they within our power,
Shall never see his pardon; for my state
Stands on* me to defend, not to debate.   requires
   (*He goes.*)

SCENE 2. A field between the two camps. Alarms. Drums.

(*The French forces, with* LEAR *and* CORDELIA, *cross the field.* EDGAR *enters with* GLOUCESTER.)

EDGAR.
  Here, father, take the shadow of this tree
  For your good host; pray that the right may thrive:
  If ever I return to you again,
  I'll bring you comfort.

GLOUCESTER.   Grace go with you, sir!
   (EDGAR *leaves. Alarm. Then a retreat is sounded, and* EDGAR *returns.*)

EDGAR.
  Away, old man; give me thy hand; away!
  King Lear hath lost, he and his daughter ta'en:
  Give me thy hand; come on.

GLOUCESTER.
  No farther, sir; a man may rot even here.

EDGAR.
  What, in ill thoughts again? Men must endure
  Their going hence, even as their coming hither: 10
  Ripeness is all: come on.

GLOUCESTER.   And that's true too.
   (*They go.*)

SCENE 3. The British camp near Dover.

(EDMUND *and his forces make a triumphal entry,
with drums and banners.* LEAR *and* CORDELIA *are
brought with them as prisoners.*)

EDMUND (*to some followers*).
  Some officers take them away: good guard,
  Until their greater pleasures first be known
  That are to censure* them.   Judge
CORDELIA (*to* LEAR).   We are not the first
  Who, with best meaning, have incurred the worst.
  For thee, oppressed king, am I cast down;
  Myself could else out-frown false fortune's frown.
  Shall we not see these daughters and these sisters?
LEAR.
  No, no, no, no! Come, let's away to prison:
  We two alone will sing like birds i' the cage:
  When thou dost ask me blessing, I'll kneel down,   10
  And ask of thee forgiveness: so we'll live,
  And pray, and sing, and tell old tales, and
    laugh
  At gilded butterflies, and hear poor rogues
  Talk of court news; and we'll talk with them too,
  Who loses and who wins; who's in, who's out;
  And take upon 's the mystery of things,
  As if we were God's spies: and we'll wear out,
  In a walled prison, packs and sects of great ones,
  That ebb and flow by the moon.
EDMUND (*to his officers*).   Take them away.
LEAR.
  Upon such sacrifices, my Cordelia,   20
  The gods themselves throw incense. Have I caught
    thee?
  He that parts us shall bring a brand from heaven,
  And fire us hence like foxes. Wipe thine eyes;

The good-years* shall devour them, flesh and   *i.e.,* disease
    fell,
Ere they shall make us weep: we'll see 'em starve
    first.
Come.
    (LEAR *and* CORDELIA *are taken away under guard.*)

EDMUND (*to an officer*). Come hither, captain; hark.
Take thou this note.
    (*Gives him a note.*) Go follow them to prison:
One step I have advanced thee; if thou dost
As this instructs thee, thou dost make thy way
To noble fortunes: know thou this, that men   30
Are as the time is: to be tender-minded
Does not become a sword: thy great employment
Will not bear question; either say thou'lt do 't,
Or thrive by other means.

CAPTAIN.   I'll do 't, my lord.

EDMUND.
About it; and write happy when thou hast done.
Mark, I say, instantly; and carry it so
As I have set it down.

CAPTAIN.
I cannot draw a cart, nor eat dried oats;
If it be man's work, I'll do it.
    (*The* CAPTAIN *goes.*)
    (*A flourish of trumpets.* ALBANY, GONERIL, REGAN
    enter, with SOLDIERS *and* ATTENDANTS.)

ALBANY (*to* EDMUND).
Sir, you have shown today your vallant strain,   40
And fortune led you well: you have the captives
That were the opposites* of this day's strife: our op-
                                             ponents
We do require them of you, so to use them
As we shall find their merits and our safety
May equally determine.

EDMUND.   Sir, I thought it fit
To send the old and miserable king
To some retention* and appointed guard;   detention
Whose age has charms in it, whose title more,

To pluck the common bosom* on his side,   sympathy
And turn our impressed lances* in our eyes   troops
Which do command them. With him I sent
   the queen;   51
My reason all the same; and they are ready
Tomorow, or at further space, to appear
Where you shall hold your session. At this time
We sweat and bleed: the friend hath lost his friend;
And the best quarrels, in the heat, are cursed
By those that feel their sharpness:
The question of Cordelia and her father
Requires a fitter place.

ALBANY.   Sir, by your patience,*   pardon my
I hold you but a subject of this war,   candor
Not as a brother.   60

REGAN.   That's as we list to grace him.
Methinks our pleasure* might have been demanded,   wishes
Ere you had spoke so far. He led our powers;
Bore the commission of my place and person;
The which immediacy* may well stand up,   closeness
And call itself your brother.   to me

GONERIL.   Not so hot:
In his own grace he doth exalt himself,
More than in your addition.*   titles you
                                                                            gave
REGAN.   In my rights,
  By me invested, he compeers the best.

GONERIL.
That were the most, if he should husband you.   70

REGAN.
Jesters do oft prove prophets.

GONERIL.   Holla, holla!
That eye that told you so looked but a-squint.

REGAN.
Lady, I am not well; else I should answer
From a full-flowing stomach.*   wrath
  (*To* EDMUND.)   General,
Take thou my soldiers, prisoners, patrimony;
Dispose of them, of me; the walls are thine:

Witness the world, that I create thee here
My lord and master.

GONERIL.   Mean you to enjoy him?

ALBANY (*to* GONERIL).

The let-alone* lies not in your good will.   prohibition

EDMUND.

Nor in thine, lord.

ALBANY.   Half-blooded fellow, yes.   80

REGAN (*to* EDMUND).

Let the drum strike, and prove my title thine.

ALBANY.

Stay yet; hear reason.
                    Edmund, I arrest thee
On capital treason; and, in thine attaint,*   impeach-
This gilded serpent.   ment
    (*Pointing to* GONERIL.) For your claim, fair sister,
I bar it in the interest of my wife;
'Tis she is sub-contracted to this lord,[118]
And I, her husband, contradict your bans.
If you will marry, make your loves to me,
My lady is bespoke.

GONERIL.   An interlude!

ALBANY.

Thou art armed, Gloucester: let the trumpet sound: 90
If none appear to prove upon thy head
Thy heinous, manifest, and many treasons,
There is my pledge;
    (*Throwing down a glove.*)
                    I'll prove it on thy heart,
Ere I taste bread, thou art in nothing* less   no respect
Than I have here proclaimed thee.

REGAN.   Sick, O, sick!

GONERIL (*aside*).

If not, I'll ne'er trust medicine.

EDMUND.

There's my exchange.
    (*Throwing down a glove.*) What in the world he is
That names me traitor, villain-like he lies:

Call by thy trumpet: he that dares approach,
On him, on you, who not? I will maintain   **100**
My truth and honor firmly.

ALBANY.

A herald, ho!

EDMUND.   A herald, ho, a herald!

ALBANY.

Trust to thy single virtue;* for thy soldiers,   *valor*
All levied in my name, have in my name
Took their discharge.

REGAN.   My sickness grows upon me.

ALBANY (*to* SOLDIERS).

She is not well; convey her to my tent.
   (REGAN *is helped off.*)
   (*A* HERALD *enters.*)
Come hither, herald—Let the trumpet sound—
And read out this.

CAPTAIN.

Sound, trumpet! (*A trumpet sounds.*)

HERALD (*reads*).

"If any man of quality or degree within the lists of   **120**
the army will maintain upon Edmund, supposed
Earl of Gloucester, that he is a manifold traitor, let
him appear by the third sound of the trumpet: he
is bold in his defense."

EDMUND.

Sound! (*First trumpet.*)

HERALD.

Again! (*Second trumpet.*)

HERALD.

Again! (*Third trumpet.*)
   (*A trumpet answers, from a distance. At this
   last trumpet call, preceded by a trumpeter,*
   EDGAR *enters, in full armor with closed visor.*)

ALBANY.

Ask him his purposes, why he appears
Upon this call o' the trumpet.

HERALD.   What are you?

Your name, your quality? And why you answer   120
This present summons?

EDGAR.   Know, my name is lost;
By treason's tooth bare-gnawn and canker-bit:*   eaten away
Yet am I noble as the adversary
I come to cope.*   cope with

ALBANY.   Which is that adversary?

EDGAR.
What's he that speaks for Edmund Earl of Gloucester?

EDMUND.
Himself: what say'st thou to him?

EDGAR.   Draw thy sword,
That, if my speech offend a noble heart,
Thy arm may do thee justice: here is mine.
Behold, it is the privilege of mine honors,*   knighthood
My oath, and my profession: I protest,   130
Maugre* thy strength, youth, place, and   in spite of
   eminence,
Despite thy victor sword and fire-new* fortune,   brand-new
Thy valor and thy heart, thou art a traitor;
False to thy gods, thy brother, and thy father;
Conspirant 'gainst this high-illustrious prince;
And, from the extremest upward* of thy head   top
To the descent and dust below thy foot,
A most toad-spotted traitor. Say thou "No,"
This sword, this arm, and my best spirits, are bent
To prove upon thy heart, whereto I speak,   140
Thou liest.

EDMUND.
       In wisdom I should ask thy name;
But, since thy outside looks so fair and warlike,
And that thy tongue some say of breeding breathes,
What safe and nicely I might well delay
By rule of knighthood, I disdain and spurn:[119]
Back do I toss these treasons to thy head;
With the hell-hated lie o'erwhelm thy heart;
Which, for they yet glance by and scarcely bruise,

This sword of mine shall give them instant way,
Where they shall rest for ever. Trumpets, speak! 150
   (*The trumpets sound.* EDMUND *and* EDGAR *fight.*
EDMUND *falls.*)

ALBANY.
Save him, save him!

GONERIL.   This is practice,* Gloucester: **trickery**
By the law of arms thou wast not bound to answer
An unknown opposite; thou art not vanquished,
But cozened and beguiled.

ALBANY.   Shut your mouth, dame,
Or with this paper shall I stop it. Hold, sir;
Thou worse than any name, read thine own evil:
   (*Gives the letter to* EDMUND.)
No tearing, lady; I perceive you know it.

GONERIL.
Say, if I do, the laws are mine, not thine:
Who can arraign me for 't?

ALBANY.   Most monstrous! Oh!
   (*To* GONERIL.)
Know'st thou this paper?

GONERIL.   Ask me not what I know.   160
   (*She goes.*)

ALBANY (*to an* OFFICER).
Go after her: she's desperate; govern her.

EDMUND.
What you have charged me with, that have I done;
And more, much more; the time will bring it out:
'Tis past, and so am I.
   (*To* EDGAR.)   But what art thou
That hast this fortune on me? If thou'rt noble,
I do forgive thee.

EDGAR.   Let's exchange charity.
   (*Takes off his helmet.*)
I am no less in blood than thou art, Edmund;
If more, the more thou hast wronged me.
My name is Edgar, and thy father's son.
The gods are just, and of our pleasant vices   170

Make instruments to plague us:
The dark and vicious place where thee he got*   begot
Cost him his eyes.

EDMUND.   Thou hast spoken right, 'tis true;
The wheel is come full circle;[120] I am here.

ALBANY (*to* EDGAR).
Methought thy very gait did prophesy
A royal nobleness: I must embrace thee:
Let sorrow split my heart, if ever I
Did hate thee or thy father!

EDGAR.   Worthy prince, I know 't.

ALBANY.
Where have you hid yourself?
How have you known the miseries of your father?   180

EDGAR.
By nursing them, my lord. List* a brief tale;   listen to
And when 'tis told, O, that my heart would burst!
The bloody proclamation to escape,
That followed me so near—O, our lives' sweetness!
That we the pain of death would hourly die
Rather than die at once!—taught me to shift
Into a madman's rags; to assume a semblance
That very dogs disdained: and in this habit
Met I my father with his bleeding rings,
Their precious stones new lost; became his guide,   190
Led him, begged for him, saved him from despair;
Never—O fault!—revealed myself unto him,
Until some half-hour past, when I was armed:
Not sure, though hoping, of this good success,
I asked his blessing, and from first to last
Told him my pilgrimage: but his flawed heart—
Alack, too weak the conflict to support—
'Twixt two extremes of passion, joy and grief,
Burst smilingly.

EDMUND.
              This speech of yours hath moved me,
And shall perchance do good: but speak you on;   200
You look as you had something more to say.

ALBANY.

   If there be more, more woeful, hold it in;
   For I am almost ready to dissolve,
   Hearing of this.

EDGAR.   This would have seemed a period*   *an end*
   To such as love not sorrow; but another,
   To amplify too much, would make much more
   And top extremity.
   Whilst I was big in clamor* came there in a man,   *lament*
   Who, having seen me in my worst estate,*   *condition*
   Shunned my abhorred society; but then, finding   210
   Who 'twas that so endured, with his strong arms
   He fastened on my neck, and bellowed out
   As he'd burst heaven; threw him on my father;
   Told the most piteous tale of Lear and him
   That ever ear received: which in recounting
   His grief grew puissant,* and the strings of life   *overpow-*
   Began to crack: twice then the trumpets sounded,   *ering*
   And there I left him tranced.*   *in a swoon*

ALBANY.   But who was this?

EDGAR.

   Kent, sir, the banished Kent; who in disguise
   Followed his enemy king, and did him service   220
   Improper for a slave.

     (*A* GENTLEMAN *enters with a bloody knife.*)

GENTLEMAN.

   Help, help, O, help!

EDGAR.   What kind of help?

ALBANY.   Speak, man.

EDGAR.

   What means that bloody knife?

GENTLEMAN.   'Tis hot, it smokes;
   It came even from the heart of—O, she's dead!

ALBANY.

   Who dead? Speak, man.

GENTLEMAN.

   Your lady, sir, your lady: and her sister
   By her is poisoned; she hath confessed it.

EDMUND.

  I was contracted to them both: all three
  Now marry in an instant.

EDGAR.   Here comes Kent.

ALBANY (*to the* GENTLEMAN).

  Produce their bodies, be they alive or dead: 230
  This judgment of the heavens, that makes us tremble,
  Touches us not with pity.
     (*The* GENTLEMAN *goes, as* KENT *enters.*)
                       O, is this he?
  The time will not allow the compliment
  Which very manners urges.

KENT.   I am come

  To bid my king and master aye good night:
  Is he not here?

ALBANY.   Great thing of us forgot!

  Speak, Edmund, where's the king? And where's
     Cordelia?
     (*The bodies of* GONERIL *and* REGAN *are borne in.*)
  See'st thou this object, Kent?

KENT.

  Alack, why thus?

EDMUND.   Yet Edmund was beloved:

  The one the other poisoned for my sake,   240
  And after slew herself.

ALBANY.

  Even so.
     (*To the* BEARERS.) Cover their faces.

EDMUND.

  I pant for life: some good I mean to do,
  Despite of mine own nature. Quickly send,
  Be brief in it, to the castle; for my writ
  Is on the life of Lear and on Cordelia:
  Nay, send in time.

ALBANY.   Run, run, O, run!

EDGAR.

  To who, my lord? Who hath the office? Send
  Thy token of reprieve.

EDMUND (*giving* EDGAR *his sword*).

  Well thought on: take my sword,   250
  Give it the captain.

ALBANY.

                   Haste thee, for thy life.

    (EDGAR *rushes out.*)

EDMUND.

  He hath commission from thy wife and me
  To hang Cordelia in the prison, and
  To lay the blame upon her own despair,
  That she fordid* herself.   destroyed

ALBANY.

  The gods defend her! Bear him hence awhile.

    (ATTENDANTS *bear* EDMUND *off.* LEAR *enters, bear-*
    ing the dead CORDELIA *in his arms.* EDGAR, *the*
    CAPTAIN, *and others follow.*)

LEAR.

  Howl, howl, howl, howl! O, you are men of
    stones:
  Had I your tongues and eyes, I'd use them so
  That heaven's vault should crack. She's gone
    forever!
  I know when one is dead, and when one lives;   260
  She's dead as earth. Lend me a looking-glass;
  If that her breath will mist or stain the stone,*   glass
  Why, then she lives.

KENT.   Is this the promised end?[121]

EDGAR.

  Or image of that horror?

ALBANY.   Fall, and cease!

LEAR.

  This feather stirs; she lives! If it be so,
  It is a chance which does redeem all sorrows
  That ever I have felt.

KENT (*kneeling*). O my good master!

LEAR.

  Prithee, away.

EDGAR.   'Tis noble Kent, your friend.

LEAR.

A plague upon you, murderers, traitors all!
I might have saved her; now she's gone for ever!   270
Cordelia, Cordelia! Stay a little. Ha!
What is 't thou say'st? Her voice was ever soft,
Gentle, and low, an excellent thing in woman.
I killed the slave that was a-hanging thee.

CAPTAIN.

'Tis true, my lords, he did.

LEAR.   Did I not, fellow?
I have seen the day, with my good biting falchion*   sword
I would have made them skip: I am old now,
And these same crosses spoil me.
    (To KENT.)   Who are you?
Mine eyes are not o' the best: I'll tell you straight.

KENT.

If fortune brag of two she loved and hated,   280
One of them we behold.[122]

LEAR.

This is a dull sight. Are you not Kent?

KENT.   The same,
Your servant Kent. Where is your servant Caius?

LEAR.

He's a good fellow, I can tell you that;
He'll strike, and quickly too: he's dead and rotten.

KENT.

No, my good lord; I am the very man—

LEAR.

I'll see that* straight.   to that

KENT.

That, from your first of difference* and decay,   change of
Have followed your sad steps.   fortune

LEAR.   You are welcome hither.

KENT.

Nor no man else: all's cheerless, dark, and deadly.   290
Your eldest daughters have fordone themselves,
And desperately* are dead.   in despair

LEAR.   Ay, so I think.

ALBANY.
He knows not what he says: and vain it is
That we present us to him.

EDGAR.   Very bootless.

(*A* CAPTAIN *enters.*)

CAPTAIN.
Edmund is dead, my lord.

ALBANY.   That's but a trifle here.
You lords and noble friends, know our intent.
What comfort to this great decay may come
Shall be applied: for us, we will resign,
During the life of this old majesty,
To him our absolute power.
    (*To* EDGAR *and* KENT.)   You, to your rights;   300
With boot, and such addition as your honors
Have more than merited. All friends shall taste
The wages of their virtue, and all foes
The cup of their deservings.
                            Cordelia   O, see, see!

LEAR.
And my poor fool is hanged![123] No, no, no life!
Why should a dog, a horse, a rat, have life,
And thou no breath at all? Thou'lt come no more,
Never, never, never, never, never!
Pray you, undo this button: thank you, sir.
Do you see this? Look on her, look, her lips,   310
Look there, look there!
    (*Dies.*)

EDGAR.   He faints! My lord, my lord!

KENT.
Break, heart; I prithee, break!

EDGAR.   Look up, my lord.

KENT.
Vex not his ghost. O, let him pass! He hates
    him much
That would upon the rack of this tough world
Stretch him out longer.[124]

EDGAR.   He is gone, indeed.

KENT.

The wonder is, he hath endured so long:
He but usurped his life.[125]

ALBANY.

Bear them from hence. Our present business
Is general woe.
 (*To* KENT *and* EDGAR.)
     Friends of my soul, you twain   319
Rule in this realm, and the gored state sustain.

KENT.

I have a journey, sir, shortly to go;
My master calls me, I must not say no.

ALBANY.

The weight of this sad time we must obey;
Speak what we feel, not what we ought to say.
The oldest hath borne most: we that are young
Shall never see so much, nor live so long.[126]
 (ATTENDANTS *take up the bodies and all leave, as
 a dead march plays.*)

Selected Commentaries

CHARLES LAMB (1775-1834)

Lamb's critical essays, along with those of his lifelong friend Coleridge, exerted a strong influence upon the revival of interest in Shakespeare and his dramatic contemporaries during the early years of the nineteenth century. Lamb was an avid reader of the Bard's works—witness his collaboration with his sister Mary in writing excellent summaries of the plots in their *Tales from Shakespeare*.

Lamb was also an inveterate theatregoer, so that he took keen delight in the triumphs of the stage. However, he did believe that Shakespeare's characters, particularly those in the greatest plays, reached their full significance as objects of contemplation and not as creatures to be heard and seen on the stage. King Lear, both the character and the play, offered Lamb convincing proof of his contention. He lamented the reduction of a king designed to create awe in the manner of a force of nature to "an old man tottering about the stage with a walking-stick." He was even more scornful of the pitiful devices used by the stage manager to create a semblance of the storm that came from the outer reaches of eternity.

We must remember that the version of the play that Lamb saw was the 1681 concoction of Nahum Tate, which held the English stage until the actor-manager Macready presented the true text in 1838. Although Tate made many absurd changes in the play, including a happy ending, he left the part of Lear largely intact. Lamb's scorn, then, is obviously directed at a production of Tate's "improvement."

In spite of these explanations for Lamb's now unpopular interdiction, critics of the play have agreed hesitatingly or even openly with his thesis that *King Lear* loses much of its power and majesty when put on the stage. Harley Granville-Barker, however, in the excerpt quoted further on from his

Prefaces to Shakespeare, takes direct issue with this opinion. He shows how much the text can gain from an expert stage production. The reader is advised to read Granville-Barker's work in connection with this essay of Lamb's.

KING LEAR ON THE STAGE
(from: *On the Tragedies of Shakespeare,* 1808)

The truth is, the Characters of Shakspeare are so much the objects of meditation rather than of interest or curiosity as to their actions, that while we are reading any of his great criminal characters,—Macbeth, Richard, even Iago,—we think not so much of the crimes which they commit, as of the ambition, the aspiring spirit, the intellectual activity, which prompts them to overleap those moral fences. Barn-well is a wretched murderer; there is a certain fitness between his neck and the rope; he is the legitimate heir to the gallows; nobody who thinks at all can think of any alleviating circumstances in his case to make him a fit object of mercy. Or to take an instance from the higher tragedy, what else but a mere assassin is Glenalvon! Do we think of any thing but of the crime which he commits, and the rack which he deserves? That is all which we really think about him. Whereas in corresponding characters in Shakspeare so little do the actions comparatively affect us, that while the impulses, the inner mind in all its perverted greatness, solely seems real and is exclusively attended to, the crime is comparatively nothing. But when we see these things represented, the acts which they do are comparatively every thing, their impulses nothing. The state of sublime emotion into which we are elevated by those images of night and horror which Macbeth is made to utter, that solemn prelude with which he entertains the time till the bell shall strike which is to call him to murder Duncan,—when we no longer read it in a book, when we have given up that vantage-ground of abstraction which reading possesses over seeing, and come to see a man in his bodily shape before our eyes actually preparing to commit a murder, if the acting be true and impressive, as I have witnessed it in Mr. K.'s performance of that part, the painful anxiety about the act, the natural longing to prevent it while it yet seems unperpetrated, the too close pressing semblance of reality, give a pain and an uneasiness which totally destroy all the delight which the words in the book convey, where the deed doing never presses upon us with the painful sense of presence: it rather seems to belong to history,—to something past and inevitable, if it has any thing to do with time at all. The sublime images, the poetry alone, is that which is present to our minds in the reading.

So to see Lear acted,—to see an old man tottering about the stage with a walking-stick, turned out of doors by his daughters in a rainy night, has nothing in it but what is painful and disgusting. We want to take him into shelter and relieve him. That is all the feeling which the acting of Lear ever produced in me. But the Lear of Shakspeare cannot be acted. The contemptible machinery by which they mimic the storm which he goes out in, is not more inadequate to represent the horrors of the real elements, than any actor can be to represent Lear: they might more easily propose to personate the Satan of Milton upon a stage, or one of Michael Angelo's terrible figures. The greatness of Lear is not in corporal dimension, but in intellectual: the explosions of his passion are terrible as a volcano: they are storms turning up and disclosing to the botton that sea, his mind, with all its vast riches. It is his mind which is laid bare. This case of flesh and blood seems too insignificant to be thought on; even as he himself neglects it. On the stage we see nothing but corporal infirmities and weakness, the impotence of rage; while we read it, we see not Lear, but we are Lear,— we are in his mind, we are sustained by a grandeur which baffles the malice of daughters and storms; in the aberrations of his reason, we discover a mighty irregular power of reasoning, immethodized from the ordinary purposes of life, but exerting its powers, as the wind blows where it listeth, at will upon the corruptions and abuses of mankind. What have looks, or tones, to do with that sublime identification of his age with that of the *heavens themselves*, when in his reproaches to them for conniving at the injustice of his children, he reminds them that "they themselves are old." What gesture shall we appropriate to this? What has the voice or the eye to do with such things? But the play is beyond all art, as the tamperings with it show: it is too hard and stony; it must have love-scenes, and a happy ending. It is not enough that Cordelia is a daughter, she must shine as a lover too. Tate has put his hook in the nostrils of this Leviathan, for Garrick and his followers, the showmen of the scene, to draw the mighty beast about more easily. A happy ending!—as if the living martyrdom that Lear has gone through,—the flaying of his feelings alive, did not make a fair dismissal from the stage of life the only decorous thing for him. If he is to live and be happy after, if he could sustain this world's burden after, why all this pudder and preparation,—why torment us with all this unnecessary sympathy? As if the childish pleasure of getting his gilt robes and sceptre again could tempt him to act over again his misused station,—as if at his years, and with his experience, any thing was left but to die.

Lear is essentially impossible to be represented on a stage.

* * *

WILLIAM HAZLITT (1778-1830)

Hazlitt's attitude toward *King Lear* is that of a romantic enthusiast. Before the tragedy he can only stand in wonder and rapture. The play stirs his emotions in the manner of a great convulsion of nature, like a tornado, for example. Producing the same sort of anguish and terror, it becomes a symbol of the tug of war between the deepest elements of our being.

THE EXPLOSIVE PASSIONS OF *King Lear*
(from: *Characters of Shakspeare's Plays*, 1817)

We wish that we could pass this play over, and say nothing about it. All that we can say must fall far short of the subject, or even of what we ourselves conceive of it. To attempt to give a description of the play itself, or of its effects upon the mind, is mere impertinence: yet we must say something. It is then the best of all Shakspeare's plays, for it is the one in which he was the most in earnest. He was here fairly caught in the web of his own imagination. The passion which he has taken as his subject is that which strikes its root deepest into the human heart; of which the bond is the hardest to be unloosed; and the cancelling and tearing to pieces of which gives the greatest revulsion to the frame. This depth of nature, this force of passion, this tug and war of the elements of our being, this firm faith in filial piety, and the giddy anarchy and whirling tumult of the thoughts at finding this prop failing it, the contrast between the fixed, immovable basis of natural affection, and the rapid, irregular starts of imagination, suddenly wrenched from all its accustomed holds and resting-places in the soul, this is what Shakspeare has given, and what nobody else but he could give. So we believe.—The mind of Lear, staggering between the weight of attachment and the hurried movements of passion, is like a tall ship driven about by the winds, buffeted by the furious waves, but that still rides above the storm, having its anchor fixed in the bottom of the sea; or it is like the sharp rock circled by the eddying whirlpool that foams and beats against it, or like the solid promontory pushed from its basis by the force of an earthquake.

The character of Lear itself is very finely conceived for the purpose. It is the only ground on which such a story could be built with the greatest truth and effect. It is his rash hate, his violent impetuosity, his blindness to everything but the dictates of his passions or affections, that produces all his misfortunes, that aggravates his impatience of them, that enforces our pity for him. The part which Cordelia bears in the scene is extremely beautiful: the story is almost told in the first words she utters. We see at once the precipice on which the poor old king stands from his own extravagant and credulous importunity, the indiscreet simplicity of her love (which, to be sure, has a little of her father's obstinacy in it), and the hollowness of her sisters' pretensions. Almost the first burst of that noble tide of passion, which runs through this play, is in the remonstrance of Kent to his royal master on the injustice of his sentence against his youngest daughter—"Be Kent unmannerly, when Lear is mad!" This manly plainness, which draws down on him the displeasure of the unadvised king, is worthy of the fidelity with which he adheres to his fallen fortunes. The true character of the two eldest daughters, Regan and Gonerill (they are so thoroughly hateful that we do not even like to repeat their names), breaks out in their answer to Cordelia, who desires them to treat their father well—"Prescribe not us our duties"—their hatred of advice being in proportion to their determination to do wrong, and to their hypocritical pretensions to do right. Their deliberate affectation of virtue adds the last finishing to the odiousness of their characters. It is the absence of this detestable quality that is the only relief in the character of Edmund the Bastard, and that at times reconciles us to him. We are not tempted to exaggerate the guilt of his conduct, when he himself gives it up as a bad business, and writes himself down "plain villain." Nothing more can be said about it. His religious honesty in this respect is admirable. One speech of his is worth a million. His father, Gloster, whom he has just deluded with a forged story of his brother Edgar's designs against his life, accounts for his unnatural behavior, and the strange depravity of the times, from the late eclipses in the sun and moon. Edmund, who is in the secret, says when he is gone—"This is the excellent foppery of the world, that when we are sick in fortune (often the surfeits of our own behavior) we make guilty of our disasters the sun, the moon, and stars: as if we were villains on necessity; fools by heavenly compulsion; knaves, thieves, and treacherous by spherical predominance; drunkards, liars, and adulterers by an enforced obedience of planetary influence; and all that we are evil in, by a divine thrusting on. An admirable evasion of whoremaster man, to lay his goatish disposition on the charge of a star! My father compounded with my mother under the Dragon's tail, and my nativity was under Ursa Major: so that it follows, I am rough and lecherous. I should have been what I am, had the maidenliest star in the firmament twinkled on my bastardising."—The whole character, its careless, light-hearted villainy, contrasted with the sullen, rancorous malignity of Regan and Gonerill, its connection with the conduct of the underplot, in which Gloster's persecution of one of his sons and the ingratitude of another form a counterpart to the mistakes and misfortunes of Lear,—his double amour with the two sisters, and the share which he has in bringing about the fatal catastrophe, are all managed with an uncommon degree of skill and power.

It has been said, and we think justly, that the third act of *Othello*, and the three first acts of *Lear*, are Shakspeare's great master-pieces in the logic of passion: that they contain the highest examples not only of the force of individual passion, but of its dramatic vicissitudes and striking effects arising from the different circumstances and characters of the persons speaking. We see the ebb and flow of feeling, its pauses and feverish starts, its impatience of opposition, its accumulating force when it has time to recollect itself, the manner in which it avails itself of every passing word or gesture, its haste to repel insinuation, the alternate contraction and dilatation of the soul, and all "the dazzling fence of controvery" in this mortal combat with poisoned weapons, aimed at the heart, where each wound is fatal. We have seen in *Othello*, how the unsuspecting frankness and impetuous passions of the Moor are played upon and exasperated by the artful dexterity of Iago. In the present play, that which aggravates the sense of sympathy in the reader, and of uncontrollable anguish in the swoln heart of Lear, is the petrifying indifference, the cold, calculating, obdurate selfishness of his daughters. His keen passions seem whetted on their stony hearts. The contrast would be too painful, the shock too great, but for the intervention of the Fool, whose well-timed levity comes in to break the continuity of feeling when it can no longer be borne, and to bring into play again the fibres of the heart just as they are rigid from over-strained excitement. The imagination is glad to take refuge in the half-comic, half-serious comments of the Fool, just as the mind under the extreme anguish of a surgical operation vents itself in sallies of wit. The character was also a grotesque ornament of the barbarous times, in which alone the tragic ground-work of the story could be laid. In another point of view it is indispensable, inasmuch as while it is a diversion to the too great intensity of our disgust, it carries the pathos to the highest pitch of which it is capable, by showing the pitiable weakness of the old king's conduct and its irretrievable consequences in the most familiar point of view. Lear may well "beat at the gate which let his folly in," after, as the Fool says, "he has made his daughters his mothers." The character is dropped in the third act to make room for the entrance of Edgar as mad Tom, which well accords with the increasing bustle and wildness of the incidents; and nothing can be more complete than the distinction between Lear's real and Edgar's assumed madness, while the resemblance in the cause of their distresses, from the severing of the nearest ties of natural affection, keeps up a unity of interest. Shakspeare's mastery over his subject, if it was not art, was owing to a knowledge of the connecting links of the passions, and their effect upon the mind, still more wonderful than any systematic adherence to rules, and anticipated and outdid all the efforts of the most refined art, not inspired and rendered instinctive by genius.

One of the most perfect displays of dramatic power is the first interview between Lear and his daughter, after the designed affronts upon him, which, till one of his knights reminds him of them, his sanguine temperament had led him to overlook. He returns with his train from hunting, and his usual impatience breaks out in his first words, "Let me not stay a jot for dinner; go, get it ready." He then encounters the faithful Kent in disguise, and retains him in his service; and the first trial of his honest duty is to trip up the heels of the officious Steward, who makes so prominent and despicable a figure through the piece . . .

The manner in which the threads of the story are woven together is almost as wonderful in the way of art as the carrying on the tide of passion, still varying and unimpaired, is on the score of nature. Among the remarkable instances of this kind are Edgar's meeting with his old blind father; the deception he practises upon him when he pretends to lead him to the top of Dover-cliff—"Come on, sir, here's the place," to prevent his ending his life and miseries together; his encounter with the perfidious Stewart, whom he kills, and his finding the letter from Gonerill to his brother upon him, which leads to the final catastrophe, and brings the wheel of Justice "full circle home" to the guilty parties. The bustle and rapid succession of events in the last scenes is surprising. But the meeting between Lear and Cordelia is by far the most affecting part of them. It has all the wildness of poetry, and all the heartfelt true of nature. The previous account of her reception of the news of his unkind treatment, her involuntary reproaches to her sister, "Shame, ladies, shame," Lear's backwardness to see his daughter, the picture of the desolate state to which he is reduced, "Alack, 'tis he; why he was met even now, as mad as the vex'd sea, singing aloud," only prepare the way and heighten our expectation of what follows, and assuredly this expectation is not disappointed when, through the tender care of Cordelia, he revives and recollects her.

CORDELIA. How does my royal lord? How fares your majesty!
LEAR. You do me wrong, to take me out of the grave:
Thou art a soul in bliss; but I am bound
Upon a wheel of fire, that mine own tears
Do scald like molten lead . . .

* * *

The concluding events are sad, painfully sad; but their pathos is extreme. The oppression of our feelings is relieved by the very interest we take in the misfortunes of others, and by the reflections to which they give birth. Cordelia is hanged in prison by the orders of the bastard Edmund, which are known too late to be countermanded, and Lear dies brokenhearted, lamenting over her.

LEAR. And my poor fool is hanged! No, no, no life:
Why should a dog, a horse, a rat, have life,
And thou no breath at all? O, thou wilt come no more,
Never, never, never, never, never!—
Pray you, undo this button: thank you, sir.—

He dies, and indeed we feel the truth of what Kent says on the occasion—

Vex not his ghost: O, let him pass! he hates him,
That would upon the rack of this rough world
Stretch him out longer.

* * *

LEO NIKOLAYEVITCH TOLSTOY (1828-1910)

Tolstoy was one of the greatest writers of all time. His works are sharply divided by a profound religious crisis occurring about the middle of his life. His early novels, like *Anna Karenina* and his panoramic *War and Peace*, stand as the summit of European prose fiction.

His essay on *King Lear* is one of the works written after he had evolved a radical religious and moral doctrine which he began to preach and to illustrate in his way of living. Its essence is that a man can gain true and abiding happiness only by stripping himself bare of all the artificialities that civilization has imposed upon him and by returning to the ways of primitive Christianity which enhances one's love of his fellow men and one's sympathy with the problems of the natural man best seen in the lives of Russian peasants. The great literary excellences were simplicity of emotion and of the language in which it found expression.

Since *King Lear* is in deadly opposition to all the aspects of Tolstoy's new creed the play offends his deepest religious instincts. The intemperance of Lear's emotions as well as the language in which they are expressed are at odds with the simplicity of the teaching of the Gospels and their language.

Tolstoy's failure to sense the magnificence of *King Lear* is proof that most of the great play is lost in translation, and particularly by a mind conditioned against all the literary assumptions of all Elizabethan dramatists.

Preference for the Old *King Leir*
(from: "On Shakespeare and the Drama," *Fortnightly Review*, 1907)

In reading any of Shakespeare's dramas whatever, I was, from the very first, instantly convinced that he was lacking in the most important, if not the only, means of portraying characters—individuality of language, *i.e.*, the style of speech of every person being natural to his character. This is absent from Shakespeare. All his characters speak, not their own, but always one and the same Shakespearean pretentious and unnatural language, in which not only they could not speak, but in which no living man ever has spoken or does speak.

No living men could or can say as Lear says—that he would divorce his wife in the grave should Regan not receive him; or that the heavens would crack with shouting; or that the winds would burst; or that the wind wishes to blow the land into the sea; or that the curled waters wish to flood the shore, as the gentleman describes the storm; or that it is easier to bear one's grief; and the soul leaps over many sufferings when grief finds fellowship; or that Lear has become childless whilst I am fatherless, as Edgar says, or use similar unnatural expressions with which the speeches of all the characters in all Shakespeare's dramas overflow.

Again, it is not enough that all the characters speak in a way in which no living men ever did or could speak—they all suffer from a common intemperance of language. Those who are in love, who are preparing for death, who are fighting, who are dying, all alike speak much and unexpectedly about subjects utterly inappropriate to the occasion, being evidently guided rather by consonances and play of words than by thoughts. They speak all alike. Lear raves exactly as does Edgar when feigning madness. Both Kent and the fool speak alike. The words of one of the personages might be placed in the mouth of another, and by the character of the speech it would be impossible to distinguish who speaks. . . .

In the older drama Leir abdicates because, having become a widower, he thinks only of saving his soul. He asks his daughters as to their love for him—that by means of a certain device he has invented he may retain his favourite daughter on his island. The elder daughters are betrothed, while the youngest does not wish to contract a loveless union with any of the neighbouring suitors whom Leir proposes to her, and he is afraid that she may marry some distant potentate.

The device which he has invented, as he informs his courtier Perillus (Shakespeare's Kent), is this, that when Cordelia tells him that she loves him more than anyone, or as much as her elder sisters do, he will tell her that she must, in proof of her love, marry the prince he will indicate on his island.

All these motives for Leir's conduct are absent in Shakespeare's play. Then, when according to the old drama Leir asks his daughters about their love to him, Cordelia does not say, as Shakespeare has it, that she will not give her father all her love, but will love her husband too, should she marry —which is quite unnatural—but simply says that she cannot express her love in words, but hopes that her actions will prove it. Goneril and Regan remark that Cordelia's answer is not an answer, and that the father cannot meekly accept such indifference; so that what is wanting in Shakespeare, i.e., the explanation of Lear's anger which caused him to disinherit his youngest daughter, exists in the old drama. Leir is annoyed by the failure of his scheme, and the poisonous words of his elder daughters irritate him still more. After the division of the kingdom between the elder daughters there follows in the older drama a scene between Cordelia and the King of Gaul, setting forth, instead of the colourless Cordelia of Shakespeare, a very definite and attractive character of the truthful, tender, and self-sacrificing youngest daughter. While Cordelia, without grieving that she has been deprived of a portion of her heritage, sits sorrowing at having lost her father's love, and looking forward to earn her bread by her labour, there comes the King of Gaul, who, in the disguise of a pilgrim desires to choose a bride from amongst Leir's daughters. He asks Cordelia why she is sad. She tells him the cause of her grief. The King of Gaul, still in the guise of a pilgrim, falls in love with her, and offers to arrange a marriage for her with the King of Gaul, but she says she will marry only a man whom she loves. The the pilgrim, still disguised, offers her his hand and heart and Cordelia confesses she loves the pilgrim and consents to marry him, notwithstanding the poverty that awaits her. Thereupon the pilgrim discloses to her that he it is who is the King of Gaul, and Cordelia marries him. Instead of this scene, Lear, according to Shakespeare, proposes to Cordelia's two suitors to take her without dowry, and one cynically refuses, whilst the other, one does not know why, accepts her. . . .

However strange this opinion may seem to worshippers of Shakespeare, yet the whole of this old drama is incomparably and in every respect superior to Shakespeare's adaptation. It is so first because it has not got the utterly superfluous characters of the villain Edmund, and unlifelike Gloucester and Edgar, who only distract one's attention; secondly, because it has not got the completely false "effects" of Lear running about the heath, his conversations with the fool and all these impossible disguises, failures to recognise and accumulated deaths; and, above all, because in this drama there is the simple, natural, and deeply touching character of Leir, and the yet more touching and clearly-defined character of Cordelia, both absent in Shakespeare. Therefore, there is in the older drama, instead of Shakespeare's long-drawn scene of Lear's interview with Cordelia and of Cordelia's unnecessary murder, the exquisite scene of the interview between Leir and Cordelia, unequalled by any in all Shakespeare's dramas.

The old drama also terminates more naturally and more in accordance with the moral demands of the spectator than does Shakespeare's, namely, by the King of the Gauls conquering the husbands of the elder sisters and Cordelia, instead of being killed, restoring Leir to his former position.

* * *

ALGERNON CHARLES SWINBURNE (1837-1909)

In his criticism Swinburne displays the fervor of the romantic poet in intensified form. He is best known for the sensu-
ousness and eroticism of his lyrics, revealed in his collection
of *Ballads and Poems*. In his essays, particularly those treating the works of Shakespeare and of other Elizabethan dramatists he is prone to the same kind of excess that often disfigures
his verse. The extract from his appreciation of *King Lear* is
an accumulation of superlatives about every aspect of the
tragedy. Since he was steeped in the Greek dramatists, it was
inevitable that he introduce the Bard into the company of
Aeschylus, Sophocles and, surprisingly, of Aristophanes.

Swinburne's essay expresses the most extreme idolatry to
be found in the wide range of Shakespearean criticism.

SHAKESPEARE, THE TRANSCENDENT DRAMATIST
(from: *A Study of Shakespeare*, 1876)

If nothing were left of Shakespeare but the single tragedy
of *King Lear*, it would still be as plain as it is now that he
was the greatest man that ever lived. As a poet, the author of
this play can only be compared with Æschylus: the Hebrew
prophets and the creator of Job are sometimes as sublime in
imagination and in passion, but always quite incomparably
inferior in imaginative intelligence. Sophocles is as noble, as
beautiful, and as kindly a thinker and a writer: but the gentle
Shakespeare could see farther and higher and wider and
deeper at a glance than ever could the gentle Sophocles.
Aristophanes had as magnificent a power of infinitely joyous
wit and infinitely inexhaustible humour: but whom can he
show us or offer us to be set against Falstaff or the Fool? It
is true that Shakespeare has neither the lyric nor the prophetic
power of the Greeks and the Hebrews: but then it must be
observed and remembered that he, and he alone among poets
and among men, could well afford to dispense even with such
transcendent gifts as these. Freedom of thought and sublimity
of utterance came hand in hand together into English speech:
our first great poet, if loftiness and splendour of spirit and of
word be taken as the test of greatness, was Christopher Mar-

lowe. From his dead hand the one man born to excel him, and to pay a due and a deathless tribute to his deathless memory, took up the heritage of dauntless thought, of daring imagination, and of since unequalled song.

The tragedy of *King Lear*, like the trilogy of the Oresteia, is a thing incomparable and unique. To compare it with *Othello* is as inevitable a temptation as to compare the *Agamemnon* with the *Prometheus* of the one man comparable with Shakespeare. And the result, for any reader of human intelligence and decent humility in sight of what is highest in the spiritual world, must always be a sense of adoring doubt and exulting hesitation. In *Othello* and in *Prometheus* a single figure, an everlasting and godlike type of heroic and human agony, dominates and dwarfs all others but those of the traitor Iago and the tyrant God. There is no Clytæmnestra in the one, and there is no Cordelia in the other. "The gentle lady married to the Moor" is too gentle for comparison with the most glorious type of womanhood which even Shakespeare ever created before he conceived and brought forth Imogen. No one could have offered to Cordelia the tribute of so equivocal a compliment as was provoked by the submissive endurance of Desdemona—"Truly, an obedient lady." Antigone herself—and with Antigone alone can we imagine the meeting of Cordelia in the heaven of heavens—is not so divinely human as Cordelia. We love her all the more, with a love that at once tempers and heightens our worship, for the rough and abrupt repetition of her nobly unmerciful reply to her father's fond and fatuous appeal. Almost cruel and assuredly severe in its uncompromising self-respect, this brief and natural word of indignantly reticent response is the key-note of all that follows—the spark which kindles into eternal life the most tragic of all tragedies in the world. All the yet unimaginable horror of the future becomes at once inevitable and assured when she shows herself so young and so untender—so young and true. And what is the hereditary horror of doom once imminent over the house of Atreus to this instant imminence of no supernatural but a more awfully natural fate? Cursed and cast out, she leaves him and knows that she leaves him in the hands of Goneril and Regan.

Coleridge, the greatest though not the first great critic and apostle or interpreter of Shakespeare, has noted "these daugh-

ters and these sisters" as the only characters in Shakespeare
whose wickedness is ultra-natural—something outside and
beyond the presumable limits of human evil. It would be well
for human nature if it were so; but is it? They are "remorse-
less, treacherous, lecherous, kindless"; hot and hard, cold
and cunning, savage and subtle as a beast of the field or the
wilderness or the jungle. But such dangerous and vicious
animals are not more exceptional than the very noblest and
purest of their kind. An Iago is abnormal: his wonderful intelligence, omnipotent and infallible within its limit and its
range, gives to the unclean and maleficent beast that he is
the dignity and the mystery of a devil. Goneril and Regan
would be almost vulgarly commonplace by comparison with
him if the conditions of their life and the circumstances of
their story were not so much more extraordinary than their
instincts and their acts. "Regan," according to Coleridge, "is
not, in fact, a greater monster than Goneril, but she has the
power of casting more venom." A champion who should
wish to enter the lists on behalf of Goneril might plead that
Regan was so much more of a Gadarean sow than her elder
sister as to be, for all we know, incapable of such passion as
flames out in Goneril at the thought of foreign banners
spread in a noiseless land.

> Where's thy drum?
> France spreads his banners in our noiseless land;
> With plumed helm thy slayer begins [his] threats;
> Whiles thou, a moral fool, sit'st still, and criest
> 'Alack, why does he so?'

Beast and she-devil as she is, she rises in that instant to the
level of an unclean and a criminal Joan of Arc. Her advo-
cate might also invoke as an extenuating circumstance the
fact that she poisoned Regan.

François-Victor Hugo, the author of the best and fullest
commentary ever written on the text of which he gave us
the most wonderful and masterly of all imaginable transla-
tions, has perhaps unwittingly enforced and amplified the
remark of Coleridge on the difference between the criminal-
ity of the one man chosen by chance and predestined by
nature as the proper paramour of either sister and the monstrosity of the creatures who felt towards him as women feel
towards the men they love. Edmund is not a more true-born

child of hell than a true-born son of his father. Goneril and
Regan are legitimate daughters of the pit; the man who excites in them such emotion as in such as they are may pass
as the substitute for love is but a half-blooded fellow from
the infernal as well as the human point of view. His last wish
is to undo the last and most monstrous of his crimes. Such a
wish would have been impossible to either of the sisters by
whom he can boast with his dying breath that Edmund was
beloved.

> I pant for life: some good I mean to do,
> Despite of mine own nature. Quickly send,
> Be brief in it, to the castle; for my writ
> Is on the life of Lear and on Cordelia:
> Nay, send in time.

The incomparable genius of the greatest among all poets
and all men approved itself incomparable for ever by the
possibly unconscious instinct which in this supreme work
induced or compelled him to set side by side the very lowest
and the very highest types of imaginable humanity. Kent and
Oswald, Regan and Cordelia, stand out in such relief against
each other that Shakespeare alone could have wrought their
several figures into one perfect scheme of spiritual harmony.
Setting aside for a moment the reflection that outside the
work of Æschylus there is no such poetry in the world, we
must remember that there is no such realism. And there is no
discord between the supreme sublimities of impassioned poetry and the humblest realities of photographic prose. In-
credible and impossible as it seems, the impression of the one
is enhanced and intensified by the impression of the other.

That Shakespeare's judgment was as great and almost as
wonderful as his genius has been a commonplace of criticism
ever since the days of Coleridge; questionable only by such
dirty and dwarfish creatures of simian intellect and facetious
idiocy as mistake it for a sign of wit instead of dullness, and
of distinction instead of degradation, to deny the sun in
heaven and affirm the fragrance of a sewer. But I do not
know whether his equally unequalled skill in the selection
and composition of material for the construction of a masterpiece has or has not been as all but universally recognised.
No more happy and no more terrible inspiration ever glori-
fied the genius of a poet than was that which bade the great-

est of them all inweave or fuse together the legend of Lear
and his daughters with the story of Gloucester and his sons.
It is possible that an episode in Sidney's *Arcadia* may have
suggested, as is usually supposed or usually repeated, the
notion or conception of this more than tragic underplot; but
the student will be disappointed who thinks to find in the
sweet and sunbright work of Sidney's pure and happy genius
a touch or a hint of such tragic horror as could only be conceived and made endurable by the deeper as well as higher,
and darker as well as brighter, genius of Shakespeare. And
this fearful understudy in terror is a necessary, an indispensable, part of the most wonderful creation ever imagined and
realised by man. The author of the Book of Job, the author
of the Eumenides, can show nothing to be set beside the
third act of *King Lear*. All that is best and all that is worst
in man might have been brought together and flashed together upon the mind's eye of the spectator or the student
without the intervention of such servile ministers as take
part with Goneril and Regan against their father. Storm and
lightning, thunder and rain, become to us, even as they became to Lear, no less conscious and responsible partners in
the superhuman inhumanity of an unimaginable crime. The
close of the *Prometheus* itself seems less spiritually and over-
poweringly fearful by comparison with a scene which is not
the close and is less terrible than the close of *King Lear*. And
it is no whit more terrible than it is beautiful. The splendour
of the lightning and the menace of the thunder serve only
or mainly to relieve or to enhance the effect of suffering and
the potency of passion on the spirit and the conscience of a
man. The sufferer is transfigured: but he is not transformed.
Mad or sane, living and dying, he is passionate and vehe-
ment, single-hearted and self-willed. And therefore it is that
the fierce appeal, the fiery protest against the social iniquities
and the legal atrocities of civilised mankind, which none before the greatest of all Englishmen had ever dreamed of daring to utter in song or set forth upon the stage, comes not
from Hamlet, but from Lear. The young man whose infinite
capacity of thought and whose delicate scrupulosity of conscience at once half disabled and half deified him could never
have seen what was revealed by suffering to an old man who
had never thought or felt more deeply or more keenly than

an average labourer or an average king. Lear's madness, at all events, was assuredly not his enemy, but his friend.

The rule of Elizabeth and her successor may have been more arbitrary than we can now understand how the commonwealth of England could accept and could endure; but how far it was from a monarchy, from a government really deserving of that odious and ignominious name, we may judge by the fact that this play could be acted and published. Among all its other great qualities, among all the many other attributes which mark it for ever as matchless among the works of man, it has this above all, that it is the first great utterance of a cry from the heights and the depths of the human spirit on behalf of the outcasts of the world—on behalf of the social sufferer, clean or unclean, innocent or criminal, thrall or free. To satisfy the sense of righteousness, the craving for justice, as unknown and unimaginable by Dante as by Chaucer, a change must come upon the social scheme of things which shall make an end of the actual relations between the judge and the cutpurse, the beadle and the prostitute, the beggar and the king. All this could be uttered, could be prophesied, could be thundered from the English stage at the dawn of the seventeenth century. Were it within the power of omnipotence to create a German or a Russian Shakespeare, could anything of the sort be whispered or muttered or hinted or suggested from the boards of a Russian or a German theatre at the dawn of the twentieth? When a Tolstoi or a Sudermann can do this, and can do it with impunity in success, it will be allowed that his country is not more than three centuries behind England in civilisation and freedom. Not political reform, but social revolution as beneficent and as bloodless, as absolute and as radical, as enkindled the aspiration and the faith of Victor Hugo, is the key-note of the creed and the watchword of the gospel according to Shakespeare. Not, of course, that it was not his first and last aim to follow the impulse which urged him to do good work for its own sake and for love of his own art: but this he could not do without delivery of the word that was in him—the word of witness against wrong done by oversight as well as by cruelty, by negligence as surely as by crime. These things were hidden from the marvellous wisdom of Hamlet, and revealed to the more marvellous insanity of Lear.

There is nothing of the miraculous in this marvel: the mere presence and companionship of the Fool should suffice to account for it; Cordelia herself is but a little more adorably worthy of our love than the poor fellow who began to pine away after her going into France and before his coming into sight of reader or spectator. Here again the utmost humiliation imaginable of social state and daily life serves only to exalt and to emphasise the nobility and the manhood of the natural man. The whip itself cannot degrade him; the threat of it cannot change his attitude towards Lear; the dread of it cannot modify his defiance of Goneril. Being, if not half-witted, not altogether as other men are, he urges Lear to return and ask his daughters' blessing rather than brave the midnight and the storm: but he cleaves to his master with the divine instinct of fidelity and love which is not, though it should be, as generally recognised in the actual nature of a cat as in the proverbial nature of a dog. And when the old man is trembling on the very verge of madness, he sees and understands the priceless worth of such devotion and the godlike wisdom of such folly. In the most fearfully pathetic of all poems the most divinely pathetic touch of all is the tender thought of the houseless king for the suffering of such a fellow-sufferer as his fool. The whirlwind of terror and pity in which we are living as we read may at first confuse and obscure to the sight of a boyish reader the supreme significance and the unutterable charm of it. But if any elder does not feel it too keenly and too deeply for tears, it is a pity that he should waste his time and misuse his understanding in the study of Shakespeare.

There is nothing in all poetry so awful, so nearly unendurable by the reader who is compelled by a natural instinct of imagination to realise and believe it, as the close of the *Choephorœ*, except only the close of *King Lear*. The cry of Ugolino to the earth that would not open to swallow and to save is not quite so fearful in its pathos. But the skill which made use of the stupid old chronicle or tradition to produce this final masterpiece of tragedy is coequal with the genius which created it. The legendary Cordelia hanged herself in prison, long after her father's death, when defeated in battle by the sons of Goneril. And this most putid and contemptible tradition suggested to Shakespeare the most dramatic and the most poetic of all scenes and all events that ever bade all men not devoid of understanding understand how much higher is the genius of man than the action of chance: how far the truth of imagination exceeds and transcends at all points the accident of fact. That an event may have happened means nothing and matters nothing; that a man such as Æschylus or Shakespeare imagined it means this: that it endures and bears witness what man may be, at the highest of his powers and the noblest of his nature, for ever.

* * *

A. C. BRADLEY (1851-1935)

The nineteenth-century analysis of the characters of Shakespeare's plays culminated in Bradley's criticism. His lectures on *Hamlet, King Lear, Macbeth* and *Othello* were first collected and published in 1904 under the title *Shakespearean Tragedy.* His usual method was to follow a character through the play scene by scene in a search for evidence upon which to base his interpretation. In applying this method to the Fool, he concludes that the strange creature is a little touched in his brain, that he is not, as many critics contend, a man as old as Lear, whose devotion to his master has been lifelong. No such enfeebled victim of senility is Lear's fool, but a frail boy.

The other excerpt from Bradley's essay represents his broodings in the role of idealistic philosopher, searching for the sources of the overpowering effects that the play makes on everyone who yields to its dark magic. The feeling which it evokes in the spectator is wonder at the monstrous wickedness of Edmund, Goneril and Regan—in short at the terrifying picture of humanity fit to be placed beside the lost creatures in Dante's *Inferno*.

SOURCES OF THE OVERPOWERING EFFECTS OF EVIL IN *King Lear*
(from: *Shakespearean Tragedy,* 1904)

How is it, now, that this defective drama so overpowers us that we are either unconscious of its blemishes or regard them as almost irrelevant? As soon as we turn to this question we recognise, not merely that *King Lear* possesses purely dramatic qualities which far outweigh its defects, but that its greatness consists partly in imaginative effects of a wider kind. And, looking for the sources of these effects, we find among them some of those very things which appeared to us dramatically faulty or injurious. Thus, to take at once two of the simplest examples of this, that very vagueness in the sense of locality which we have just considered, and again that excess in the bulk of the material and the number of figures, events and movements, while they interfere with the clearness of vision, have at the same time a positive value for imagination. They give the feeling of vastness, the feeling not of a scene or particular place, but of a world; or, to speak more accurately, of a particular place which is also a world. This world is dim to us, partly from its immensity, and partly because it is filled with gloom; and in the gloom shapes approach and recede, whose half-seen faces and motions touch us with dread, horror, or the most painful pity,—sympathies and antipathies which we seem to be feeling not only for them but for the whole race. This world, we are told, is called Britain; but we should no more look for it in an atlas than for the place, called Caucasus, where Prometheus was chained by Strength and Force and comforted by the daughters of Ocean, or the place where Farinata stands erect in his glowing tomb, "Come avesse lo Inferno in gran dispitto."

Consider next the double action. It has certain strictly dramatic advantages, and may well have had its origin in purely dramatic considerations. To go no further, the secondary plot fills out a story which would by itself have been somewhat thin, and it provides a most effective contrast between its personages and those of the main plot, the tragic strength and stature of the latter being heightened by comparison with the slighter build of the former. But its chief value lies elsewhere, and is not merely dramatic. It lies in the fact—in Shakespeare without a parallel—that the sub-plot simply repeats the theme of the main story. Here, as there, we see an old man "with a white beard." He, like Lear, is affectionate, unsuspicious, foolish, and self-willed. He, too, wrongs deeply a child who loves him not less for the wrong. He, too, meets with monstrous ingratitude from the child whom he favours, and is tortured and driven to death. This repetition does not simply double the pain with which the tragedy is witnessed: it startles and terrifies by suggesting that the folly of Lear and the ingratitude of his daughters are no accidents or merely individual aberrations, but that in that dark cold world some fateful malignant influence is abroad, turning the hearts of the fathers against their children and of the children against their fathers, smiting the earth with a curse, so that the brother gives the brother to death and the father the son, blinding the eyes, maddening the brain, freezing the springs of pity, numbing all powers except the nerves of anguish and the dull lust of life.

Hence too, as well as from other sources, comes that feeling which haunts us in *King Lear*, as though we were witnessing something universal,—a conflict not so much of particular persons as of the powers of good and evil in the world. And the treatment of many of the characters confirms this feeling. Considered simply as psychological studies few of them, surely, are of the highest interest. Fine and subtle touches could not be absent from a work of Shakespeare's maturity; but with the possible exception of Lear himself, no one of the characters strikes us as psychologically a *wonderful* creation, like Hamlet or Iago or even Macbeth; one or two seem even to be somewhat faint and thin. And, what is more significant, it is not quite natural to us to regard them from this point of view at all. Rather we observe a most unusual circumstance. If Lear, Gloster and Albany are set apart, the rest fall into two distinct groups, which are strongly, even violently, contrasted: Cordelia, Kent, Edgar, the Fool on one side, Goneril, Regan, Edmund, Cornwall, Oswald on the other. These characters are in various degrees individualised, most of them completely so; but still in each group there is a quality common to all the members, or one spirit breathing through them all. Here we have unselfish and devoted love, there hard self-seeking. On both sides, further, the common quality takes an extreme form; the love is incapable of being chilled by injury, the selfishness of being softened by pity; and, it may be added, this tendency to extremes is found again in the characters of Lear and Gloster, and is the main source of the accusations of improbability directed against their conduct at certain points. Hence the members of each group tend to appear, at least in part, as varieties of one species; the radical differences of the two species are emphasized in broad hard strokes; and the two are set in conflict, almost as if Shakespeare, like Empedocles, were regarding Love and Hate as the two ultimate forces of the universe.

The presence in *King Lear* of so large a number of characters in whom love or self-seeking is so extreme, has another effect. They do not merely inspire in us emotions of unusual strength, but they also stir the intellect to wonder and speculation. How can there be such men and women? we ask ourselves. How comes it that humanity can take such absolutely opposite forms? And, in particular, to what omission of elements which should be present in human nature, or, if there is no omission, to what distortion of these elements is it due that such being as some of these come to exist? This is a question which Iago (and perhaps no previous creation of Shakespeare's) forces us to ask, but in *King Lear* it is provoked again and again. And more, it seems to us that the author himself is asking this question. "Then let them anatomise Regan, see what breeds about her heart. Is there any cause in nature that makes these hard hearts?"—the strain of thought which appears here seems to be present in some degree throughout the play. We seem to trace the tendency which, a few years later, produced Ariel and Caliban, the tendency of imagination to analyse and abstract, to decompose human nature into its constituent factors, and then to construct beings in whom one or more of these factors is absent or atrophied or only incipient. This, of course, is a tendency which produces symbols, allegories, personifications of qualities and abstract ideas; and we are accustomed to think it quite foreign to Shakespeare's genius, which was in the highest degree concrete. No doubt in the main we are right here; but it is hazardous to set limits to that genius. The Sonnets, if nothing else, may show us how easy it was to Shakespeare's mind to move in a world of "Platonic" ideas; and, while it would be going too far to suggest that he was employing conscious symbolism or allegory in *King Lear*, it does appear to disclose a mode of imagination not so very far removed from the mode with which, we must remember, Shakespeare was perfectly familiar in Morality plays and in the *Fairy Queen*.

This same tendency shows itself in *King Lear* in other forms. To it is due the idea of monstrosity—of beings, actions, states of mind, which appear not only abnormal but absolutely contrary to nature; an idea, which, of course, is common enough in Shakespeare, but appears with unusual frequency in *King Lear*, for instance in the lines:

> Ingratitude, thou marble-hearted fiend,
> More hideous when thou show'st thee in a child
> Than the sea-monster!

or in the exclamation,

> Filial ingratitude!
> Is it not as this mouth should tear this hand
> For lifting food to't?

It appears in another shape in that most vivid passage where Albany, as he looks at the face which had bewitched him, now distorted with dreadful passions, suddenly sees it in a new light and exclaims in horror:

> Thou changed and self-cover'd thing, for shame,
> Bemonster not thy feature. Were't my fitness
> To let these hands obey my blood,
> They are apt enough to dislocate and tear
> Thy flesh and bones: howe'er thou art a fiend,
> A woman's shape doth shield thee.

It appears once more in that exclamation of Kent's, as he listens to the description of Cordelia's grief:

> It is the stars,
> The stars above us, govern our conditions;
> Else one self mate and mate could not beget
> Such different issues.

(This is not the only sign that Shakespeare had been musing over heredity, and wondering how it comes about that the composition of two strains of blood or two parent souls can produce such astonishingly different products.)

This mode of thought is responsible, lastly, for a very striking characteristic of *King Lear*—one in which it has no parallel except *Timon*—the incessant references to the lower animals and man's likeness to them. These references are scattered broadcast through the whole play as though Shakespeare's mind were so busy with the subject that he could hardly write a page without some allusion to it. The dog, the horse, the cow, the sheep, the hog, the lion, the bear, the wolf, the fox, the monkey, the pole-cat, the civet-cat, the pelican, the owl, the crow, the chough, the wren, the fly, the butterfly, the rat, the mouse, the frog, the tadpole, the wall-newt, the water-newt, the worm—I am sure I cannot have completed the list, and some of them are mentioned again and again. Often, of course, and especially in the talk of Edgar as the Bedlam, they have no symbolical meaning; but not seldom, even in his talk, they are expressly referred to for their typical qualities—"hog in sloth, fox in stealth, wolf in greediness, dog in madness, lion in prey." "The fitchew nor the soiled horse goes to't With a more riotous appetite." Sometimes a person in the drama is compared, openly or implicitly, with one of them. Goneril is a kite: her ingratitude has a serpent's tooth: she has struck her father most serpent-like upon the very heart: her visage is wolvish: she has tied sharp-toothed unkindness like a vulture on her father's breast: for her husband she is a gilded serpent: to Gloster her cruelty seems to have the fangs of a boar. She and Regan are dog-hearted: they are tigers, not daughters: each is an adder to the other: the flesh of each is covered with the fell of a beast. Oswald is a mongrel, and the son and heir of a mongrel: ducking to everyone in power, he is a wag-tail: white with fear, he is a goose. Gloster, for Regan, is an in-grateful fox: Albany, for his wife, has a cowish spirit and is milk-liver'd: when Edgar as the Bedlam first appeared to Lear he made him think a man a worm. As we read, the souls of all the beasts in turn seem to us to have entered the bodies of these mortals; horrible in their venom, savagery, lust, deceit-fulness, sloth, cruelty, filthiness; miserable in their feebleness, nakedness, defencelessness, blindness; and man, "consider him well," is even what they are. Shakespeare, to whom the idea of the transmigration of souls was familiar and had once been material for jest, seems to have been brooding on humanity in the light of it. It is remarkable, and somewhat sad, that he seems to find none of man's better qualities in the world of the brutes (though he might well have found the prototype of the self-less love of Kent and Cordelia in the dog whom he so habit-ually maligns); but he seems to have been asking himself whether that which he loathes in man may not be due to some strange wrenching of this frame of things, through which the lower animal souls have found a lodgment in human forms, and there found—to the horror and confusion of the thinking mind—brains to forge, tongues to speak, and hands to act, enormities which no mere brute can conceive or execute. He shows us in *King Lear* these terrible forces bursting into monstrous life and flinging themselves upon those human beings who are weak and defenceless, partly from old age, but partly because they *are* human and lack the dreadful undivided energy of the beast. And the only comfort he might seem to hold out to us is the prospect that at least this bestial race, strong only where it is vile, cannot endure: though stars and gods are powerless, or careless, or empty dreams, yet there must be an end of this horrible world:

> It will come;
> Humanity must perforce prey on itself
> Like monsters of the deep.

The influence of all this on imagination as we read *King Lear* is very great; and it combines with other influences to convey to us, not in the form of distinct ideas but in the manner proper to poetry, the wider or universal significance of the spectacle presented to the inward eye. But the effect of theatrical exhibition is precisely the reverse. There the poetic atmosphere is dissipated; the meaning of the very words which create it passes half-realised; in obedience to the tyranny of the eye we conceive the characters as mere particular men and women; and all that mass of vague suggestion, if it enters the mind at all, appears in the shape of an allegory which we immediately reject. A similar conflict between imagination and sense will be found if we consider the dramatic centre of the whole tragedy, the Storm-scenes. The temptation of Othello and the scene of Duncan's murder may lose upon the stage, but they do not lose their essence, and they gain as well as lose. The Storm-scenes in *King Lear* gain nothing and their very essence is destroyed. It is comparatively a small thing that the theatrical storm, not to drown the dialogue, must be silent whenever a human being wishes to speak, and is wretchedly inferior to many a storm we have witnessed. Nor is it simply that, as Lamb observed, the corporal presence of Lear, "an old man tottering about the stage with a walking-stick," disturbs and depresses that sense of the greatness of his mind which fills the imagination. There is a further reason, which is not expressed, but still emerges, in these words of Lamb's: "the explosions of his passion are terrible as a volcano: they are storms turning up and disclosing to the bottom that sea, his mind, with all its vast riches." Yes, "they are *storms*." For imagination, that is to say, the explosions of Lear's passion, and the bursts of rain and thunder, are not, what for the senses they must be, two things, but manifestations of one thing. It is the powers of the tormented soul that we hear and see in the "groans of roaring wind and rain" and the "sheets of fire"; and they that, at intervals almost more overwhelming, sink back into darkness and silence. Nor yet is even this all; but, as those incessant references to wolf and tiger made us see humanity "reeling back into the beast" and ravening against itself, so in the storm we seem to see Nature herself convulsed by the same horrible passions; the "common mother,"

> Whose womb immeasurable and infinite breast
> Teems and feeds all,

turning on her children, to complete the ruin they have wrought upon themselves. Surely something not less, but much more, than these helpless words convey, is what comes to us in these astounding scenes; and if, translated thus into the language of prose, it becomes confused and inconsistent, the reason is simply that it itself is poetry, and such poetry as cannot be transferred to the space behind the foot-lights, but has its being only in imagination. Here then is Shakespeare at his very greatest, but not the mere dramatist Shakespeare.

And now we may say this also of the catastrophe, which we found questionable from the strictly dramatic point of view. Its purpose is not merely dramatic. This sudden blow out of the darkness, which seems so far from inevitable, and which strikes down our reviving hopes for the victims of so much cruelty, seems now only what we might have expected in a world so wild and monstrous. It is as if Shakespeare said to us: "Did you think weakness and innocence have any chance here? Were you beginning to dream that? I will show you it is not so."

I come to a last point. As we contemplate this world, the question presses on us What can be the ultimate power that moves it, that excites this gigantic war and waste, or, perhaps, that suffers them and overrules them? And in *King Lear* this question is not left to *us* to ask, it is raised by the characters themselves. References to religious or irreligious beliefs and feelings are more frequent than is usual in Shakespeare's tragedies, as frequent perhaps as in his final plays. He introduces characteristic differences in the language of the different persons about fortune or the stars or the gods, and shows how the question What rules the world? is forced upon their minds. They answer it in their turn: Kent, for instance:

> It is the stars,
> The stars above us, govern our condition:

Edmund:

> Thou, nature, art my goddess; to thy law
> My services are bound:

and again,

> This is the excellent foppery of the world, that, when we are sick in fortune—often the surfeit of our own behaviour—we make guilty of our disasters the sun, the moon and the stars; as if we were villains by necessity, fools by heavenly compulsion, . . . and all that we are evil in by a divine thrusting on:

Gloster:

> As flies to wanton boys are we to the gods;
> They kill us for their sport;

Edgar:

> Think that the clearest gods, who make them honours
> Of men's impossibilities, have preserved thee.

Here we have four distinct theories of the nature of the ruling power. And besides this, in such of the characters as have any belief in gods who love good and hate evil, the spectacle of triumphant injustice or cruelty provokes questionings like those of Job, or else the thought, often repeated, of divine retribution. To Lear at one moment the storm seems the messenger of heaven:

> Let the great gods,
> That keep this dreadful pother o'er our heads,
> Find out their enemies now. Tremble, thou wretch,
> That hast within thee undivulged crimes. . . .

At another moment those habitual miseries of the poor, of which he has taken too little account, seem to him to accuse the gods of injustice:

> Take physic, pomp;
> Expose thyself to feel what wretches feel,
> That thou mayst shake the superflux to them
> And show the heavens more just;

and Gloster has almost the same thought. Gloster again, thinking of the cruelty of Lear's daughters, breaks out,

> but I shall see
> The winged vengeance overtake such children.

The servants who have witnessed the blinding of Gloster by Cornwall and Regan, cannot believe that cruelty so atrocious will pass unpunished. One cries,

> I'll never care what wickedness I do,
> If this man come to good;

and another,

> if she live long,
> And in the end meet the old course of death,
> Women will all turn monsters.

Albany greets the news of Cornwall's death with the exclamation,

> This shows you are above,
> You justicers, that these our nether crimes
> So speedily can venge;

and the news of the deaths of the sisters with the words,

> This judgment of the heavens, that makes us tremble,
> Touches us not with pity.

Edgar, speaking to Edmund of their father, declares

> The gods are just, and of our pleasant vices
> Make instruments to plague us,

and Edmund himself assents. Almost throughout the latter half of the drama we note in most of the better characters a preoccupation with the question of the ultimate power, and a passionate need to explain by reference to it what otherwise would drive them to despair. And the influence of this pre-occupation and need joins with other influences in affecting the imagination, and in causing it to receive from *King Lear* an impression which is at least as near of kin to the *Divine Comedy* as to *Othello*.

For Dante that which is recorded in the *Divine Comedy* was the justice and love of God. What did *King Lear* record for Shakespeare? Something, it would seem, very different. This is certainly the most terrible picture that Shakespeare painted of the world. In no other of his tragedies does humanity appear more pitiably infirm or more hopelessly bad. What is Iago's malignity against an envied stranger compared with the cruelty of the son of Gloster and the daughters of Lear? What are the sufferings of a strong man like Othello to those of helpless age? Much too that we have already observed—the repetition of the main theme in that of the under-plot, the comparisons of man with the most wretched and the most horrible of the beasts, the impression of Nature's hostility to him, the irony of the unexpected catastrophe—these, with much else, seem even to indicate an intention to show things at their worst, and to return the sternest of replies to that question of the ultimate power and those appeals for retribution. Is it an accident, for example, that Lear's first appeal to something beyond the earth,

> O heavens,
> If you do love old men, if your sweet sway
> Allow obedience, if yourselves are old,
> Make it your cause:

is immediately answered by the iron voices of his daughters, raising by turns the conditions on which they will give him a humiliating harbourage; or that his second appeal, heart-rending in its piteousness,

> You see me here, you gods, a poor old man,
> As full of grief as age; wretched in both:

is immediately answered from the heavens by the sound of the breaking storm? Albany and Edgar may moralise on the divine justice as they will, but how, in the face of all that we see, shall we believe that they speak Shakespeare's mind? Is not his mind rather expressed in the bitter contrast between their faith and the events we witness, or in the scornful rebuke of those who take upon them the mystery of things as if they were God's spies? Is it not Shakespeare's judgment on his kind that we hear in Lear's appeal,

> And thou, all-shaking thunder,
> Smite flat the thick rotundity o' the world!
> Crack nature's moulds, all germens spill at once,
> That make ingrateful man!

and Shakespeare's judgment on the worth of existence that we hear in Lear's agonised cry, "No, no, no life!"?

Beyond doubt, I think, some such feelings as these possess us, and, if we follow Shakespeare, ought to possess us, from time to time as we read *King Lear*. And some readers will go further and maintain that this is also the ultimate and total impression left by the tragedy. *King Lear* has been held to be profoundly "pessimistic" in the full meaning of that word, —the record of a time when contempt and loathing for his kind had overmastered the poet's soul, and in despair he pronounced man's life to be simply hateful and hideous. And if we exclude the biographical part of this view, the rest may claim some support even from the greatest of Shakespearean critics since the days of Coleridge, Hazlitt and Lamb. Mr. Swinburne, after observing that *King Lear* is "by far the most Aeschylean" of Shakespeare's works, proceeds thus:

"But in one main point it differs radically from the work and the spirit of Aeschylus. Its fatalism is of a darker and harder nature. To Prometheus the fetters of the lord and enemy of mankind were bitter; upon Orestes the hand of heaven was laid too heavily to bear; yet in the not utterly infinite or everlasting distance we see beyond them the promise of the morning on which mystery and justice shall be made one; when righteousness and omnipotence at last shall kiss each other. But on the horizon of Shakespeare's tragic fatalism we see no such twilight of atonement, such pledge of reconciliation as this. Requital, redemption, amends, equity, explanation, pity and mercy, are words without a meaning here.

> As flies to wanton boys are we to the gods;
> They kill us for their sport.

Here is no need of the Eumenides, children of Night everlasting; for here is very Night herself." ...

The theatrical fool or clown (we need not distinguish them here) was a sore trial to the cultured poet and spectator in Shakespeare's day. He came down from the Morality plays, and was beloved of the groundlings. His antics, his songs, his dances, his jests, too often unclean, delighted them, and did something to make the drama, what the vulgar, poor or rich, like it to be, a variety entertainment. Even if he confined himself to what was set down for him, he often disturbed the dramatic unity of the piece; and the temptation to "gag" was too strong for him to resist. Shakespeare makes Hamlet object to it in emphatic terms. The more learned critics and poets went further and would have abolished the fool altogether. His part declines as the drama advances, diminishing markedly at the end of the sixteenth century. Jonson and Massinger exclude him. Shakespeare used him—we know to what effect —as he used all the other popular elements of the drama; but he abstained from introducing him into the Roman plays, and there is no fool in the last of the pure tragedies, *Macbeth*.

But the Fool is one of Shakespeare's triumphs in *King Lear*. Imagine the tragedy without him, and you hardly know it. To remove him would spoil its harmony, as the harmony of a picture would be spoiled if one of the colours were extracted. One can almost imagine that Shakespeare, going home from an evening at the Mermaid, where he had listened to Jonson fulminating against fools in general and perhaps criticising the Clown in *Twelfth Night* in particular, had said to himself: "Come, my friends, I will show you once for all that the mischief is in you, and not in the fool or the audience. I will have a fool in the most tragic of my tragedies. He shall not play a little part. He shall keep from first to last the company in which you most object to see him, the company of a king. Instead of amusing the king's idle hours, he shall stand by him in the very tempest and whirlwind of passion. Before I have done you shall confess, between laughter and tears, that he is of the very essence of life, that you have known him all your days though you never recognised him till now, and that you would as soon go without Hamlet as miss him."

The Fool in *King Lear* has been so favourite a subject with good critics that I will confine myself to one or two points on which a difference of opinion is possible. To suppose that the Fool is, like many a domestic fool at that time, a perfectly sane man pretending to be half-witted, is surely a most prosaic blunder. There is no difficulty in imagining that, being slightly touched in the brain, and holding the office of fool, he performs the duties of his office intentionally as well as involuntarily: it is evident that he does so. But unless we suppose that he *is* touched in the brain we lose half the effect of his appearance in the Storm-scenes. The effect of those scenes (to state the matter as plainly as possible) depends largely on the presence of three characters, and on the affinities and contrasts between them; on our perception that the differences of station in King, Fool, and beggar-noble, are levelled by one blast of calamity; but also on our perception of the differences between these three in one respect,—viz. in regard to the peculiar affliction of insanity. The insanity of the King differs widely in its nature from that of the Fool, and that of the Fool from that of the beggar. But the insanity of the King differs from that of the beggar not only in its nature, but also in the fact that one is real and the other simply a pretence. Are we to suppose then that the insanity of the third character, the Fool, is, in this respect, a mere repetition of that of the second, the beggar,—that it too is *mere* pretence? To suppose this is not only to impoverish miserably the impression made by the trio as a whole, it is also to diminish the heroic and pathetic effect of the character of the Fool. For his heroism consists largely in this, that his efforts to outjest his master's injuries are the efforts of a being to whom a responsible and consistent course of action, nay even a responsible use of language, is at the best of times difficult, and from whom it is never at the best of times expected. It is a heroism something like that of Lear himself in his endeavour to learn patience at the age of eighty. But arguments against the idea that the Fool is wholly sane are either needless or futile; for in the end they are appeals to the perception that this idea almost destroys the poetry of the character.

This is not the case with another question, the question

whether the Fool is a man or a boy. Here the evidence and the grounds for discussion are more tangible. He is frequently addressed as "boy." This is not decisive; but Lear's first words to him, "How now, my pretty knave, how dost thou?" are difficult to reconcile with the idea of his being a man, and the use of this phrase on his first entrance may show Shakespeare's desire to prevent any mistake on the point. As a boy, too, he would be more strongly contrasted in the Storm-scenes with Edgar as well as with Lear; his faithfulness and courage would be even more heroic and touching; his devotion to Cordelia, and the consequent bitterness of some of his speeches to Lear, would be even more natural. Nor does he seem to show a knowledge of the world impossible to a quick-witted though not whole-witted lad who had lived at Court. The only serious obstacle to this view, I think, is the fact that he is not known to have been represented as a boy or youth till Macready produced *King Lear*.

But even if this obstacle were serious and the Fool were imagined as a grown man, we may still insist that he must also be imagined as a timid, delicate and frail being, who on that account and from the expression of his face has a boyish look. He pines away when Cordelia goes to France. Though he takes great liberties with his master he is frightened by Goneril, and becomes quite silent when the quarrel rises high. In the terrible scene between Lear and his two daughters and Cornwall (II. iv. 129-289), he says not a word; we have almost forgotten his presence when, at the topmost pitch of passion, Lear suddenly turns to him from the hateful faces that encompass him:

> You think I'll weep;
> No, I'll not weep:
> I have full cause of weeping; but this heart
> Shall break into a hundred thousand flaws
> Or ere I'll weep. O fool, I shall go mad.

From the beginning of the Storm-scenes, though he thinks of his master alone, we perceive from his words that the cold and rain are almost more than he can bear. His childishness comes home to us when he runs out of the hovel, terrified by the madman and crying out to the King "Help me, help me," and the good Kent takes him by the hand and draws him to his side. A little later he exclaims, "This cold night will turn us all to fools and madmen"; and almost from that point he leaves the King to Edgar, speaking only once again in the remaining hundred lines of scene. In the shelter of the "farm-house" (III. vi.) he revives, and resumes his office of love; but I think that critic is right who considers his last words significant. "We'll go to supper i' the morning," says Lear; and the Fool answers "And I'll go to bed at noon," as though he felt he had taken his death. When, a little later, the King is being carried away on a litter, the Fool sits idle. He is so benumbed and worn out that he scarcely notices what is going on. Kent has to rouse him with the words,

> Come, help to bear thy master,
> Thou must not stay behind.

We know no more. For the famous exclamation "And my poor fool is hanged" unquestionably refers to Cordelia; and even if it is intended to show a confused association in Lear's mind between his child and the Fool who so loved her (as a very old man may confuse two of his children), still it tells us nothing of the Fool's fate. It seems strange indeed that Shakespeare should have left us thus in ignorance. But we have seen that there are many marks of haste and carelessness in *King Lear;* and it may also be observed that, if the poet imagined the Fool dying on the way to Dover of the effects of that night upon the heath, he could perhaps convey this idea to the audience by instructing the actor who took the part to show, as he left the stage for the last time, the recognised tokens of approaching death.

* * *

HARLEY GRANVILLE-BARKER (1877-1946)

Barker was one of the most intelligent among the scores of modern producers of Shakespeare's plays. In his role of critic he was concerned with a discovery of the particular values of *King Lear* in its adaptation to the demands of the stage. His analysis of this tragedy is a direct answer to Lamb's contention that *King Lear* loses most of its imaginative reach when crowded into the confines of a stage. Barker makes clear the additional value of the great scenes in terms of stagecraft.

He points out that the sound of the words spoken in the dialogue is as important as their meaning; and the full significance of a scene is enhanced by what we see. This is strikingly true when we actually see Lear kneeling down like a child at his bedside to offer the prayer for the

> Poor naked wretches, wheresoe'er you are,
> That bide the pelting of this pitiless storm

In these ways Barker succeeds in showing how an experienced and imaginative director can enhance the effectiveness of scene after scene in the text, by adapting each of them to the resources of the stage.

ADVANTAGES ACCRUING TO THE TEXT OF *King Lear* WHEN STAGED
(from: *Prefaces to Shakespeare*, Vol. I, 1946)

If the play, with the invocation of the curse upon Goneril, entered an arena of anarchy and darkness, Lear himself is to pass now from personal grievance to the taking upon him, as great natures may, the imagined burden of the whole world's sorrow—and if his nature breaks under it, what wonder! And Shakespeare brings about this transition from malediction to martyrdom with great art, by contrivance direct and indirect, by strokes broad and subtle; nor ever—his art in this at its greatest—does he turn his Lear from a man into an ethical proposition. The thing is achieved—as the whole play is achieved—in terms of humanity, and according to the rubric of drama.

Lear comes back with Gloucester; the well-meaning Gloucester, whose timid tact is the one thing least likely to placate him. He is struggling with himself, with the old tyrannic temper, with his newfound knowledge of himself, with his body's growing weakness. He is like a great oak tree, torn at the roots, blown this way and that. When the half-veiled insolence of Regan's and Cornwall's greeting must, one would think, affront him, a pathetic craving for affection peeps through. When he once more finds refuge in irony, it is to turn the edge of it against himself. But with four quick shocks—his sudden recall of the outrage upon his servant, the sound of a trumpet, the sight of Oswald, the sight of

Goneril—he is brought to a stand and to face the realities arrayed against him. This must be made very plain to us. On the one side stand Goneril and Regan and Cornwall in all authority. The perplexed Gloucester hovers a little apart. On the other side is Lear, the Fool at his feet, and his one servant, disarmed, freed but a minute since behind him. Things are at their issue. His worst errors, after all, have partaken of nobility; he has scorned policy. He has given himself, helpless, into these carnal hands. He will abide, then, as nobly the fate he has courted. Note the single touch of utter scorn for the cur Cornwall, who, the moment looking likely, takes credit for those stocks.

> I set him there, sir; but his own disorders
> Deserved much less advancement.
>   You! Did you!

But all consequences he'll abide, even welcome, he'll abjure his curses, run from one ingrate daughter to the other, implore and bargain, till the depth is sounded and he stands at last surrendered, and level in his helplessness and deprivation with the least of his fellow-men.

> GONERIL.   Hear me, my lord,
>   What need you five-and-twenty, ten, or five,
>   To follow in a house where twice so many
>   Have a command to tend you?
> REGAN.   What need one?
> LEAR. O! reason not the need; our basest beggars
>   Are in the poorest thing superfluous:
>   Allow not nature more than nature needs,
>   Man's life is cheap as beast's. . . .
>   But, for true need—
>   You heavens, give me that patience, patience I need!
>   You see me here, you gods, a poor old man
>   As full of grief as age, wretched in both!

"O! reason not the need . . ."! This abandoning of the struggle and embracing of misfortune is a turning point of the play, a salient moment in the development of Lear's character, and its significance must be marked. He is now at the nadir of his fortunes; the tragic heights are at hand.

It may be thought that by emphasizing so many minor points of stagecraft the great outlines of play and character will be obscured. But while Shakespeare projects greatly, asking from his interpreters a simplicity of response, lending them greatness by virtue of this convention that passes the play's material through the sole crucible of their speech and action, he yet saves them alive, so to speak—not stultified in an attempt to overpass their own powers nor turned to mere mouthpieces of mighty lines—by constant references to the commonplace (we noted more of them in discussing the methods of the dialogue). He invigorates his play's action by keeping its realities upon a battleground where any and every sort of stroke may tell.

Thus there now follows the tense passage in which Goneril, Regan and Cornwall snuff the impending storm and find good reason for ill-doing. What moralists! Regan with her

> O! sir, to wilful men,
> The injuries that they themselves procure
> Must be their schoolmasters.

Cornwall, with his

> Shut up your doors, my lord; 'tis a wild night:
> My Regan counsels well; come out of the storm.

This is surely the very voice—though the tones may be harsh—of respectability and common sense? And what a prelude to the "high engender'd battles" now imminent! Before battle is joined, however, the note of Kent is interposed to keep the play's story going its more pedestrian way and to steady us against the imaginative turmoil pending. This use of Kent is masterly; and, in the storm-scenes themselves, the contrasting use of the Fool, feeble, fantastic, pathetic, a foil to Lear, a foil to the storm—what more incongruous sight conceivable than such a piece of Court tinsel so drenched and buffeted!—is more than masterly.

But it is upon Lear's own progress that all now centers, upon his passing from that royal defiance of the storm to the welcomed shelter of the hovel. He passes by the road of patience:

> No, I will be the pattern of all patience;
> I will say nothing.

of—be it noted—a thankfulness that he is at last simply

a man

> More sinn'd against than sinning . . .

to the humility of

> My wits begin to turn.
> Come on, my boy. How dost, my boy? Art cold?
> I am cold myself. Where is this straw, my fellow?
> The art of our necessities is strange
> That can make vile things precious. Come, your hovel. . . .

and, a little later yet, mind and body still further strained towards breaking point, to the gentle dignity, when Kent would make way for him—to the more than kingly dignity of

> Prithee, go in thyself: seek thine own ease.
> This tempest will not give me leave to ponder
> On things would hurt me more. But I'll go in:
> In, boy; go first.

Now comes the crowning touch of all:

> I'll pray, and then I'll sleep.

In the night's bleak exposure he kneels down, like a child at bedtime, to pray.

> Poor naked wretches, wheresoe'er you are,
> That bide the pelting of this pitiless storm,
> How shall your houseless heads and unfed sides,
> Your loop'd and window'd raggedness, defend you
> From seasons such as these? O, I have ta'en
> Too little care of this! Take physic, pomp;
> Expose thyself to feel what wretches feel,
> That thou mayst shake the superflux to them,
> And show the heavens more just.

To this haven of the spirit has he come, the Lear of unbridled power and pride. And how many dramatists, could they have achieved so much, would have been content to leave him here! Those who like their drama rounded and trim might approve of such a finish, which would leave us a play more compassable in performance no doubt. But the wind of a harsher doctrine is blowing through Shakespeare. Criticism, as we have seen, is apt to fix upon the episode of the storm as the height of his attempt and the point of his dramatic defeat; but it is this storm of the mind here beginning upon which he expends skill and imagination most recklessly till inspiration has had its will of him; and the drama of desperate vision ensuing it is hard indeed for actors to reduce to the positive medium of their art—without reducing it to ridicule. The three coming scenes of Lear's madness shows us Shakespeare's art at its boldest. They pass beyond the needs of the plot, they belong to a larger synthesis. Yet the means they employ are simple enough; of a kind of absolute simplicity, indeed.

The boldest and simplest is the provision of Poor Tom, that living instance of all rejection. Here, under our eyes, is Lear's new vision of himself.

> What! have his daughters brought him to this pass?
> Could'st thou save nothing? Did'st thou give them all?

Side by side stand the noble old man, and the naked, scarce human wretch.

> Is man no more than this? Consider him well. Thou owest the worm no silk, the beast no hide, the sheep no wool, the cat no perfume. Ha! here's three on's are sophisticated; thou art the thing itself; unaccommodated man is no more but such a poor, bare, forked animal as thou art. Off, off, you lendings! Come; unbutton here.

Here is a volume of argument epitomized as only drama can epitomize it, flashed on us by word and action combined. And into this, one might add, has Shakespeare metamorphosed the didactics of those old Moralities which were the infancy of his art.

> What! hath your grace no better company?

gasps poor Gloucester, bewailing at once the King's wrongs and his own, as he offers shelter from the storm. But Lear, calmness itself now, will only pace up and down, arm in arm with this refuse of humanity:

> Noble philosopher, your company.

—nor will he seek shelter without him. So they reach the outhouse, all of his own castle that Gloucester dare offer. What a group! Kent, sturdy and thrifty of words; Gloucester, tremulous; the bedraggled and exhausted Fool; and Lear, magnificently courteous and deliberate, keeping close company with his gibbering fellow-man.*

They are in shelter. Lear is silent; till the Fool—himself never overfitted, we may suppose, in body or mind for the rough and tumble of the world—rallies, as if to celebrate their safety, to a semblance of his old task. Edgar, for his own safety's sake, must play Poor Tom to the life now. Kent has his eyes on his master, watching him—at what new fantastic trick? The old king is setting two joint-stools side by side; they are Regan and Goneril, and the Fool and the beggar are to pass judgment upon them.

The lunatic mummery of the trial comes near to something we might call pure drama—as one speaks of pure mathematics or pure music—since it cannot be rendered into other terms than its own. Its effect depends upon the combination of the sound and meaning of the words and the sight of it being brought to bear as a whole directly upon our sensibility. The sound of the dialogue matters almost more than its meaning. Poor Tom and the Fool chant antiphonally; Kent's deep and kindly tones tell against the higher, agonized, weakening voice of Lear. But the chief significance is in the show. Where Lear, such a short while since, sat in his majesty, there sit the Fool and the outcast, with Kent whom he banished beside them; and he, witless, musters his failing strength to beg justice upon a joint-stool. Was better justice done, the picture ironically asks, when he presided in majesty and sanity and power?

But what, as far as Lear is concerned, is to follow? You cannot continue the development of a character in terms of lunacy—in darkness, illuminated by whatever brilliant flashes of lightning. Nor can a madman well dominate a play's action. From this moment Lear no longer is a motive force; and the needs of the story—the absolute needs of the character—would be fulfilled if, from this exhausted sleep upon the poor bed in the outhouse, he only woke to find Cordelia at his side. But Shakespeare contrives another scene

* And Kent is unknown to Lear and Edgar to his father, as we shall sufficiently remember.

of madness for him, and one which lifts the play's argument to a yet rarer height. It is delayed; and the sense of redundancy is avoided partly by keeping Lear from the stage altogether for a while, a short scene interposed sufficiently reminding us of him.

His reappearance is preluded—with what consonance!—by the fantastically imaginative episode of Gloucester's fall from the cliff. There also is Edgar, the aura of Poor Tom about him still. Suddenly Lear breaks in upon them.* The larger dramatic value of the ensuing scene can hardly be overrated. For in it, in this encounter between mad Lear and blind Gloucester, the sensual man robbed of his eyes, and the despot, the light of his mind put out, Shakespeare's sublimation of the two old stories is consummated. No moral is preached to us. It is presented as it was when king and beggar fraternized in the storm and beggar and Fool were set on the bench of justice, and we are primarily to *feel* the significance. Yet this does not lack interpretation; less explicit than when Lear, still sane, could read the lesson of the storm, clearer than was the commentary on the mock trial. It is Edgar here that sets us an example of sympathetic listening. His asides enforce it, and the last one:

> O! matter and impertinency mixed,
> Reason in madness!

will reproach us if we have not understood. The train of fancies fired by the first sight of Gloucester, with its tragically comic

> Ha! Goneril with a white beard!

(Goneril, disguised, pursuing him still!) asks little gloss.

> They flattered me like a dog. . . . To say 'Ay' and 'No' to everything I said! . . . When the rain came to wet me once and the wind to make me chatter, when the thunder would not peace at my bidding, there I found 'em, there I smelt 'em out. Go to, they are not men o' their words; they told me I was everything; 'tis a lie, I am not ague-proof.

---

* *Mad,* says the stage direction, and no more; the usual *fantastically dressed with wild flowers* is Capel's addition. But something of the sort is justified by Cordelia's speech in the earlier scene. And the dramatic purpose of them is plain: to emphasize the contrast between this and our last sight of him amid the barren wildness of the heath and the storm.

Gloucester's dutiful

> Is't not the king?

begins to transform him in those mad eyes. And madness sees a Gloucester there that sanity had known and ignored.

> I pardon that man's life: What was thy cause?
> Adultery?
> Thou shalt not die: die for adultery! No:
> The wren goes to't, and the small gilded fly
> Does lecher in my sight.
> Let copulation thrive; for Gloucester's bastard son
> Was kinder to his father than my daughters
> Got 'tween the lawful sheets.

Gloucester knows better; but how protest so to the mere erratic voice? Besides which there is only the kindly stranger-peasant near. A slight unconscious turn of the sightless eyes toward him, a simple gesture—unseen—in response from Edgar, patiently biding his time, will illuminate the irony and the pathos.

Does the mad mind pass logically from this to some uncanny prevision of the ripening of new evil in Regan and Goneril? Had it in its sanity secretly surmised what lay beneath the moral surface of their lives, so ready to emerge?

> Behold yon simpering dame
> Whose face between her forks presageth snow;
> That minces virtue and does shake the head
> To hear of pleasure's name;
> The fitchew, nor the soiled horse, goes to't
> With a more riotous appetite.

But a man—so lunatic logic runs—must free himself from the tyrannies of the flesh if he is to see the world clearly:

> Give me an ounce of civet, good apothecary, to sweeten my imagination.

And then a blind man may see the truth of it, so he tells the ruined Gloucester:

> Look with thine ears: see how yond justice rails upon yond simple thief. Hark in thine ear: change places, and,

> handy-dandy, which is the justice, which is the thief? Thou
> hast seen a farmer's dog bark at a beggar? . . . And the crea-
> ture run from the cur? There thou might'st behold the great
> image of authority; a dog's obeyed in office.

It is the picture of the mock trial given words. But with a
difference! There is no cry now for vengeance on the
wicked. For what are we that we should smite them?

> Thou rascal beadle, hold thy bloody hand!
> Why dost thou lash that whore? Strip thine own back;
> That hotly lust'st to use her in that kind
> For which thou whip'st her. The usurer hangs the cozener.
> Through tattered clothes small vices do appear;
> Robes and furr'd gowns hide all. Plate sin with gold,
> And the strong lance of justice hurtless breaks;
> Arm it in rags, a pigmy's straw doth pierce it.

Shakespeare has led Lear to compassion for sin as well as
suffering, has led him mad to where he could not hope to
lead him sane—to where sound common sense will hardly
let us follow him:

> None does offend, none, I say, none.

To a deep compassion for mankind itself.

> I know thee well enough; thy name is Gloucester;
> Thou must be patient; we came crying hither:
> Thou know'st the first time that we smell the air
> We wawl and cry. I will preach to thee: mark. . . .
> When we are born, we cry that we are come
> To this great stage of fools.

This afterpart of Lear's madness may be redundant, then,
to the strict action of the play, but to its larger issues it is
most germane. It is perhaps no part of the play that Shakespeare set out to write. The play that he found himself writing would be how much the poorer without it!

The simple perfection of the scene that restores Lear to
Cordelia one can leave unsullied by comment. What need of
any? Let the producer only note that there is reason in the
Folio's stage direction:

> Enter Lear in a chair carried by servants.

For when he comes to himself it is to find that he is royally
attired and as if seated on his throne again. It is from this
throne that he totters to kneel at Cordelia's feet. Note, too,
the pain of his response to Kent's

> In your own kingdom, sir.
> Do not abuse me.

Finally, Lear must pass from the scene with all the ceremony
due to royalty; not mothered—please!—by Cordelia.

Cordelia found again and again lost, what is left for Lear
but to die? But for her loss, however, his own death might
seem to us an arbitrary stroke; since the old Lear, we may
say, is already dead. Shakespeare, moreover, has transported
him beyond all worldly issues. This is, perhaps, why the
action of the battle which will seemingly defeat his fortunes
is minimized. What does defeat matter to him—or even victory? It is certainly the key to the meaning of the scene
which follows. Cordelia, who would "out-frown false fortune's frown," is ready to face her sisters and to shame them
—were there a chance of it!—with the sight of her father's
wrongs. But Lear himself has no interest in anything of the
sort.

> No, no, no, no! Come, let's away to prison.
> We two alone will sing like birds i' the cage:
> When thou dost ask me blessing, I'll kneel down,
> And ask of thee forgiveness: so we'll live,
> And pray, and sing, and tell old tales, and laugh
> At gilded butterflies, and hear poor rogues
> Talk of court news. . . .

He has passed beyond care for revenge or success, beyond
even the questioning of rights and wrongs. Better indeed to
be oppressed, if so you can be safe from contention. Prison
will bring him freedom.

> Upon such sacrifices, my Cordelia,
> The gods themselves throw incense. Have I caught thee?
> He that parts us shall bring a brand from heaven
> And fire us hence like foxes. Wipe thine eyes;
> The good years shall devour them, flesh and fell,
> Ere they shall make us weep: we'll see 'em starve first.

Lear's death, upon one ground or another, is artistically inevitable. Try to imagine his survival; no further argument will be needed. The death of Cordelia has been condemned as a wanton outrage upon our feelings and so as an aesthetic blot upon the play. But the dramatic mind that was working to the tune of

> As flies to wanton boys are we to the gods;
> They kill us for their sport.

was not likely to be swayed by sentiment. The tragic truth about life, to the Shakespeare that wrote *King Lear*, included its capricious cruelty. And what meeter sacrifice to this than Cordelia? Besides, as we have seen, he must provide this new Lear with a tragic determinant, since "the great rage . . . is kill'd in him," which precipitated catastrophe for the old Lear. And what but Cordelia's loss would suffice?

We have already set Lear's last scene in comparison with his first; it will be worth while to note a little more particularly the likeness and the difference. The same commanding figure; he bears the body of Cordelia as lightly as ever he carried robe, crown and scepter before. All he has undergone has not so bated his colossal strength but that he could kill her murderer with his bare hands.

> I kill'd the slave that was a-hanging thee.
> Tis true, my lords, he did.

says the officer in answer to their amazed looks. Albany, Edgar, Kent and the rest stand silent and intent around him; Regan and Goneril are there, silent too. He stands, with the limp body close clasped, glaring blankly at them for a moment. When speech is torn from him, in place of the old kingly rhetoric we have only the horrible, half human

> Howl, howl, howl, howl!

Who these are, for all their dignity and martial splendor, for all the respect they show him, he neither knows nor cares. They are men of stone and murderous traitors; though, after a little, through the mist of his suffering, comes a word for Kent. All his world, of power and passion and will, and the wider world of thought over which his mind in its ecstasy had ranged, is narrowed now to Cordelia; and she is dead in his arms.

Here is the clue to the scene; this terrible concentration upon the dead, and upon the unconquerable fact of death. This thing was Cordelia; she was alive, she is dead. Here is human tragedy brought to its simplest terms, fit ending to a tragic play that has seemed to outleap human experience. From power of intellect and will, from the imaginative sweep of madness, Shakespeare brings Lear to this; to no moralizing nor high thoughts, but just to

> She's gone for ever.
> I know when one is dead and when one lives;
> She's dead as earth. Lend me a looking-glass;
> If that her breath wll mist or stain the stone,
> Why, then she lives.

Lacking a glass, he catches at a floating feather. That stirs on her lips; a last mockery. Kent kneels by him to share his grief. Then to the bystanders comes the news of Edmund's death; the business of life goes forward, as it will, and draws attention from him for a moment. But what does he heed? When they turn back to him he has her broken body in his arms again.

> And my poor fool is hang'd. No, no, no life!
> Why should a dog, a horse, a rat, have life,
> And thou no breath at all? Thou'lt come no more,
> Never, never, never, never, never!
> Pray you, undo this button; thank you, sir.
> Do you see this? Look on her, look, her lips,
> Look there, look there!

* * *

OSCAR JAMES CAMPBELL (1879-   )

Professor Campbell, formerly the head of the English Department at Columbia University, is now a Professor Emeritus. He is one of the editors of the Bantam Shakespeare.

THE SALVATION OF LEAR
(from: the *Annual Tudor and Stewart Lecture of Johns Hopkins University*, delivered on April 30, 1948)

The *Tragedy of King Lear* moves to its catastrophe on a higher plane than any other of Shakespeare's great tragedies. Most critics of the play have sensed its wider moral range and its greater sublimity. And in their efforts to apprehend what has been called the "metaphysical meaning" of the action and to convey its essence to their readers, they have lavishly expended all the resources of their vocabularies. Yet they have succeeded only in invoking a sense of grandeur both for the unlocalized space which serves as the stage for Lear's woes and for the nature of his conflicts. Their utterances have been oracular rather than precise.

The violent double action of the play, which hurries the mind to the double catastrophe as on an irresistible torrent, constitutes in itself one of the greatest of all tragic themes. As Hazlitt remarked, it is one of the "great master-pieces in the logic of passion." Yet though most critics are agreed that the things that happen on the stage are but the symbols of some profound inner meaning, they have found no common ground on which to base their interpretations.

The romantic critics were content to express their wonder at the sense of infinitude which the play inspired. Lamb's verdict that "The Lear of Shakespeare cannot be acted" is familiar to everyone. He believed that an actor "might more easily propose to impersonate the Satan of Milton or one of Michael Angelo's terrible figures." Schlegel, for his part, finds that the action of the play represents "a great insurrection in the moral world . . . and that the horror it awakens is akin to that which would be felt were the heavenly bodies to rush away from their appointed course." Gervinus is less cosmic but hardly more precise when he writes "while other tragedies treat of single passions, this tragedy deals with passion in general."

Professor Tucker Brooke in an essay entitled "King Lear on the Stage" takes a view so widely different from these that he must have been consciously framing a paradox. His view is that the play is far from suffering from excessive grandeur; indeed, when visually presented, it manifests to us situations of less than tragic proportion. It is really a bürger-liches Trauerspiel (a bourgeois tragedy)—the story of family squabbling and jealous self-seeking—an exhibition of the detested petty vice of selfishness.

More recent critics have employed their own far-sought terms to express the conviction that Shakespeare designed *King Lear* to be a tragedy of universal significance. But in their attempts to explain the cosmic symbolism of the play most of them are as vague as the romanticists. Many modern commentators are convinced that Shakespeare in this tragedy depicts evil as a monstrous daemonic force. Once caught in its iron grip, so Shakespeare seems to say, man is as pitiful and helpless a creature as is Lear in the grip of the terrible storm on the heath. But if the drama were only an expression of blind and tragic fatalism, it could not produce the sense of sublimity that all thoughtful readers of the play feel. It must possess a more positive moral or religious significance than this.

For *King Lear* is, in my opinion, a sublime morality play, the action of which is set against a back-drop of eternity. Lear's problem and his career resemble those of the central figure in the typical morality play, who is variously called Genus Humanum, Mankind or Everyman. And the action of Shakespeare's play is his greatly modified version of man's endless search for true and everlasting spiritual values, rewarded, in this case, by their final discovery just before he must answer Death's awful summons. *The Tragedy of King Lear* differs, however, from the usual Morality first, in being cast in a much deeper tragic mould and second, in presenting the salvation of Mankind not in orthodox theological terms nor even in strictly Christian terms. For Lear is not so much an erring Christian as a completely unstoical man and he is converted to a state of mind which is a mixture of Stoic insight and Christian humility. Furthermore, the methods by which his conversion and redemption are accomplished are similar to those advocated by the great stoic philosophers.

I realize, of course, that stoicism was an eclectic philosophy which changed at least in emphasis in the long course of its development from the time of Zeno in the fourth century B.C. to its adoption in Rome. . . . The Stoics whose writings are of importance to us are Seneca, Plutarch, Epictetus and Marcus Aurelius. It was the practical moral philosophy of these stoics of the Roman Empire that influenced the Renaissance and English thinkers of the sixteenth and seventeenth century.

This is not the place to review even the major tenets of later stoicism. It is sufficient to mention one or two of its controlling ideas which will appear in our study of Lear. The stoics believed

1. That there are only two kinds of men, the completely wise and good and the completely unwise and bad.

2. That no outward calamity is a misfortune, but a divine instrument for the development and training of a man in virtue.

3. That the good man gives Reason his undivided devotion and rejects passion and even emotion as a disease of the intellect.

4. That the good life be sought in the soul (the God within) where it can be untouched by those vicissitudes of Fortune which are beyond human control.

5. That the good man must therefore (a) resign himself to the will of the Universe, (b) treat his fellow men with forbearance and humility, and (c) willingly accept his Destiny.

These main tenets of stoicism, were well known in Elizabethan and Jacobean England. . . .

It is not surprising then that Shakespeare in his version of the Summoning of Everyman should have put a stoical unwise or bad man in the place of the Christian sinner, particularly when we remember that Shakespeare definitely sets his play in pre-Christian times and that stoicism was probably the only pagan philosophy with which he was familiar. In fusing these two alien elements, one a product of mediaeval piety, the other a Renaissance recovery of a classical philosophy, Shakespeare was illustrating what some modern critics believe to be the distinguishing feature of baroque art.

However, before we seek to establish the truth of this conception of the play's structure, we should perhaps ask how Shakespeare came to transform the old and very popular tale of King Lear and his three daughters into a sublime apotheosis of a rigid and emotionally barren form of moral instruction.

Shakespeare's source, an old chronicle history play entitled *The True Chronicle History of King Leir and his three daughters* is constructed on no such pattern. To be sure Leir and his faithful retainer have a few perilous adventures while making their way from Ragan's manor to Cordella's army. But the play ends not in Leir's death, but with his restoration to the throne and his reassumption of all the powers and glories of his high office. Moreover the character of this Leir is utterly unlike Shakespeare's Lear, for the former is no slave of anger or of any other passion. His daughters do outrageously harass him. "But he, the mirror of mild patience, puts up all wrong and never gives reply." Naturally this Leir never yields to extravagant fits of frenzy. Nor does he banish his faithful retainer—Perillus—who has not the impulse to plain-speaking, along with the fidelity, which is Kent's most striking characteristic.

Shakespeare and his audiences of course were familiar with morality plays and also with the conventional homilies and didactic tales—which the preachers found effective *exempla.* . . .

Lear, then, in many respects resembles mankind of the traditional sermon and morality play. Like him, the old King has finished his work in the world, and can therefore devote all his attention to preparation for death. He then seeks to discover who are his real friends, through whose companionship he can face death without fear. But he makes the fatal mistake of thinking that he can buy affection. Goneril and Regan, representing worldly goods and those insubstantial human relationships which are precariously cemented only by favors granted, grievously disappoint him. He suffers shattering disillusionment when he sees that their love has been an illusion, that they have been attached only to his power and possessions. The discovery that as soon as he strips himself of these, his ungrateful daughters scorn and reject him, reduces him to anger and despair. They cannot give him that spiritual security without which he will be unable to meet death bravely. Although Cordelia has in terms of favors received the least reason to love her father, it is nevertheless she who sustains and inspires him to the end. As the embodiment of unselfish, spiritual love she makes his death a transfiguration.

Lear, then, is like mankind of both the Morality and homiletic tradition in that he has devoted his energies to the accumulation and worship of ephemeral possessions and to the pursuit of merely secular satisfactions. But he has erred not because he has deviated from the Christian's straight path to Heaven but because he has flouted all the Stoic's rules for the attainment of wisdom.

When we first see Lear, he is the typical unwise man, for he has disobeyed all the Stoic's rules for right conduct. He values his kingship not for the responsibilities it places upon him but for the possessions and outward shows which attend it. Indeed he has run so directly counter to the injunction to detach himself from the things of this world that he has come to value even love only as it can serve his vanity.

Moreover he is the complete slave of the most violent and uncontrollable of his passions—anger. In his unbridled anger he is as far as may be from the Stoic ideal of "Keeping an unruffled temper, an unchanging mien and the same cast of countenance in every condition of life." . . . Reason, according to the Stoics, being identical with Nature and the will of God, was the one safe guide to every sort of human action, and Lear's conduct during the first two acts of the play insults reason in every respect. In particular all his actions run directly counter to the Stoic's advice to old men. "There is nothing," writes Cicero, "against which old age should be more carefully on guard than surrendering to listlessness and violence." . . . Plutarch develops this maxim and applies it to a man engaged in public affairs in his essay entitled "Whether an Aged Man Ought to Manage Public Affairs." His view is that men who in old age cease to play their traditional part in affairs of state are guilty of sloth and cowardice. Instead of indulging their appetite for indolence they should put their wisdom and experience into the service of their country. In his very first speech Lear announces his intention of ignoring this article of the Stoic faith:

> Know we have divided
> In three our kingdom; and 'tis our fast intent
> To shake all cares and business from our age;
> Conferring them on younger strengths, while we
> Unburden'd, crawl toward death.

Before he has finished his abdication speech, he repeats for emphasis, his intention of giving up "rule" and "the cares of state." The division of his territory among his daughters is but an inevitable consequence of his decision to ignore one of the most solemn of Stoic injunctions.

Lear's actions in the first scene of the play thus show him to be so completely the slave of his uncontrolled emotions that he can neither follow the guidance of reason nor subordinate his impulses to the demands of moral obligation. His two elder daughters realize that their father's craving for flattery has drowned his reason and so they truckle to his senile vanity. But Cordelia, oblivious of the turbulent state of her father's mind, directs her reply to his buried reason and so unleashes only a torrent of anger. The terrifying burst of wrath erases from his mind every trace of justice, of judgment and of wisdom. He throws to the winds his carefully planned scheme for turning his abdication into a pageant of adulation. Even low cunning must yield to anger. Thus does Lear illustrate the folly and wickedness of a truant from Stoicism. He has obviously forgotten all the Stoic exhortations to self-knowledge and self-control. Goneril and Regan are not surprised at their father's violence and folly. Goneril reminds her sister that "The best and soundest of his time hath been but rash" (Even during the best years of his life, when his mind was soundest, he always acted in a headlong fashion). And Regan answers, "He hath ever but slenderly known himself." As a slave of passion Lear is in desperate need of liberation; as a pilgrim who "unburthened" has begun "to crawl toward death," he needs desperately to discover the right way to salvation.

All the clashes with his unfilial daughters which follow his abdication are further exhibitions of unstoical conduct. His wrath explodes at their every attempt to strip him of the hundred knights who form his body guard. Intemperate insistence on retaining these symbols of luxury and pride is a combination of impulses which the stoics stigmatized as evil. . . . Frustrated in his efforts to retain these things which the Stoics despised, he violently turns from the satisfaction of these condemned appetites and begins his frantic search for the truth that will free him from his slavery to passion. Thereafter he shows his abhorrence of passion by the violence of his anathemas against lust, one of the impulses which most surely degrades man because it most completely submerges reason.

On his pilgrimage he is accompanied by two companions, and commentators, both of whom are creatures of Cynic-Stoic primitivism introduced into Elizabethan literature by way of Roman satire. These two are Kent, the Stoic plain man, and the Fool, or the wise innocent—each a child of Nature. Kent follows the rules for the proper Cynic behavior, as defined among others by Epictetus; that is, "the exercise of the right and duty to rebuke evil in others." . . . Kent's explanation of his own conduct stamps him as the approved frank speaker. He says to Cornwall:

> Sir, 'tis my occupation to be plain . . .

and he tells everyone the truth bluntly in scorn of the consequences. When Lear banishes Cordelia, Kent persists in urging him to reverse his doom in spite of the old man's threats. He cries

> Be Kent unmannerly
> When Lear is mad.
>   To plainness honour's bound
> When majesty falls to folly.

His plainness when turned upon obsequious time-servers like Oswald becomes enormously violent figurative vituperation:

> A plague upon your epileptic visage.
> Smile you my speeches as I were a fool?
> Goose, an I had you upon Sarum Plain,
> I'ld drive ye cackling home to Camelot.

(This is probably a double allusion to the geese of Somersetshire and to vanquished knights.) Kent's plain speaking, an expression of his devotion to his Master, ironically has the effect of increasing rather than allaying Lear's passions. The fool's strange mixture of irrelevance and wisdom is similarly ironical. His efforts to outjest his master's woes only increase their poignancy, for he keeps Lear reminded of his folly in surrendering the rule of his kingdom to his wicked daughters:

> *Fool* I have us'd it (singing), ever since thou madest
> thy daughters thy mother; for when thou gavest them the
> rod, and put'st down thine own breeches,

(Sings) Then they for sudden joy did weep,
      And I for sorrow sung.
      That such a King should play bo-peep,
      And go the fools among.
Prithee, nuncle, keep a schoolmaster that can teach thy fool to lie. I would fain learn to lie.

In a situation turned topsy turvy by unleashed passions, plain speaking in the Cynic-Stoic manner is utterly ineffectual. It only intensifies Lear's mental turmoil. Here, as elsewhere in the play, Shakespeare insists that the Stoic way to salvation from turbulent and unworthy emotion is psychologically unsound—that passion cannot be conquered by force of Reason, but only by the substitution for the destructive emotion of a stronger and nobler passion. In other words, erring man can be freed from attachment to the ephemeral treacherous values of this world only by utter devotion to the eternal blessings of the spirit.

When Shakespeare sends Lear accompanied by Kent and the Fool out upon the barren heath to be tormented by the storm blown from Eternity, he enormously extends the canvas of the Morality play. Lear's endurance of such terrible suffering as the storm brings him is an essential part of both the Christian and the Stoical scheme for salvation. The Stoic believed that adversity purifies, that outward calamity is a divine instrument for teaching the wise man to be indifferent to external conditions, so that he may confine his efforts to exercising the powers of his soul. This is not unlike the Christian doctrine that sinful man is made fit for Heaven by passing through the torments of purgatory. However, even though it be difficult to establish a precise difference between the two forms of salvation, largely because the Roman Stoics endowed the severe principles of Stoicism with an emotion akin to religious conviction, still Lear's purgatorial experiences result in a form of salvation more Christian than Stoical. Earlier in the play Lear had appealed to Nature as his "dear goddess." It is natural then that he should flee to her for comfort when human aid failed him.

The chaotic Nature to which Lear flees is utterly unlike that predicated by the Stoics. Far from being an expression of cosmic harmony established and controlled by reason, it is a revelation of universal discord. That is, the storm on the heath corresponds to the chaos in Lear's nature, in that at this moment both the microcosm and the macrocosm are utterly beyond the control of reason. They have both become expressions of disruptive energy. In no corner of such a chaos of natural forces can the poor old wanderer of the dark find peace, security or moral value. Driven to insane rage by the failure of his quest, Lear enacts a mad version of Stoical reformation. If it be true, as the philosophers say, that all external possessions smother the spirit, he will follow their teaching to its bitter end by casting away the last remnants of such superfluities—the clothes that cover his nakedness. By tearing them off perhaps he may be able to discover what place in her realm Nature can offer to pure unaccommodated man. Lear cries

Thou ow'st the worm no silk, the beast no hide, the sheep no wool, the cat no perfume. . . . Thou art the thing itself: unaccommodated man is no more but such a poor, bare, forked animal as thou art. Off, off, you lendings! Come, unbutton here.

But the answer that Nature gives is negative, even derisive. Instead of appearing as a kind mother able to protect and foster her favorite child, she looses all her malevolence upon his bare body.

In the course of this mad experiment, Lear meets Gloucester's good son Edgar who is now disguised as Tom, a bedlam beggar, that is, a poor harmless insane fellow who has been allowed to beg on the roads in order to collect money to pay for his keep in the mad house. Lear asks this grotesque creature, "What is your study." Edgar's answer is, "How to prevent the fiend and to kill vermin," a reply which means, as Joseph Wood Krutch once pointed out, how to attain comfort of body and peace of mind. Yet in the situation in which he finds himself, neither he nor Lear can attain either blessing. The rain continues to drench them both and the wind to lash them. "Tom's a'cold" and Lear's wits are crazed. Nature proves to be no kind fostering mother to unaccommodated man, but a relentless enemy. Lear's frantic search cannot end on the heath. To the will of the natural universe thus revealed Lear cannot resign himself. . . .

The Roman Stoics, sensing the moral corruption of the times and the oppression of tyrannical government, counseled complete retirement from active life and attention only to self-examination. The thoughtful men of Shakespeare's day were rendered pessimistic by their belief in the decay of the world, the disarrangement in nature and the worthlessness of man, calamities from which there was no escape. Man's intimate relation to Nature involved him in her inevitable progress toward degeneration.

Yet the suffering Lear is now enduring begins to show itself as purgatorial. It forces him to realize his own humanity and awakens the philanthropic disposition which was the attitude the Stoics cultivated toward their fellow men. Lear expresses his conversion to this ethical position in very famous lines:

> Poor naked wretches, whereso'er you are,
> That bide the pelting of this pitiless storm,
> How shall your houseless heads and unfed sides,
> Your loop'd and window'd raggedness, defend you
> From seasons such as these? O, I have ta'en
> Too little care of this! Take physic, pomp;
> Expose thyself to feel what wretches feel,
> That thou mayst shake the superflux to them
> And show the heavens more just.

A. C. Bradley says that these lines mark the redemption of Lear. But they report only his first hesitant step in that direction, for the old man's moment of humility is fleeting; it has no immediate effect upon his conduct or upon his madness.

The real redemption of Lear comes when he awakens from the delusions of his frenzied mind to discover Cordelia and her unselfish enduring love. The mere sight of her kills "the great rage" in him, the unstoical emotional turmoil from which all his sins and sufferings have sprung. Now he is calmly receptive to the healing power of Christian love. For he has not arrived at utter indifference to external events, at that complete freedom from emotion, the disease of the intellect, which produces true stoic content. On the contrary Lear finds his peace in an active emotion—in all absorbing love. That it is which at last renders him independent of circumstance. Even shut within the narrow walls of a prison, he can now find utter peace and happiness if only Cordelia and her love be with him there:

> Come, let's away to prison.
> We two alone will sing like birds i' th' cage.
>
> . . . .
>
> And pray, and sing, and tell old tales, and laugh
> At gilded butterflies, . . .
>
> . . . .
>
> And take upon 's the mystery of things,
> As if we were God's spies; and we'll wear out,
> In a walled prison, packs and sects of great ones,
> That ebb and flow by th' moon.
>
> . . . .
>
> Upon such sacrifices, my Cordelia,
> The gods themselves throw incense.

This speech shows that Lear's ideals have come full circle. In the first scene of the play he showed himself so exclusively devoted to the external shows of his position that he had come to value even love only in so far as it augmented his earthly glory. But his passage through purgatory has made him realize that, beside love, all the baser uses of this world seem utterly unprofitable. Even the packs and sects (conspiracies and factions) of great ones, to which he used to pay all his allegiance, seem wholly insignificant.

If Lear's reunion with Cordelia brings about his salvation, one may well ask why Shakespeare snatches her so suddenly from him? And why does he put Lear to death so soon? The answers to the two questions are closely related. It is not what the earthly creature Cordelia *is*, but what she *represents* that is important for the meaning of the play. It is her spirit not her bodily presence that redeems her father. . . . And she is hanged, as Christ was crucified, so that mankind might be saved.

For since this is a sublime morality play its action prepares Lear not for a life of Stoic tranquillity on this earth, but for the heavenly joy of a redeemed soul. The meaning of Cordelia's execution comes to Lear slowly and painfully. At first he is filled with despair at losing her:

> Thou'lt come no more
> Never, never, never, never, never.

But suddenly he makes the blessed discovery that Cordelia is not dead after all, that the breath of life still trembles on her lips:

> Do you see this? Look on her, look, her lips,
> Look there! look there!

In the joy of this discovery the old man's heart breaks in a
spasm of ecstasy. For only to earthbound intelligence is Lear
pathetically deceived in thinking poor Cordelia alive. Those
familiar with the pattern of the morality play realize that
Lear has discovered in her unselfish God-like love the one
companion who is willing to go with him through Death up
to the throne of the Everlasting Judge. This knowledge en-
ables Lear to meet Death in a state of rapture.

This interpretation of *King Lear* has been concerned only
with its formal structure and largely confined to an analysis
of the central plot. Shakespeare also incorporated into his
play a second or echo plot in which the situation both
parallels that of Lear and offers a contrast to it. It tells the
story of a different round of sin, purgation and salvation.
Gloucester, the central figure in this part of the play, sins in
begetting his bastard son Edmund and in treating him with
a sniggering sort of contempt. His punishment comes
through his son's treachery against his father and his legitimate half-brother Edgar. Gloucester fatuously believes his
false son's calumnies against the faithful Edgar and so becomes the villain's victim, is condemned as a traitor, and has
his eyes put out. With the loss of his physical sight the eyes
of his mind are opened. Then, conscious of his awful guilt,
he falls into a state of utter despair and tries to kill himself.
But after Edgar has thwarted his attempt, he at last recog-
nizes the difference between good and evil and dies from the
strain of their conflict in his nature:

> his flawed heart
> . . . .
> Twixt two extremes of passion, joy and grief,
> Burst smilingly.

Like Lear, Gloucester dies at peace and in hope (note the
word "smilingly"). Like Lear, too, he is saved by contrition from eternal darkness, but through a different purgatorial progress. His road to salvation is much more like the
way described and urged by scores of Protestant preachers.
It has led through sin, consciousness of guilt, despair leading

to an impulse toward suicide, contrition, repentance, to salvation.

Even if the basic form of King Lear be that of a morality play upon which has been grafted a view of the unwise man of stoic morality, we must not expect to find in the drama either the stiff schematism or the obvious ethical teaching of the naive morality play. The bare outlines of the dramatic type have been overlaid and often obscured by the fullness of the plot and the intricacies of the relationship between the characters. The personifications of the mediaeval play have grown into human beings as complicated and unpredictable as men and women usually are. Finally, the simple stage on which the morality was set suggested a high road between two villages, while Shakespeare's poetic imagination persuades us that the action of *King Lear* takes place on a vast darkling plain, swept by trade-winds from eternity.

* * *

LILY BESS CAMPBELL (1883-   )

Dr. Campbell, one of the most widely and favorably known of contemporary American Shakespeare scholars, has been for many years a professor of English in the University of California at Los Angeles. Her knowledge of Renaissance literature of the passions, their origin, their display, and their effects has enabled her to show the intimate connection between these conceptions and their illustration in Shakespeare's tragedies. Indeed, she finds the plays perfect mirrors of the Renaissance anatomy of the passions.

King Lear, A Tragedy of Wrath in Old Age
(from: *Shakespeare's Tragic Heroes Slaves of Passion,* 1939)

There was in Shakespeare's day an old and firmly founded philosophy of anger, finding its sources in ancient medicine and ancient philosophy and in the mediaeval makings-over of those ancient sources as well. According to this philosophy, pride or self-esteem is the condition in which anger takes its rise, vengeance becomes its immediate object, and some slight, real or imagined, is its cause. Anger is folly;

anger brings shame in its train. The sequence of passions is pride, anger, revenge, and unless madness clouds the reason altogether, shame. Anger hurts him who feels it even more than it hurts the one on whom he seeks revenge. In its train are shame on the one hand and rage, fury, frenzy, and madness on the other, not to speak of death and eternity in the reckoning. It is the most pernicious, the most destructive of passions; it has in it indeed something of the essence of all passions. And the feeble and the old are its most likely victims.

As we have seen, anger is not paired with any other passion in the table of passions. Patience is the complementary virtue of anger, but there is no complementary vice of excess or defect. Because it stands alone in the table of passions, it is therefore studied alone in *King Lear*.

In connection with the study of the passion of anger, however, Shakespeare has presented several of the problems of what I have termed practical philosophy, all of them problems such as can be most appropriately considered in connection with anger. The first is the problem of old age, for as we have seen, the feeble and the old are more subject to anger than are others, and the particular aspect of the problem of age which concerned Shakespeare at this time would seem to have been that which was treated by Plutarch under the title *Whether an aged Man Ought to Manage publike affaires*. Specifically Plutarch wrote:

But forasmuch as men ordinarily alledge many causes and pretenses, for to colour and cover their sloth & want of courage to undertake the businesse and affaires of State, & among others, as the very last, and as one would say, that which is of the sacred line & race, they tender unto us old age, & suppose they have found now one sufficient argument to dull or turne backe the edge, and to coole the heat of seeking honor thereby, in bearing us in hand & saying: That there is a certein convenient & meet end limited, not only to the revolution of yeeres, proper for combats and games of proofe, but also for publike affaires and dealings in State.

Such an attitude, Plutarch affirms, is really the result of sloth and voluptuousness. In reality the aged man should give his experience and wisdom to the state, and he is being led by "sloth & want of courage" or by voluptuousness when he lays down his burdens.

Thus Lear enters with his explanation:

> Know that we have divided
> In three our kingdom; and 't is our fast intent
> To shake all cares and business from our age,
> Conferring them on younger strengths, while we
> Unburden'd crawl toward death.

And he concludes his speech by restating his intention and then appealing to his daughters:

> Tell me, my daughters,—
> Since now we will divest us both of rule,
> Interest of territory, cares of state,—
> Which of you shall we say doth love us most,
> That we our largest bounty may extend
> Where nature doth with merit challenge?

It is apparent that Lear here is divesting himself of cares which he no longer wishes to carry. And it is equally apparent that he is doing it not in the interest of the recipients of his benefits but because he seeks release from duties that are burdensome.

With his appeal to his daughters to proclaim who loves him most, the King demonstrates the difficulties of another problem which was of great interest to the Renaissance philosophers and which they found well stated in another essay of Plutarch, *How a man may discerne a flatterer from a friend*. Self-love, Plutarch says, subjects a man to flattery, for he likes to have his good opinion of himself sustained. It is difficult to tell the flatterer from the friend, but the basis of judgment is to be found in the fact that the flatterer applies himself to appeal to the passions of the one concerned, while the friend makes his appeal not to passion but to reason. Many specific differences are further to be observed, of course. The flatterer is inconstant, the friend constant; the flatterer always says and does what will give pleasure, the friend does not hesitate to give pain, to offer rebuke or correction, when it is necessary; the flatterer is always ready to speak, the friend is often silent; the flatterer is over-ready and excessive in his promises, the friend is temperate and just and reasonable; the flatterer bustles about but is not ready with genuine service, the friend will dissuade from unjust action but will serve even at great cost to himself.

The excessive and passionate speeches of Goneril and Regan are wordy speeches recited in answer to Lear's appeal; they are in all essentials the speeches of flatterers. But Lear, happy in his self-love, demands still more from his "joy, his youngest daughter":

> . . . what can you say to draw
> A third more opulent than your sisters?

Cordelia's reply is the appropriate one for the friend. She can say nothing that will draw a richer third of the kingdom. And to her father's hasty warning she can only add:

> Unhappy that I am, I cannot heave
> My heart into my mouth: I love your Majesty
> According to my bond; no more nor less.

Then she speaks further a speech closely resembling that of Desdemona to her father, a speech that is clearly an appeal to reason rather than passion:

> Good my lord,
> You have begot me, bred me, lov'd me: I
> Return those duties back as are right fit;
> Obey you, love you, and most honour you.
> Why have my sisters husbands, if they say
> They love you all?

And she proclaims the fact that when she marries, she will give her husband half her care and duty.

That it is self-love that makes a man susceptible to flattery is shown in the next speech, but the speech indicates much more than a susceptibility to flattery. In self-love and injured self-esteem anger takes its rise, as we have seen. To Cordelia's tempered and reasonable speech, the aged King breaks out at once in intemperate and almost frenzied anger:

> Let it be so; thy truth, then, be thy dower!
> For, by the sacred radiance of the sun,
> The mysteries of Hecate, and the night;
> By all the operation of the orbs
> From whom we do exist, and cease to be;

> Here I disclaim all my paternal care,
> Propinquity and property of blood,
> And as a stranger to my heart and me
> Hold thee, from this, forever. The barbarous Scythian,
> Or he that makes his generation messes
> To gorge his appetite, shall to my bosom
> Be as well neighbour'd, piti'd, and reliev'd,
> As thou my sometime daughter.

Then it is that another friend dares to speak to dissuade from unjust action, but the good Kent's interruption is checked by Lear's

> Come not between the dragon and his wrath.
> I lov'd her most, and thought to set my rest
> On her kind nursery.

And thus in the beginning of his wrath we see Lear demonstrating what we know to have been an accepted principle, that a man is angered by an injury to his self-esteem, that he is soonest angered when that respect in which he has thought himself most worthy seems to be disregarded, that he is soonest angry with friends, with those who have previously treated him becomingly and now change, and with those who do not appreciate his kindness. Cordelia, most loved and most loving heretofore, to whom he intended the greatest favours, is at once the easy victim of the aged Lear. And as is the manner of the angry man, he at once seeks to have revenge, to show his power, and to injure the one from whom he conceives himself to have received an injury. At once he adds to the dowers of his two flattering daughters all the third that should have been Cordelia's. It must be noted, however, that while he gives away the burdens of the state, he retains

> The name, and all the addition to a king;

and thus we see that pride will still be panoplied with the trappings of a king. His monthly progress between the divided halves of his kingdom with his extensive retinue evidently pleases him as he pictures it. His pride and self-esteem are so mingled with his anger and his desire for revenge in this speech that they become one.

Again Kent will show that he is a true friend by attempting to check the rashness of his king, but Lear again rebuffs him:

> The bow is bent and drawn; make from the shaft.

Now Kent becomes the man of righteous anger, angry not at the doer, but at the deed; further, he is the true friend opposing himself to the flatterer as he replies:

> . . . be Kent unmannerly
> When Lear is mad. What wouldst thou do, old man?
> Think'st thou that duty shall have dread to speak
> When power to flattery bows?

And he begs Lear to check his "hideous rashness", even as he pleads the love of Cordelia. And even to the King's threat of his life, he will not yield his right to try to protect him from himself. Even as the King lays his hand upon his sword, Kent exclaims again:

> Kill thy physician, and thy fee bestow
> Upon the foul disease. Revoke thy gift;
> Or, whilst I can vent clamour from my throat,
> I'll tell thee thou dost evil.

And now, just as Lear has turned in his pride to try to revenge himself for the injury to his self-esteem inflicted by Cordelia's refusal to offer flattering vows and promises, he turns likewise at once in pride and outrageous anger to revenge himself on his most loyal friend, who likewise has refused to play the part of flatterer but has instead insisted upon trying to save him from evil and folly by telling him the truth. At once Lear shows his power in ordering the faithful Kent to turn his "hated back" upon his kingdom by the sixth day, the forfeit of his life to be exacted if he fail to accept his brutal banishment.

Then the angry King turns to scoff again at Cordelia. To Burgundy he offers her as

> Unfriended, new-adopted to our hate,
> Dower'd with our curse, and stranger'd with our oath,

and France he beseeches to avert his love

> . . . a more worthier way
> Than on a wretch whom Nature is asham'd
> Almost to acknowledge hers.

Finally, to Cordelia's plea that he explain to her suitors that his changed attitude is not the result of murder or unchastity on her part, he replies:

> Better thou
> Had not been born than not to have pleas'd me better.

But Cordelia is as temperate in her sorrow as in her love, and to France's injunction to bid her sisters farewell, "though unkind," even to her father's final rebuffs, she replies only by indicating that she knows what sort of persons she is leaving her father with, and she departs sounding almost like a daughter of the good Polonius:

> Time shall unfold what plighted cunning hides;
> Who covers faults, at last shame them derides.
> Well may you prosper!

That Lear's anger has led him to a course that is both evil and foolish is at once evident in the discussion between Goneril and Regan that follows the departure of Cordelia. It is apparent that Lear has always been something of a problem at home, and that, in this fatal outburst of anger, he has but shown the results of a temperament given to habitual anger. Goneril observes:

> You see how full of changes his age is; the observation we have made of it hath not been little. He always lov'd our sister most; and with what poor judgement he hath now cast her off appears too grossly.

To which daughter's wisdom Regan adds:

> 'Tis the infirmity of his age; yet he hath ever but slenderly known himself.

And Goneril reasons well:

> The best and soundest of his time hath been but rash; then must we look from his age to receive not alone the imperfections of long-engraffed condition, but therewithal the unruly waywardness that infirm and choleric years bring with them.

Regan instances this "inconstant start" of Kent's unjust banishment, and Goneril arrives at the main point that something must be done, for

if our father carry authority with such disposition as he bears, this last surrender of his will but offend us.

And they proceed to remove the sting from the adder.

It is thus apparent that we have in Lear the habitually wrathful man, advanced by years to that age when his self-esteem takes offence suddenly, easily, without reason and without regard to justice. He is indeed the slave of habitual wrath.

The second scene of the first act of *Lear* repeats the same philosophical themes that were introduced in the first scene. Again a father is moved by a sense of injured self-esteem to anger which demands revenge, and seeks to find revenge in an immediate use of power to hurt the one who is supposed to be the author of the injury. Again a father is moved by the flattery of an undeserving child to cast off the loyal child and prefer the flatterer in his place. And again there enters the question of old age and its continued guidance of affairs. . . .

King Lear as the tragedy of wrath, then, was planned as a tragedy of old age. In Lear and Gloucester Shakespeare represented old men bestowing benefits unjustly, led by flattery to give unwisely, led by anger to withhold unjustly and to seek revenge for imagined slights. Both the evil and the folly of their anger are brought out. The evil lay in their inflicting evil on others. The folly lay in the evil they brought upon themselves. Even Kent, the friend and loyal follower, is led in anger to go beyond the command of reason in his treatment of Oswald and hence to bring further misfortune on the King. Cornwall is killed in an angry fight with his servant, but the servant is also killed for his righteous anger. The whole is a welter of passion. But the picture is relieved by Cordelia, who cannot be moved by passion; by Edgar, who acts as reason dictates even in the guise of a madman; and by Albany, who at the last is the calm arbiter of the "gor'd state".

The play at times becomes inarticulate, but its meaning can never be in doubt.

Notes

TEXTS: In 1608 Nathaniel Butler and John Busby, though not very reputable printers, issued an apparently authorized quarto of *King Lear*. However, the text is in so many places corrupt that it is probable that the printers set it up from a copy in which many pages were illegible. The editors of the First Folio apparently based their text on an independent and better manuscript owned by their company. The quarto contains about 300 lines not in the Folio, and the latter 100 lines not in the quarto. There is a second quarto, also dated 1608, which was really printed in 1619 by Pavier, when he planned to publish a pirated collected edition of a number of Shakespeare's plays. Just why he gave the quarto a fictitious date, no one really knows.

DATE: *King Lear* was probably written in 1605. We know that it was performed before the court at Whitehall on December 26, 1606, and one piece of evidence leads us to believe that the tragedy was composed and first produced the year before. In May 1605, the old *King Leir*, which had been entered in the *Stationers' Register* nine years before, was at length published, almost surely in order to capitalize on renewed interest in the Lear story aroused by Shakespeare's drama and perhaps also to trap unwary purchasers into the belief that this *King Leir* was the recent stage hit. How long before May 1605, *King Lear* had first appeared we are unable to say. We do know that it cannot have been composed before the printing of Harsnet's *Declaration of Popish Impostures* in 1603, for from that work Shakespeare took the fantastic names of the devils supposed to haunt Poor Tom.

SOURCE: The principal source of the central plot of the tragedy is an anonymous old play called *The True Chronicle History of King Leir and His Three Daughters*—first entered in the *Stationers' Register* in 1594, but probably written some years earlier. The story is a folk tale, a variant of the Cinderella legend, which Geoffrey of Monmouth made a recognized part of English history by inserting it into his *Historia Regum Britonum* (1136).

In addition to the old play, Shakespeare was familiar with versions of the tale to be found in Holinshed's *Chronicles*, *The Mirror for Magistrates*, and *The Faerie Queene*. The adventures of Gloucester and his two sons copy those of the Blind King of Paphlagonia, a character in Sidney's *Arcadia*. Edgar's feigned madness is Shakespeare's invention, as is the love of Lear's two wicked daughters for Edmund.

* * *

ACT I, SCENE 1

1. Lines 5–6
for equalities are so weighed, that curiosity in neither can make choice of either's moiety. The shares are so evenly balanced that careful examination cannot determine which is the larger part.

2. Line 54
Where nature doth with merit challenge. Where my natural love and your merit lay equal claim to my generosity.

3. Line 57
Dearer than eye-sight, space, and liberty. Space means freedom from imprisonment; liberty means freedom of action.

4. Line 112
mysteries of Hecate. Hecate was the Greek deity of the lower world, of witchcraft, and of magic. The "mysteries" were the secret rites by which she was worshiped and appeased.

5. Line 118
The barbarous Scythian. The Scythians inhabited a region in southern Russia. From classical times they were regarded as unalloyed barbarians.

6. Line 123
Come not between the dragon and his wrath. The dragon was the traditional crest of the ancient British kings.

7. Lines 125–6
    and thought to set my rest
On her kind nursery.
"Set my rest" is a term used in the card game of Primero. In a player's mouth, it means "I stand pat." 'Rest' may also suggest to Lear the repose he looks forward to obtaining after he has thrown off the cares of kingship.

8. Line 181
   > By Jupiter,
   > *This shall not be revoked.*

   Jupiter was the Roman equivalent of the Greek Jove, the king of the gods.

9. Line 201
   that little seeming substance. That which has only the appearance of being genuine.

10. Lines 241–2
    > *Love is not love*
    > *When it is mingled with regards that stand*
    > *Aloof from the entire point.*

    That is when it is joined to considerations that have nothing to do with the essence of the matter.

11. Lines 280–1
    > *who hath received you*
    > *At fortune's alms.*

    That is when fortune was doling out petty gifts.

12. Line 282
    And well are worth the want that you have wanted. And well deserve the lack of that affection (from your husband) which you have lacked.

ACT I, SCENE 2

13. Line 109
    I would unstate myself, to be in a due resolution. I would give up all the privileges of my rank to be sure.

14. Lines 114–16
    though the wisdom of nature can reason it thus and thus, yet nature finds itself scourged by the sequent effects. Though science can explain phenomena like eclipses of the sun and moon, we suffer from their effects.

15. Lines 133–4
    treachers, by spherical predominance. Traitors because of the controlling influence of some star.

16. Line 148
    with a sigh like Tom o' Bedlam. Bedlam was Bethlehem Hospital, the London insane asylum. Some of the less crazy inmates were released and allowed to wander about the countryside, begging for money to pay for their keep.

ACT I, SCENE 4

17. Line 18

and to eat no fish. Kent promises to be a faithful Protestant and not one of those disloyal fish-eating Roman Catholics. (This is an obvious anachronism, since there were no Protestants in King Lear's time.)

18. Line 108

here's my coxcomb. The coxcomb was a hood worn by the court jester. It was crested with a piece of red cloth shaped like the comb of a cock.

19. Line 112

an thou canst not smile as the wind sits, thou'lt catch cold shortly. If you cannot take sides with the faction in power, you will find yourself in trouble.

20. Line 117

How now, nuncle! Nuncle—a contraction of mine uncle— was a term used by licenced fools in addressing their superiors.

21. Line 123

Take heed, sirrah; the whip. Fools that took too many liberties in their tilting at their masters were punished by being whipped.

22. Line 126

Truth's a dog must to kennel; he must be whipped out, when Lady the brach may stand by the fire and stink. Lady was a common name for a bitch, brach a bitch hound. Here she stands for flattery as compared with truth. While truth is banished, flattery may make herself comfortable at home, no matter how offensive it may be.

23. Lines 166–70

if I had a monopoly out, they would have part on 't: and ladies too, they will not let me have all fool to myself; they'll be snatching. This is the Fool's attack on the royal patents granted to favorites of the sovereign to be sole dealers in certain commodities. The Fool declares that if he were granted such a monopoly, the courtiers who helped him to secure it would be demanding their share of the loot.

24. Line 170

Give me an egg, nuncle, and I'll give thee two crowns. Give me an egg; then after I have eaten it, I will give you the two halves of the shell. The clown intimates that Lear has done just that in dividing his kingdom.

25. Line 176
thou borest thy ass on thy back o'er the dirt. The Fool
refers to a popular fable of the stupid man who did just
that, instead of having the beast carry him.

26. Lines 181–2
Fools had ne'er less wit in a year;
For wise men are grown foppish.
Fools were never less in demand than they are this year,
for wise men are now taking their place by being foppish.

27. Line 191
Then they for sudden joy did weep. According to Kittredge,
the Fool, in this stanza, is adapting an old song first printed
in Rollins' *Old English Ballads:*
> Some men for sudden joy do weep,
>   And some in sorrow sing;
> Whenas they are in danger deep,
>   To put away mourning.

28. Line 230
in the tender of a wholesome weal. In our care for a sound
commonwealth.

29. Lines 232–3
Which else were shame, that then necessity
Will call discreet proceeding.
Which otherwise would be shameful, but which the demands
(of the situation) would force one to call prudent action
(discreet proceeding).

30. Line 245
Whoop, Jug! I love thee. Whenever the Fool fears that one
of his sallies has been too impertinent, he takes refuge in
pure nonsense, like the above, which he hopes will raise a
laugh.

31. Lines 265–6
              epicurism and lust
Make it more like a tavern or a brothel.
In Shakespeare's day even the intelligent had a false conception of Epicurean philosophy. They thought it advocated
voluptuousness.

32. Lines 282–3
Ingratitude . . . .
More hideous when thou show'st thee in a child
Than the sea-monster!
Some editors see here a possible reference to the hippopota-

mus, which while not a monster of the sea, had a reputation for ingratitude. More likely the reference is to any sea monster of classical mythology.

33. Line 290
That, like an engine, wrenched my frame of nature. Engine meant any powerful piece of mechanism; here the rack, a well-known instrument of torture.

34. Line 321
Blasts and fogs upon thee! Fogs and mists were supposed to be laden with pestilence.

35. Line 322
The untented woundings of a father's curse. A "tent" was a small roll of lint used to probe and cleanse wounds. So the phrase means a wound too deep to be cleansed.

36. Line 338
take the fool with thee. According to Kittredge, the phrase besides its literal meaning was a farewell gibe: "Good-by, take the fool that you are with you."

37. Lines 352–3
Let me still take away the harms I fear,
Not fear still to be taken.
Let me always get rid of what I fear will harm me, rather than live in fear of harm to come.

ACT I, Scene 5
38. Line 15
Shalt see thy other daughter will use thee kindly. The Fool in this ironical speech puns on "kindly" meaning (1) "with kindness," and (2) "according to her nature."

ACT II, Scene 1
39. Line 36
I have seen drunkards
Do more than this in sport.
An Elizabethan gallant, particularly if he was flushed with wine, on occasions cut his arm so that he could mix his blood with wine and drink the mixture to his lady's health.

40. Lines 74–9
I'd turn it all
To thy suggestion, plot, and damned practice:
And thou must make a dullard of the world,
If they not thought the profits of my death

Were very pregnant and potential spurs
To make thee seek it.
I would turn everything you, Edmund, might accuse me of against you by ascribing it to your wicked plotting; and you must think the world dull indeed if it did not see the benefits you stood to derive from my (Edgar's) death would be so great as to make you seek it.

41. Line 114
How in my strength you please. Using my authority in any way that you please.

ACT II, SCENE 2

42. Lines 9–10
If I had thee in Lipsbury pinfold, I would make thee care for me. A pinfold was a pen in which stray cattle were held. Nares defines "Lipsbury pinfold" as the "enclosure adjacent to my teeth, that is in my jaws," hence, in my clutches.

43. Lines 13–25
This passage is full of insulting epithets, the full meaning of which heighten their power.
three-suited. Three suits a year and no more were the usual allotment of a man servant.
hundred-pound gentleman. Such a man was possessed of only meager property.
worsted-stocking. Not a gentleman, because gentlemen wore only silk stockings.
glass-gazing. Always looking at himself in a glass.
lily-livered. One with no blood in his liver and therefore cowardly.
action-taking. One who goes to law to gain protection from an enemy, instead of meeting him, like a man, in combat.
superserviceable. A servant who serves his master beyond the limits of honor, for example, one who acts as a procurer for him.
one-trunk-inheriting. One all of whose possessions could be contained in one trunk.

44. Line 35
I'll make a sop o' the moonshine of you. I will stab you so full of holes that the moonlight will permeate you until you will seem to be soaked in it.

45. Line 36
barber-monger. A constant visitor to a barber.

46. Line 39
take vanity the puppet's part. Lady Vanity was frequently a character in the imitated morality plays acted by puppets.

47. Line 69
Thou whoreson zed! Thou unnecessary letter! Zed or z is an unnecessary letter because its sound can usually be expressed by *s.*

48. Line 73
Spare my gray beard, you wagtail? A wagtail is a bird who appears ridiculously active from the continual jerking up and down of its tail.

49. Lines 80–1
Like rats, oft bite the holy cords a-twain
Which are too intrinse t' unloose.
The holy cords, the sacred bonds that tie the members of a family together, form too intricate a knot to be unloosed.

50. Line 84
turn their halcyon beaks. It was widely believed that if the halcyon (kingfisher) was hung up by the legs it could serve as a weathervane, turning with the wind in such a way that its beak would always point in the direction from which the wind came.

51. Line 87
your epileptic visage. Oswald's attempted smile is so distorted by his fright that his face resembles that of a man in a fit.

52. Line 90
I'd drive ye cackling home to Camelot. Camelot (the site of King Arthur's court) was a fortified hill near Cadbury. In the nearby moors there were flocks of geese.

53. Lines 103–4
            constrains the garb
Quite from his nature.
Forces him to assume a bearing of saucy roughness, completely at odds with his real nature.

54. Line 114
            like the wreath of radiant fire
On flickering Phoebus' front.
Phoebus was one of the names of the Olympian god Apollo, who, among other services he rendered to mankind, was the bringer of light and so became the Sun God. The language

of the speech parodies the way of talking affected by the obsequious (ducking) courtiers just referred to.

55. Lines 129–31
For him attempting who was self-subdued;
And, in the fleshment of this dread exploit,
Drew on me here again.

"Attempting who was self-subdued" means attacking one who made no defense. To "flesh" a dog was to make him ferocious by feeding him raw meat.

56. Line 161
Will not be rubbed nor stopped. In bowling, a rub was anything that deflected the ball from its straight course.

57. Lines 168–9
Thou out of heaven's benediction comest
To the warm sun!

The proverb describes a typical case of bad judgment, *i.e.*, of a man who on a hot day leaves a comfortable place in the shade for exposure to the hot sun.

58. Lines 172–3
Nothing almost sees miracles
But misery.

This phrase has received different interpretations. (1) "When we are in despair, it is only relief that seems miraculous"; (2) "When we are in despair, any relief seems miraculous."

ACT II, Scene 3

59. Line 1
I heard myself proclaimed. This refers to Gloucester's measures for his apprehension (see 2/1/82 ff.).

60. Lines 9–21
my face I'll grime with filth
... That's something yet: Edgar I nothing am.

This passage enumerates the actions of Bedlam beggars, one of whom Edgar was pretending to be. Bedlam was Bethlehem Hospital, a London institution in which lunatics were placed. When they recovered some of their wits, they were allowed to wander about the countryside to beg for money to pay for their keep. These creatures sometimes punctured their arms to show how little attention they gave to physical pain. They preferred to frequent places remote from any village, like insignificant (pelting) farms or sheepcotes and mills. "Turlygood" was a name which these beggars applied to themselves. It seems to fit the whining tone they adopted when begging. Edgar says, "For poor Tom whom I impersonate, there may be some hope for a future. As the real Edgar, I have no chance of escaping death."

ACT II, SCENE 4

61. Line 7
cruel garters. The Fool is punning on "crewel," meaning "worsted."

62. Line 9
monkeys [are tied] by the loins. Pet monkeys were thus tied, usually to a bed post.

63. Lines 56–7
O, how this mother swells up toward my heart!
Hysterica passio.
"Mother," a name for hysteria, was supposed to be produced by wind rising from the stomach to cloud the brain and cause dizziness.

64. Lines 68 ff.
We'll set thee . . . In this string of wise sayings the Fool reminds Lear that his fortunes are at a low ebb. They also tell Kent how much wiser he (the Fool) is than he (Kent).

65. Lines 85–6
The knave turns fool that runs away;
The fool no knave, perdy.
The knave who run away from his master is a fool; the Fool (I) who remains faithful is no knave. Perdy is a mild oath (per Dieu).

66. Lines 123–8
as the cockney did to the eels when she put 'em i' the paste alive; she knapped 'em o' the coxcombs with a stick, and cried 'Down, wantons, down!' 'Twas her brother that, in pure kindness to his horse, buttered his hay. This is obviously a London cook who did not know how to cook eels. She does not realize that they must be killed before being cooked. When they tried to escape from the dish she hit them on their heads, crying "Down, little darlings, down." And it must have been a brother of hers who thought that putting butter on hay would be a kindness to his horse.

67. Lines 133–4
I would divorce me from thy mother's tomb,
Sepulchring an adultress.
Lear says that if Regan had not been glad to see him, he
would be forced to think that her mother's tomb had been
the tomb of an adultress.

68. Line 165
Strike her young bones. Commentators have given "young
bones" two meanings: (1) Goneril's youthful figure; (2) her
unborn child.

69. Lines 267–8
       our basest beggars
Are in the poorest thing superfluous.
Even the most wretched beggars have among their meager
possessions things that they do not actually need.

ACT III, SCENE 1

70. Line 15
And bids what will take all.
"Take all" is the cry of the gambler when he stakes his last
penny. Hence it is a gesture of desperation.

71. Lines 16–7
        who labors to out-jest
His heart-struck injuries.
who tries by means of jests to offset the injuries inflicted on
the king.

ACT III, SCENE 2

72. Lines 8–9
Crack nature's molds, all germens spill at once,
That make ingrateful man!
The molds that Nature uses in forming men.

73. Lines 27 ff.
The cod-piece that will house, etc. If a man will beget children before he has a house for them, both will live a louse-
infested life, as do beggars when they marry. The cod-piece
was an appendage worn in the front of men's breeches. It
was a cant word for male genitals.

74. Lines 31 ff.
The man that makes his toe
  What he his heart should make . . .

The man who puts his heart where his toe is will get a corn on his heart instead of on his toe. That would give him so severe a heartache that he could not sleep at night.

75. Lines 58–9
                    and cry
These dreadful summoners grace.
Summoners were the police of Ecclesiastical Courts.

76. Lines 70–1
The art of our necessities is strange,
That can make vile things precious.
The art alluded to here is that of alchemy, which essayed to turn base metals into gold.

77. Line 76
Must make content with his fortunes fit. Must be contented with whatever fortune brings him.

78. Line 95
This prophecy Merlin shall make; for I live before his time. According to legend, King Lear was a contemporary of King Joash of Israel. Consequently he lived long before the time of Merlin, the great magician of Arthurian legend. Shakespeare here is making a joke on one of his anachronisms, for the first time in any of his plays.

ACT III, Scene 4
79. Line 37
Fathom and half. Edgar talks like a sailor taking soundings in a storm threatening to swamp his ship.

80. Lines 51–64
Who gives anything to Poor Tom . . . I have him now—and there—and there again, and there. Edgar, impersonating a Bedlam beggar, tries to establish his insanity by pretending that he is the unresisting slave of the devil, who has led him through all sorts of dangers, and who has tempted him to suicide in some of the ways Edgar describes. Then his wretchedness gains the upper hand of his fear of the devil and he prays to be protected from natural calamities, including infection (taking), and finally from the attack of fleas, at which he snatches in the final lines of his mad monologue.

81. Line 75
Should have thus little mercy on their flesh? Edgar has stuck thorns or skewers into the flesh of his arms to make his pretended madness seem real.

82. Lines 76–7

> 'twas this flesh begot
> *Those pelican daughters.*

It was believed that fledgling pelicans fed on their mother's blood.

83. Lines 82–104

Take heed o' the foul fiend: obey thy parents
. . . Dolphin, my boy, my boy, sessa! Let him trot by.

Edgar begins this long speech solemnly as if he were trying to remember the Ten Commandments. Later he confesses that he has been guilty of each of the seven deadly sins: Pride, Sloth, Envy, Gluttony, Wrath, Greed, and Lust. He indicates each one with a revealing phrase: Pride ("proud in heart and mind"); Gluttony ("wine loved I deeply"); Lust ("served the lust of my mistress' heart"); Sloth ("hog in sloth"). Traditionally, the lion stands for pride; the serpent for envy; the unicorn for wrath; the bear, and not the hog, for sloth; the fox for covetousness; the swine for greed; and the scorpion for lust.

wore gloves in my cap. For a gallant to wear his mistress' glove in his hat was to pay her an obvious compliment and attention. The act of darkness is of course sexual intercourse.

Dolphin, my boy, my boy, sessa! Let him trot by.

Edgar is quoting a ballad or song ridiculing the French Dauphin. Then he imagines he hears a trotting horse approaching, to which he calls "Sessa," *i.e.,* "Come on."

84. Line 120

This is the foul fiend Flibbertigibbet. Flibbertigibbet is one of the dancing devils described in Harsnet's *Declaration of Popish Impostures,* Shakespeare's source of all the grotesque spirits to which Tom refers. This includes Smulkin (line 146), and Modo and Mahu (line 149). The verse beginning with "Saint Withold footed thrice the old" was probably recited as a charm to ward off the incubus.

85. Lines 187–9

> *Child Rowland to the dark tower came,*
> *His word was still—Fie, foh, and fum,*
> *I smell the blood of a British man.*

This passage is probably a snatch from some lost ballad. "Child" describes a candidate for knighthood. Tom starts to give the "child's" watchword and then breaks off into "Fie, foh, and fum" which everyone in the audience will recognize as a speech of the Giant in Jack, the Giant-Killer, a most inappropriate motto for any aspirant for knighthood. The speech is an example of Tom's feigned confusion.

ACT III, SCENE 6

86. Stage direction
Most modern editions locate this scene in "a farmhouse near Gloucester's castle." Common sense about stage practice suggests, however, that if at the end of Act III, Scene 4, we see them from the outside of a farm building going in, and now in Act III, Scene 6, we see them next (with no suggestion of lapse of time) from the inside of a farm building coming in, the building they are entering is the same one. This is one of the clearest examples in Shakespeare of his anticipation of "cinematic" technique.

87. Line 8
and tells me Nero is an angler in the lake of darkness. This is an allusion to Rabelais. Nero is described as a fiddler.

88. Line 13
for he's a mad yeoman that sees his son a gentleman before him. A yeoman was a small landed proprietor, one step lower in rank than a gentleman.

89. Line 22
It shall be done; I will arraign them. Lear imagines that two joint stools represent his daughters, whom he is arraigning. He casts Edgar as one of the judges, the Fool as another; and, seeing that he has given Kent no role to play, he remembers that he, too, can be cast as a Justice of the Peace. The line "Wantest thou eyes at trial, madam?" is addressed by Edgar to one of the daughters, the meaning being: If you wish to have spectators at your trial, the fiend who stands there glaring at you can make one. When Lear's illusion fades, he thinks the culprits are fleeing from the Court and berates the Judge for permitting them to escape.

90. Line 27
Come o'er the bourn, Bessy, to me. This is the first line of an old ballad in which a lover urges his sweetheart to come across the brook to him.

91. Lines 31–3
The foul fiend haunts poor Tom in the voice of a nightingale. Hopdance cries in Tom's belly for two white herring.

The Fool has evidently sung the preceding two lines. Collier says the lines were part of an old song. Hopdance, the name of another devil, is taken, like all the other fiends that haunt poor Tom, from Harsnets.

92. Line 79
Poor Tom, thy horn is dry. There are two explanations of Tom's horn, both understanding it as an appeal for drink. One explanation is that a Bedlam beggar wore about his neck a horn that he blew when he came to an almshouse. The beggar poured the drink into his horn into which he had put a stopper. The second explanation makes "horn" mean "bottle."

93. Line 117
He childed as I fathered! His children are to him as my father is to me.

94. Line 120
In thy just proof, repeals and reconciles thee. The proof that you are guiltless restores you to favor.

ACT III, Scene 7

96. Line 13
farewell, my lord of Gloucester. In this sentence "Gloucester" is Edmund, who has been given the title as a reward for his treachery. In line 15 "Gloucester" is the old Earl.

96. Lines 26-7
Shall do a courtesy to our wrath, which men
May blame, but not control.
Our power will act in accordance with the anger we feel. That action you cannot stop though you may find it blameworthy.

97. Lines 53-4
I am tied to the stake, and I must stand the course. The figure is drawn from the "sport" of bear-baiting. The animal was tied to a stake and set upon by fierce dogs. Gloucester develops the figure by saying, "I must stand and take the attack of the dogs."

98. Line 57
               nor thy fierce sister
In his anointed flesh stick boarish fangs.
Lear, like all English kings, was anointed by consecrated oil

at his coronation. This ceremony made it sacrilege to lay hands on him.

99. Lines 65–6
All cruels else subscribed: but I shall see
The winged vengeance overtake such children.
All creatures, even the wildest animals, except you, gave way to their need for shelter from the storm. Gloucester expects to see the vengeance of the gods swoop down, like birds of prey, on Lear's daughters.

ACT IV, SCENE 1

100. Lines 11–12
World, world, O world!
But that thy strange mutations make us hate thee,
Life would not yield to age.
If it were not for the tricks of fortune that make us hate the world, we would not age.

101. Lines 22–3
Our means secure us, and our mere defects
Prove our commodities.
Prosperity gives us a false sense of security, while the things we lack make us realize the true nature of life.

102. Lines 69–73
heavens, deal so still!
Let the superfluous and lust-dieted man,
That slaves your ordinance, that will not see
Because he doth not feel, feel your power quickly;
So distribution should undo excess.
Continue to treat men who have become overconfident in their prosperity as you have me. Let the man who has more than he needs, all that he lusts for—who makes heaven's will subservient to his own, quickly feel your power (as I have). Thus men will learn how to distribute their excess in such a way that no one will be in want.

ACT IV, SCENE 2

103. Line 21
Wear this. (Gives him a favor.)
The duel between Edmund and Edgar is conducted as though it were a part of a chivalric tournament. Goneril gives to

Edmund—as her champion—a favor (usually a glove or a
ribbon to wear, as a token of love and support).

104. Lines 32–3
That nature, which contemns its origin,
Cannot be bordered certain in itself.
A nature which holds its own origin, that is, paternity, in
contempt can have no definite restraints in its own character.

105. Line 39
Filths savor but themselves. Everything tastes filthy to the
filthy.

106. Lines 62–3
Thou changed and self-covered thing, for shame,
Be-monster not thy feature.
Thou transformed creature, covering thy real fiend's nature
with a woman's form, don't allow thy whole appearance to
be changed into that of a monster.

107. Line 68
Marry, your manhood now. What a fine specimen of manhood you now are.

108. Lines 84–6
But being widow, and my Gloucester with her,
May all the building in my fancy pluck
Upon my hateful life.
But Regan being a widow, may pull down all the structures
created by my imagination (the plan to marry Edmund) and
make a hateful ruin of my life.

ACT IV, Scene 4

109. Lines 3–4
Crowned with rank fumiter and furrow-weeds,
With burdocks, hemlock, nettles, cuckoo-flowers.
Crowded with luxuriant fumitory (earth-smoke), flowers
growing in the furrows of a plowed field, and flowers growing when the cuckoo is abroad, that is, in April and May—
perhaps cowslips.

ACT IV, Scene 6

110. Line 15
Hangs one that gathers samphire, dreadful trade! Samphire
was an aromatic herb; when pickled it became a popular

relish with meat. Men lowered by ropes gathered it from the face of cliffs.

111. Line 29

> fairies and gods
> *Prosper it with thee!*

Hidden treasure guarded by fairies was supposed to increase miraculously when in the possession of its finder.

112. Lines 86 ff.

Nature's above art in that respect. There's your press-money. That fellow handles his bow like a crow-keeper: draw me a clothier's yard. Look, look, a mouse! Peace, peace; this piece of toasted cheese will do 't. There's my gauntlet; I'll prove it on a giant. Bring up the brown bills. O, well flown, bird! I' the clout, i' the clout: hewgh! Give the word.

This incoherent speech displays Lear's mind at the top of its confusion. He veers rapidly from one imagined situation to another.

Nature's above art in that respect. That is, in the matter of a king's being above the law. Lear turns upside down a philosophical proverb: "Art improves on nature," to assert that the king's authority comes by nature which no art can modify. Lear first imagines that he is recruiting soldiers: *press-money* is the sum paid to a recruit upon enlistment. He then madly thinks that he is taking part in a contest in archery. He remarks that one of the archers handles his bow awkwardly, like a crow-keeper, that is, a boy who scares away crows. He asks for an arrow of standard size, that is, one that was a cloth-yard in length. He produces an imaginary gauntlet, a sign that he is willing to put his case to the test of a combat. The *brown bills* he asks for are pikes that have been treated with a brown substance to prevent rusting. He then imagines that one of the contestants has hit the clout, the center of the target: the bird is the arrow, the clout is the bull's eye. *Hewgh!* is Lear's imitation of the whizzing of the arrow. He then thinks that an intruder is seeking to gain entrance to the contest and demands that he give the word, that is, the countersign.

113. Line 125

Down from the waist they are Centaurs. A centaur was a fabulous lustful creature—the upper half man, the lower half horse.

114. Line 158
And, handy-dandy, which is the justice, which is the thief?
"Handy-dandy" was a formula in a children's game. It means,
which hand will you take? That is, what is your choice?

115. Lines 242–9
Good gentleman, go your gait . . . chill be plain with you.
Edgar casts his speech in the stage rustic dialect. It was based
on the Somersetshire dialect.

ACT IV, SCENE 7

116. Stage directions
The Globe edition places this scene inside a tent with Lear
lying in bed asleep. It seems clear however that Lear is not
present during the early part of the scene. See for example
Cordelia's question, "How does the King?" and the Doctor's
answer, "Madam, sleeps well." And again, Cordelia's question,
"Is he arrayed?" We have therefore adapted the directions as
they appear, later in the scene, in the first Folio: "Enter
Lear in a chair carried by servants." Since Lear must be
brought from some sheltered place and returned to it, it
seemed suitable to place the action before the tent rather
than in it.

117. Lines 35–6
        to watch—poor perdu!—
With this thin helm?
A "perdu" was a soldier on an isolated post of great danger.
Helm stands for helmet, that is, protection for the head, in
this instance hair.

ACT V, SCENE 3

118. Line 86
'Tis she is sub-contracted to this lord. Regan's contract to
marry Edmund is invalid unless Goneril's pre-contract to
marry the same man is abrogated, which Albany (as Goneril's
husband) forbids. Albany's appeal to legality in this situation
is elaborate irony.

119. Lines 144–5
What safe and nicely I might well delay
By rule of knighthood, I disdain and spurn.
According to the rule of Knighthood, Edmund was not
bound to accept a challenge from an anonymous opponent.

But he scorns to delay the duel by taking advantage of this law.

120. Line 174

The wheel is come full circle. That is, as a bastard I began life at the lowest point on Fortune's revolving wheel. It took me to the top but now that the revolution has been completed, I am at the bottom again.

121. Lines 263–4

KENT: *Is this the promised end?*

EDGAR: *Or image of that horror?*

ALBANY: *Fall, and cease!*

"The promised end" is Doom's Day. Albany says, "Let it come and all things cease to be."

122. Lines 280–1

If fortune brag of two she loved and hated,
One of them we behold.

No more than two men experienced such violent ups and downs of fortune and one of them is Lear.

123. Line 305

And my poor fool is hanged! Lear here uses "fool" as a term of affection and refers to Cordelia not to the court fool, who disappeared for once and all on a line that is taken to express an anticipation of his death: "And I'll go to bed at noon."

124. Lines 314–5

That would upon the rack of this tough world
Stretch him out longer.

The rack was an instrument of torture in Shakespeare's time. The victim was bound to a frame and levers applied to stretch his joints.

125. Line 317

He but usurped his life. He seized and kept control of his life, that is, he lived longer than the normal life span.

126. Lines 325–6

The oldest hath borne most: we that are young
Shall never see so much, nor live so long.

The meaning is: "Even if we were to live as long as have Lear and Gloucester, we should not experience so much misery as theirs." Thus Albany fulfills his function of calm arbiter of the events of this tragedy and that of prophet of the new social structure he expects to build on the ruins of the old.

Bibliography

I. REFERENCE

BARTLETT, JOHN. *Concordance to Shakespeare*. London: Macmillan Co., 1960. An invaluable reference book, containing a complete verbal index to words, phrases, and passages in all the plays and poems.

BROOKE, C. F. TUCKER. *Shakespeare of Stratford*. New York: 1926. This volume, a handbook for students, gives the reader a brief, scholarly survey of the essential facts about the dramatist and his work.

COLLIER, J. P. and W. C. HAZLITT. *Shakespeare's Library: A Collection of the Romances, Novels, Poems, and Histories Used by Shakespeare in the Composition of His Works*. 2nd ed. 6 vols. London: 1875.

HALLIDAY, FRANK E. *A Shakespeare Companion 1500–1950*. New York: Funk and Wagnalls Co., 1950. An alphabetized list of critics, actors, plays, etc., and their relation to Shakespeare: an indispensable reference book.

HOLINSHED. *Shakespeare's Holinshed: The Chronicle and the Historical Plays*. Compared by W. G. Boswell-Stone. rev. ed. London: 1907.

———. *Holinshed's Chronicle as Used in Shakespeare's Plays*. ed. Allardyce and Josephine Nicoll. New York: Everyman's Library, E. P. Dutton & Co., 1927.

INGLEBY, CLEMENT. M. *Shakespeare's Century of Praise*. London: 1870. A history of opinion on Shakespeare and his work from 1591 to 1693. This contains a source of information about the contemporary and early reputation of the Bard.

———. *Shakespeare Allusion Book: A Collection of Allusions to Shakespeare*. Rev., re-ed., rearranged. 2 vols. New York: Oxford University Press, 1932. These volumes bring the reputation of Shakespeare first reported in *Shakespeare's Century of Praise* down to the year 1932.

KÖKERITZ, HELGE. *Shakespeare's Pronunciation*. New Haven: Yale University Press, 1953. The latest authoritative work on this important subject.

KÖKERITZ, HELGE, and CHARLES TYLER PROUTY. (eds.). *Shakespeare, William. Shakespeare's First Folio.* Facsimile ed. New Haven: Yale University Press, 1954. A photographic facsimile of the First Folio edition of Shakespeare's plays. An introduction on the printing of the Folio, playwriting, and the printing practices of Shakespeare's day prepared by Mr. Prouty.

SCHMIDT, ALEXANDER. *Shakespeare Lexicon.* 3rd ed. 2 vols. Berlin: 1902. The only complete dictionary of the English words, phrases and constructions occurring in all the Poet's works.

II. SHAKESPEARE'S LIFE

ALEXANDER, PETER. *Shakespeare's Life and Art.* London: James Nisbet & Co., Ltd., 1939. Many important and new insights into the relation of Shakespeare's life to his art.

BRANDES, GEORG M. C. *William Shakespeare: A Critical Study.* Translated by William Archer. London: William Heinemann Ltd., 1902. A "life" by one of the most famous literary critics of the nineteenth century.

CHAMBERS, SIR EDMUND K. *William Shakespeare: A Study of Facts and Problems.* 2 vols. New York: Oxford University Press, 1930. A thorough assemblage of all the important facts of Shakespeare's life by the most rigorous scholar in the field.

CHUTE, MARCHETTE. *Shakespeare of London.* New York: E. P. Dutton & Co., 1949. An excellent biography of Shakespeare. It contains a bibliography.

LEE, SIR SIDNEY. *A Life of William Shakespeare.* 4th ed. New York: Macmillan Co., 1929. For years the most authoritative account of the Poet's life.

VAN DOREN, MARK. *Shakespeare.* New York: Doubleday and Co., Inc., 1953. This is an appreciation, particularly of the poetry in all Shakespeare's plays, by a sensitive critic, who is himself a poet.

III. SHAKESPEARE'S TIMES

JENKINS, ELIZABETH. *Elizabeth the Great.* New York: Coward-McCann, Inc., 1959. The most recent American biography, a distinguished piece of scholarship and literary skill.

NEALE, JOHN E. *Queen Elizabeth.* New York: Harcourt, Brace and Co., Inc., 1934. The authoritative biography.

RALEIGH, SIR WALTER. *Shakespeare's England: An Account of the Life and Manners of His Age.* 2 vols. Oxford: 1917. A complete account of the habits, interests and activities of the people during Shakespeare's lifetime.

STEEHOLM, CLARA and HARDY. *James I of England*. New York: Crown Publishers, Inc., 1938. A lively and acute account of James's personal life and kingship.

TILLYARD, E. M. W. *The Elizabethan World Picture*. New York: Macmillan Co., 1944. The authoritative account of the geography—celestial and earthly—and the organization of the world as the Elizabethan pictured it.

IV. SHAKESPEARE'S THEATRE

ADAMS, JOHN C. *The Globe Playhouse: Its Design and Equipment*. rev. ed. New York: Barnes & Noble, 1961. The most widely approved description of the theatre for which most of Shakespeare's plays were written.

BECKERMAN, BERNARD. *Shakespeare at the Globe* (1599–1609). New York: The Macmillan Co., 1962. The most recent and best study of all the elements of the production of Shakespeare's plays by his company at the Globe Theatre. By the Director of the Theatre at Hofstra College.

CHAMBERS, SIR EDMUND K. *The Elizabethan Stage*. 4 vols. Oxford: 1923. The most complete account of the subject extant.

HARBAGE, ALFRED. *Shakespeare's Audience*. New York: Columbia University Press, 1941. An important account of the size and character of the typical audience when Shakespeare's plays were mounted at the Globe.

HOTSON, LESLIE. *Shakespeare's Wooden O*. New York: Macmillan Co., 1960.

JOSEPH, BERTRAM L. *Elizabethan Acting*. New York: Oxford University Press, 1951. The best book on the subject. The author's thesis is that the performance of the Elizabethan actor was the same as that of the orator in the uses of voice, face, body, hands and feet.

NICOLL, ALLARDYCE. "Studies in the Elizabethan Stage since 1900." *Shakespeare Studies* 1 (1948), pp. 1-16.

SPRAGUE, ARTHUR C. *Shakespeare and the Actor's Stage Business in His Plays* (1660-1905). Cambridge: Harvard University Press, 1944. Expertly selected examples of the "business" of famous actors in crucial scenes of the plays. *Hamlet, Macbeth, Julius Caesar* and *Romeo and Juliet* are all treated.

STOPES, CHARLOTTE C. *Burbage and Shakespeare's Stage*. London: 1913. The most thorough account of the Poet's relation to James, Richard and Cuthbert Burbage and the theatres in which Shakespeare's plays were acted.

V. GENERAL CRITICISM

BRADBY, ANNE. ed. *Shakespeare Criticism 1919–1935*. New York: Oxford University Press, 1936.

BRADLEY, A. C. *Shakespearean Tragedy*. London: Macmillan Co., 1904; New York: St. Martin's Press, Inc., 1955. The author gives memorable expression to the essential features of nineteenth-century criticism, i.e., the emphasis on the characters. An indispensable volume for understanding this one aspect of Shakespeare's work. It deals with *Hamlet, Othello, King Lear* and *Macbeth*.

CAMPBELL, LILY B. *Shakespeare's Tragic Heroes*. New York: Cambridge University Press, 1930. This excellent study interprets the tragedies as expressions of Elizabethan psychology. Each one dramatizes a sickness of the soul: *Hamlet*, grief; *Othello*, jealousy; *King Lear*, wrath in old age.

CHARLTON, H. B. *Shakespearian Comedy*. New York: Macmillan Co., 1938.

——. *Shakespearian Tragedy*. New York: Cambridge University Press, 1930.

GRANVILLE-BARKER, H. *Prefaces to Shakespeare*. 2 vols. Princeton: University Press, 1946. The author explains his ideas of the proper staging and acting of *Hamlet, King Lear, The Merchant of Venice, Antony and Cleopatra* and *Cymbeline*.

MOULTON, RICHARD G. *Shakespeare as a Dramatic Artist*. 3rd ed. New York: Oxford University Press, 1929. This book is one of the best accounts of Shakespeare's methods in constructing his plays.

SMITH, D. N. (ed.). *Shakespeare Criticism: A Selection*. New York: Oxford University Press, 1916.

SPURGEON, CAROLINE F. E. *Shakespeare's Imagery and What It Tells Us*. New York: Cambridge University Press, 1935.

STAUFFER, DONALD. *Shakespeare's World of Images*. New York: W. W. Norton and Co., 1949. This book is a study of Shakespeare's formulation of ideas and moral attitudes in a single character, or in the tension established among two or more characters.

VI. KING LEAR

CLEMEN, W. H. *The Development of Shakespeare's Imagery*. Cambridge: Harvard University Press, 1951. Imagery is Lear's most characteristic form of utterance.

COLERIDGE, SAMUEL TAYLOR. *Lectures and Notes on Shakespeare.* London: 1818. Many reprints. Coleridge's comments provide the best and the most influential philosophical understanding of the play.

DOWDEN, EDWARD. *Shakespeare: A Critical Study of His Mind and Art.* London and New York: 1874. "The ethics of *King Lear* are Stoical ethics. Ethical principles radiate through the play, their chief function being to present a vision of human life, to free, amuse, and dilate."

DRAPER, JOHN W. "The Occasion of King Lear," *Studies in Philology.* 1937, pp. 176-185.

FREUD, SIGMUND. "The Theme of the Three Caskets," *Complete Psychological Works,* vol. 12. London: Hogarth Press, 1958, pp. 289-301. "Cordelia is the goddess of Death."

HAZLITT, WILLIAM. *Characters in Shakespeare's Plays.* London: 1817. Many reprints.

HUDSON, H. N. *Lectures on Shakespeare,* vol. 2. New York: Baker and Scribner, 1848.

JAMES, D. G. *The Dream of Learning, and Essay on the Advancement of Learning in Hamlet and King Lear.* London: Oxford University Press, 1951. "Lear feels that he is the source of his daughters' evil. Hence his forbearance and his struggle for patience."

JOHNSON, SAMUEL (Walter Raleigh, Ed.). *Johnson on Shakespeare.* London: Oxford University Press, 1940, pp. 154-162. "There is no scene that does not contribute to the aggravation of the distress or conduct of the action, and scarce a line which does not conduce to the progress of the scene."

KERNODLE, GEORGE H. "The Symphonic Form of King Lear," *Elizabethan Studies and Other Essays, in Honor of George F. Reynolds.* Boulder: University of Colorado Press, 1945, pp. 185-191. An acute analysis of the structure of the play.

KNIGHT, G. WILSON. *The Shakespearean Tempest.* London: Methuen Co., 1953. "The tempest is Shakespeare's persistent image of evil and turmoil." Knight analyzes the part played by the tempest in both Lear's mind and the terrible disturbance in Nature.

LAMB, CHARLES. *On Shakespeare's Tragedies.* London: 1808. Many reprints.

MASEFIELD, JOHN. *William Shakespeare.* New York: Henry Holt and Co., 1911.

MURRY, JOHN MIDDLETON. *Shakespeare.* London: Jonathan Cape Ltd., 1936. "The theme of the play is the Death of Self and the birth of Divine Love."

ORWELL, GEORGE. "Lear, Tolstoy and the Fool," *Shooting an Elephant and Other Essays*. New York: Harcourt, Brace & Co., 1950. This is an answer to Tolstoy's "impartial criticism." "Perhaps Tolstoy chose this play to attack because he was aware of the similarity between Lear's story and his own. He completely fails to deal with Shakespeare as a poet."

SPURGEON, CAROLINE F. E. *Shakespeare's Imagery and What It Tells Us*. London and New York: Cambridge University Press, 1935. The author finds that all the images in the play are those of agonized bodily movement and strain.

STOLL, ELMER EDGAR. *Art and Artifice in Shakespeare: A Study of Dramatic Contrast and Illusion*. New York: Macmillan Co., 1933. This is a good example of Stoll's rigorously historical and objective criticism. He asserts: "A stage play is not a riddle, and Shakespeare's least of all. Structure must not be turned into psychology. Shakespeare is concerned with emotional effect, even at the expense of character."

SWINBURNE, CHARLES ALGERNON. *A Study of Shakespeare*. London: Chatto and Windus, 1902. "It [*King Lear*] is by far the most Aeschylean of his works, the most elemental and primeval, the most oceanic and Titanic in conception."

TOLSTOY, LEO (V. Thertkoff, trans.). "On Shakespeare and the Drama," *Fortnightly Review*. 1906, pp. 963-983; 1907, pp. 62-91. Tolstoy believes that the language is pompous and characterless and that the drama is absurd, producing only aversion and weariness.

The painting on the cover of this
edition is by Leo and Diane Dillon,
who drew their inspiration
from medieval woodcuts.